Praise for *The Lolita Effect* and Dr. M. Gigi Durham

∞

"University of Iowa professor M. Gigi Durham has written an excellent analysis on our culture's pervasive fascination with little girls: *The Lolita Effect: The Media Sexualization of Young Girls and What We Can Do about It*. In the book, which should be required reading for parents, Durham argues that there is a link between the constant stream of highly sexualized images of young girls in the media and the increase in child pornography and sexual violence against young girls and women worldwide. While one may not explicitly cause the other, she writes, sexualizing young girls to sell movies, TV shows, magazines and clothes makes it an acceptable part of mainstream culture."

—*St. Louis Post Dispatch*

"Educational, informative, and extremely relatable."   —*Feminist Review*

"*The Lolita Effect* makes alarmingly clear that Lolita, the flirty, 12-year-old protagonist of Vladimir Nabokov's novel Lolita, has grown into cultural shorthand for 'prematurely, even inappropriately sexual, little girl. She offers helpful, if generalized, discussions on how [myths of sexuality] came into being, their pervasiveness in the media, and why they have so much appeal for girls, capping each discussion with talking point designed to help parents engage with their kids...*The Lolita Effect* does not advocate censorship, but Durham does want adults to more actively and consciously monitor the sexualized products and images that mass media encourage children to consume. This will help prevent Lolita from taking hold of girls, thus keeping Lolita the stuff of fiction, where she belongs."

—*Ms. Magazine*

"Durham takes pains to show that she is no prude or censor...she sees a vast gulf between healthy female sexuality and the one dictated by 'hooker chic'...her book offers dozens of helpful specific ideas for rendering it less potent... As my daughter hurtles toward adolescence, I am grateful for such strategies. It's good to know I can do something more useful than shout 'You'll wear that out of the house over my dead body!'"

—*Washington Post Book World*

"*The Lolita Effect* is a disturbing but important look at a phenomenon that is happening right under our noses."   —*ForeWord Magazine*

"In a world rife with 5-year-olds prancing around in t-shirts that plaster 'Little Miss Naughty' across undeveloped chests and teenagers looking up to 'role models' like Paris Hilton and Lindsey Lohan, it's hard to know where to begin a conversation—both among adults, and between adults and children—about the sexualization of cotemporary girls. University of Iowa journalism professor M. Gigi Durham provides an excellent starting point...Chapter by chapter, Durham tackles fives 'myths of the sexy girl in mainstream media', and each chapters conclusion offers tips toward engaging girls in converstion about the cultural pressures on and around them...What Durham espouses is worth repeating, and parents navigating the unpredictability of teenage hormones will likely be glad they came to the table prepared."   *—Bitch Magazine*

"Durham offers an arsenal of statistics and examples to demonstrate that drawing young girls into sexual culture ism in part, a backlash against feminism. As adult women gain more influence in the public square, girls—naïve and easily manipulated—become a more appealing image of female sexuality for a media culture that has enshrined 'sex sells' as its motto. *The Lolita Effect* becomes a powerful tool for those wanting to challenge the objectification of the vulnerable among us."   *—Christianity Today*

"[*The Lolita Effect*] shows how toxic our culture is in dealing with girls' sexuality, and how parents and teachers can turn it around. Durham's book is worthwhile...[she] has a lot to offer...the problems Durham points to are real and pervasive, and her arguments deserve attention...[she] has identified a problem ...and her suggestions for parents are worth reading."   *—Olympian*

"We've all seen it—the tiny T-shirts with sexually suggestive slogans, the four-year-old gyrating to a Britney Spears song, the young boy shooting prostitutes in his video game—and University of Iowa journalism professor Durham has had enough. In her debut book, she argues that the media—from advertisements to *Seventeen* magazine—are circulating damaging myths that distort, undermine and restrict girls' sexual progress.... Durham offers practical suggestions for overcoming these falsehoods, including sample questions for parents and children. In a well-written and well-researched book, she exposes a troubling phenomenon and calls readers to action."   *—Publishers Weekly*

THE
Lolita
EFFECT

THE MEDIA SEXUALIZATION OF YOUNG
GIRLS AND WHAT WE CAN DO ABOUT IT

M. GIGI DURHAM, PH.D.

THE OVERLOOK PRESS
New York

To my daughters

Sonali and Maya

Who have made me think so carefully,
intensely, and lovingly about these issues

First published in paperback in the United States in 2009 by
The Overlook Press, Peter Mayer Publishers, Inc.

NEW YORK:
141 Wooster Street
New York, NY 10012

Cataloging-in-Publication Data is available from the Library of Congress

Book design and type formatting by Bernard Schleifer
Manufactured in the United States of America
ISBN 978-1-59020-215-9
2 4 6 8 10 9 7 6 5 3 1

Contents

Today's children and young men and women have sexual identities that spiral around paper and celluloid phantoms: from *Playboy* to music videos to the blank torsos in women's magazines, features obscured and eyes extinguished, they are being imprinted with a sexuality that is mass produced, deliberately dehumanizing and inhuman.

—NAOMI WOLF, *The Beauty Myth*

Introduction to the Paperback Edition

In April 2008, 15-year-old Disney icon Miley Cyrus caused a sensation by posing nude for *Vanity Fair* magazine. And just as she'd finished baring all for Annie Liebovitz's camera, *The Lolita Effect* rolled off the presses and into bookstores.

I was instantly bombarded with phone calls and emails from reporters from all over the world. What did I have to say about Miley's photo shoot? Was photographer Annie Leibovitz a child pornographer? Were six-year-olds around the world going to be corrupted by this wanton display? In an instant, I had to work out a complex situation in the form of a sound bite that would explain the photographs, and the widespread discomfort with them, to the public at large.

In many ways, the event was a focal point for the raging debates about girls, sexuality, and the media that have been plaguing parents and pundits for years now. The public reaction to the photographs was a perfect, graphic illustration of the dichotomies we're caught in: dichotomies that define girls' sexuality as either "good" or "bad;" that claim an underage girl must be either asexual or a slut; that charge that if adults acknowledge that girls are sexual, we must be either libertines or perverts.

But of course Miley Cyrus' sexuality, like any young girl's, is a far more complex issue than these easy binaries would allow us to recognize.

In writing *The Lolita Effect*, I was seeking to challenge the binaries and find a way to acknowledge and embrace sexuality as a normal, healthy and vital part of girls' development, while calling attention to the distorted and exploitative ways in which it is represented and manipulated by the commercial media. In the case of the notorious Miley Cyrus photo shoot, there were many dimensions to consider: at fifteen, the girl was in a transitional moment of puberty, at a life stage where she was exploring her sexuality, so the outrage at her "loss of innocence" was wholly misplaced. At the same time, sexual development is a sensitive and significant process, one that's best dealt with in safe and private spaces. The public exploitation of her body was, to my mind, problematic. Then there were legal questions, especially as very similar images of girls are deemed child pornography and banned from publication. There were other issues at stake: the aesthetic value of the photographs, which raised the difficulty of distinguishing between pornography and erotica, as well as the ethical question of whether aesthetics trumps any social obligation to protect children. Finally, there was Miley's abashed apology to the world a few days after the photo shoot, in which she confessed, "Now, seeing the photographs and reading the story, I feel so embarrassed." The apology indicated that she had not been in control of the situation: in the end, a variety of adults had connived to use her body for their own commercial motives, a situation in which no young girl should ever be placed.

So there were critiques to be made of the *Vanity Fair* photographs, but none of them were simple or morally unambiguous. It's impossible to take a basic "good" or "bad" stance on matters of sexuality, because so much rests on the cultural and social construction and representation of sexuality, which is itself neither good nor bad, but simply a fact of human existence, to be handled with thoughtfulness and care.

Because of our oversimplication of these matters, we are not doing a good job of helping girls to understand and handle their sex lives in responsible and self-protective ways—we have distressingly high rates of teen pregnancy and STDs, and a cultural horror of dealing matter-of-factly with the issue of sex, especially sex and youth. At the same time, we revel in a media environment that capitalizes on narrow, restrictive, regressive and often harmful definitions of sex, and any critique of them is dismissed as prudishness or censorship.

So *The Lolita Effect* was my attempt to sort through these thickets and offer a way to approach these issues calmly and analytically, with a view to finding ethical solutions to the problems, yet without calls for censorship or religious repression. I wanted to develop strategies that all of us who care about girls could adopt, in collaboration with girls themselves, whose voices have been muted through all these moral debates and panics. For me, the tried-and-true feminist tradition of "consciousness raising" was central to finding truly empowering approaches to girls' sexuality.

I hoped that by reading *The Lolita Effect*, girls as well as the adults who loved them—parents, teachers, counselors, coaches—would form communities of critique that could stand against the insidious and inimical anti-girl assaults from the mainstream media. I wanted to liberate the powerful, activist techniques and theories of media scholarship from the pages of obscure academic journals and make them available to people whose lives they could change.

And I think it's worked. Shortly after *The Lolita Effect* was published, I got an email from a fourteen-year-old girl. "I always knew that the media influenced many aspects of my life," she wrote, "but after reading your book, I have realized just how much the media controls everything; from what I wear, to what movies I see.... I had no idea what kind of messages [the media] send to the world and women in general. After reading your book, I have decided to make a conscious effort to not support groups that are homophobic or send messages encouraging mistreatment of women."

Just that one message would have been enough for me: reaching one teenage girl, catalyzing her consciousness-raising and spurring her activism on behalf of women would mean that *The Lolita Effect* had fulfilled its mission. But the emails, telephone calls and face-to-face responses I've gotten from girls, women and men all over the country and the world are showing me that *The Lolita Effect*'s core messages about truly empowered female sexuality have been reaching many people in crucial, life-transforming ways.

This really matters to me. After years of publishing research articles on this topic in academic journals, I wanted to go public with my findings. I was inspired by an essay by the British sociologist Stuart Hall in which he described cultural studies as "a practice which aims to make a difference in the world." That view is right in line with feminist scholarship, which is also deeply connected to activism on behalf of women. And it's in line with the highest ideals of journalism, which at its best is all about promoting social justice. These three modes of writing, and the ethics underlying them all, have shaped who I am as an author.

I was anxious about many things when the book was first published, and my deepest anxiety was that I might be misunderstood. In the era of abstinence-only, prurient yet prissy sexuality in which the book took shape, I thought I might be seen as an anti-sex crusader who saw sex as a danger to girls, when really the opposite is true: I think sex is a truly marvelous part of being human, and of growing up, and I want girls to know and understand their bodies in accurate, healthy, and positive ways as they grow into adults. But my fears were baseless: so far, no one has misunderstood my position or categorized me as falling into a polarized political camp on the issue of sex. I've talked with supportive people on both ends of the political spectrum and found points of agreement and solidarity with them. Preventing sexual harm to girls—giving them the tools to take charge of their sex lives when they have a complete understanding of their sexual rights, responsibilities, and risks—should be nonpartisan social goal.

It's a goal made more difficult when media critique is brought into play: the specter of censorship haunts all such endeavors. My argument has always been that critique is not censorship: more public discussion of media content is, in fact, the opposite of censorship. Another difficulty in critiquing media culture is that it seems innocuous, even silly. How can anyone take advertising or TV sitcoms or little plastic dolls seriously? They're just entertainment, and everyone knows they're fictions, so why get exercised about them?

But there is growing empirical evidence that the media do influence children's behaviors, and a few months after my book came out, a study in the medical journal *Pediatrics*, based on a national survey of over 2,000 teenagers, found a direct correlation between children's exposure to sexual content on television and teen pregnancy rates. "Television plays a role in shaping adolescent reproductive health outcomes," the study unequivocally reported. Other recent research has also revealed links between sexual content in the media and early sexual activity. Given this, it is imperative that we take the media seriously as factors that profoundly impact our children's lives. "Just turn it off" is not a good response, either— it's an ostrich move that is doomed to fail, because we can't keep our kids in bubbles forever. This doesn't mean that adults shouldn't monitor and limit kids' media consumption, for of course they should, or that adults shouldn't take media corporations to task for their lack of thoughtful and diverse programming, for media must be held accountable by consumers. But it does mean that adults also need to be keenly attuned to their children's media habits so that they can communicate with them about the distinctions between media fictions and the real world.

The good news is that kids are natural critics, and showing them how to be active, analytical media consumers, rather than passive audiences, is like teaching fish to swim: they take to it with gusto and glee. And, as one of my students pointed out to me, "once that light-bulb goes on, it never goes off."

In the process of sharing media literacy skills with kids, we learn them ourselves, and these are skills we all need in today's media-flooded environment. I've been told that while teen girls are sharing *The Lolita Effect* at slumber parties, moms and dads are talking about it at barbecues and cocktail parties, recognizing their own media blinders and learning how to evaluate their own relationships with corporate marketing and messages.

Though *The Lolita Effect* refers specifically to the mediated myths about girls' sexuality, the overriding issue at stake is the blurring distinction between girlhood and adulthood. This is a gendered issue, because it's girls—not boys—whose sexuality is being so insistently touted by the media. And this blurring is a gradual elision that we should be alert to, because little girls are not capable of making good sexual decisions before they have reached psychological and emotional maturity. The media coach us to chuckle about French maid outfits in toddler sizes, or Hooters t-shirts for pre-teens, or pole-dancing kits sold as toys, but these are symbolic markers of our cultural normalization of young girls projecting a very adult sexuality. We need to learn the difference between a sexual consciousness that is appropriate for a child, and an adult eroticism that may in fact jeopardize the child's safety, wellbeing and holistic development. We need to be alert enough to challenge the myths that pervade our media, because they have reached a point where we seem to no longer recognize their hazards.

The more I talk with parents, teachers, counselors and girls, the more I realize that we all need to share responsibility for remaking our societies into places where girls can flourish—where sexuality is neither a taboo nor a bacchanal, but a fact of life that can be handled with intelligence and clarity.

Sometimes this seems like an unreachable goal, but I take inspiration from Margaret Mead, the anthropologist whose work offers us insights into what a healthy, culturally sanctioned adolescent sexuality might look like. "Never doubt," she wrote, "that a small group of thoughtful, committed citizens can change the world. Indeed, it is the only thing that ever has." I hope *The Lolita Effect* will similarly inspire my readers to join hands to change the world for girls.

—Meenakshi Gigi Durham
Iowa City
December2008

THE

Lolita

EFFECT

Preface

The Lolita Effect begins with the premise that children are sexual beings. As they mature, they deserve to be furnished with factual, developmentally appropriate, and useful information about sex and sexuality. They need safe environments and lots of room in which to grow and learn about sex in ways that benefit them in the long term. This is especially important for girls, because for so long girls' sexuality has been repressed, controlled, and punished in ways that have curbed and subjugated them in this crucial domain.

So the starting point for this book is the fact that sex and sexuality are normal, natural, and, at best, wonderful aspects of being alive, and that the diverse range of expressions of sexual feelings can be both inspiring and valid. At the same time, it is important to recognize childhood as a time of learning and growth, and to acknowledge that caring adults have a responsibility to guide children toward healthy, fulfilled, and capable adult lives.

Right now, the media aren't doing much to contribute to this goal as far as sex is concerned; in fact, they are mishandling and distorting girls' sexuality. This book homes in on the ways that the mainstream corporate media construct sex and sexuality in ways that actually limit and hamper girls' healthy sexual development. This is what I have dubbed "The Lolita Effect"— the distorted and delusional set of myths about girls' sexuality that circulates widely in our culture and throughout the world, that works to limit, undermine , and restrict girls' sexual progress. In this book, I aim to give parents, educators, media audiences, and advocates the tools to recognize and respond proactively to these myths so that we can work together in the best interests of the girls who look to us for guidance.

In today's media-saturated environment, children are bombarded with images and messages about sex and sexuality at very early ages. Unfortunately, there's lots of evidence that the messages they're getting about sex are harmful rather than helpful. Because children are engaging in sexual activity at earlier ages, rates of teen pregnancy are rising in the United States and elsewhere, and the incidence of sexually transmitted diseases among teenagers is extremely high. And child sexual abuse is too common—the World Health Organization estimates that 25 percent of all girls and 8 percent of boys have been subjected to some form of sexual abuse; in the United States, an estimated 20 percent of boys and 25 percent of girls have been sexually molested.

Because it's so clear that we aren't doing a good job of ensuring children's sexual safety and well-being, I hope to open up a discussion about how we can do better to confront the problematic and manipulative ideas about sex that circulate in commercial popular culture.

From that position, this book is not about censoring, ignoring, or repressing discussions about sex. On the contrary, it's about galvanizing more open and active dialogues about sexuality, especially girls' sexuality. Everyone is sexual, and the range of ways in which sexuality is expressed and experienced is diverse and multifaceted. It is crucial to recognize that sexual feelings, curiosities, and responses begin very early in life, and that our best move is to support and nurture young people as they develop sexually, intellectually, psychologically, and in other ways. In many ways we aren't doing a good job of differentiating healthy sexuality from damaging and exploitative sexuality. And we aren't always thinking about what's appropriate at different developmental stages: what kids can handle, how best to present sexual information to them, and how to guide them through the complicated and precarious terrain of sex.

In general, we are squeamish about talking directly and rationally about sex, even though we are only too happy to indulge in the prurient, voyeuristic, and titillating versions of sex that proliferate in popular culture and mainstream media. Our puritanical but passive attitude is at the root of our problems. We've got to tackle this issue head-on. We need to talk about it, to gain some critical distance from the media that surround us, and to find more productive, progressive, and positive ways to think about girls and sex—ways that are good for them and good for society as a whole. And we need to do this in collaboration with girls, who are bright, thoughtful, and crucial participants in this discussion. They don't need "rescuing" from sex. Rather, they need our respect and attention as they explore what should be a healthy and natural part of their lives as they become adults.

This really matters, because the media, which are driven by profit and ratings, aren't in the business of respecting or advocating for girls. As far as the media industries go, cultivating consumers as early as possible is a central goal. That's why we're seeing increasingly adult content being aimed at very young children; that's why the dolls sold to preschoolers look exactly like the half-dressed women in music videos and soft-core men's magazines, and why toddlers' fashions are almost indistinguishable from those of teenagers. Marketers call this "KGOY," or "Kids Getting Older Younger": that's where the developmental differences among children are blurred by the media through strategies geared toward creating consumer bases as early as possible. But it's we must remember that children aren't in charge of this trend, even though media managers and marketers want us to believe they are. This phenomenon originates from corporate command centers seeking to maximize their reach and profits. And it's changing the landscape of childhood.

This is why, in this book, I use the term "girls" broadly, to span an age range from preschool to the late teens. Even though girls at different developmental ages process and cope with media messages about sex and sexuality differently, the messages themselves are reaching across very diverse age groups: toddlers see R-rated films; preschoolers watch MTV; grade-school children tune in to Victoria's Secret fashion shows; everyone gets on the Internet. In Vladimir Nabokov's novel *Lolita*, he rhapsodizes about nine- to fourteen-year-old girls as inhabiting a special category of "nymphets," and in general I am thinking of this age range as I write. But the borders of girlhood have extended beyond these margins. And our concept of a "girl" is necessarily unclear. Those of us who are in frequent contact with girls know this to be true.

While this book is pro-girl, in a way, it's also pro-media. The media are part of our lives, and they enrich and enliven them. In general, the mainstream media are in the business of providing programming that both captivates audiences and attracts advertisers; their goals are mundanely mercenary rather than actively malicious. But the fallout can be quite serious. One dimension of becoming an active and critical media consumer is to talk back to the media, to lead them toward engaging responsibly with their audiences and finding more enlightened ways to make their profits. Another is being a responsible consumer. We have to know how to control our media environment and how to use the media in ways that better our lives, instead of allowing the media free rein over both public and private spaces. This book represents a step in that direction.

∞

This book began more than a decade ago, when I first began studying girls' media and the audiences they're trying to reach. Along the way, many amazing people have supported and mentored me, encouraging me to ask questions, go out into the field, publish my findings, and take committed stands on women's issues and human rights. They kept me focused on the real-world goals of cultural studies. I could not have written this book without their backing and affirmation.

I have been fortunate to have parents who believed in gender equity and girls' progress, though they came from a culture in which these things are not guaranteed or easily justified. My first teachers were my parents, V. R. Venugopal and Jaya Venugopal; they supported my passion for writing (even though they never thought it was a viable career path!), they tolerated my rebellious and nonconformist nature, and most of all they instilled in me a lifelong love of reading. My girlhood was spent in the company of two brothers, Narendar ("Buddy") and Ravinder ("Ticky"), whose perspectives, analytical minds, and affection unquestionably helped me to become the person I am. My parents-in-law, Frank E. Durham and Darla Rushing, have always understood what my work meant to me and unconditionally celebrated their unconventional, feminist daughter-in-law; and my extended family—Byron and Karen Durham, Caroline Durham, Susie Davies, and Sonali Roy Venugopal—have unfailingly cheered me on. This book could not have happened without my family's unstinting love and encouragement.

My first awareness of sexual assault and social inequities came from Claire Walsh and Debbie Burke at the University of Florida's Sexual Assault Recovery Service. These thoughtful, brilliant, and activist women first ignited my own commitment to working to end sexual violence against women and to understanding the media's role in our sexual lives, and I owe them a great deal.

My feminist consciousness was fostered by the Women's Studies Program at the University of Texas at Austin, where I found a warm and friendly academic home for my burgeoning interest in gender, sexuality, and youth culture. I am forever grateful to Lucia Gilbert for her kindness, mentorship, and inspiration—she will always be my intellectual role model. Thanks, too, to Christine Williams for believing in my work, to Steve Reese for understanding and affirming my interest in feminist scholarship about adolescent girls, and to many others who were on the University of Texas faculty when I was there—D. Charles Whitney, Craig Watkins, Janet Staiger, Horace Newcomb, Tom Schatz, Don Heider, Max McCombs, and many others—for offering me so much validation and encouragement in this unusual, and often marginalized, line of study.

I began this book when I received a Career Development Award from the University of Iowa and a residency at the Obermann Center for Advanced Studies, in the fall of 2006. The Obermann Center proved to be an intellectual haven—the energetic and enlightening discussions I had with the other scholars in residence were invaluable to this project. Many thanks to Obermann's director, Jay Semel, for providing an environment where creativity and scholarship can flourish, and to everyone who talked with me about the ideas in this book: Michelle Scherer, Carin Green, Connie Berman, Russell Valentino, Mark Sidel, David Klemm, Bruce Spencer, and, especially, Peter Manning and Susan Scheckel, who read early drafts of the proposal and who managed to be thoughtful critics, cheerleaders, and friends, all at once.

The Feminist Scholarship Division of the International Communication Association has been another intellectual home to me ever since I was a graduate student. The brilliant and vital women in that organization continue to be my friends, colleagues, and inspirations: I owe so much to Dafna Lemish, Sharon Mazzarella, Radhika Parameswaran, Norma Pecora, and Linda Steiner. Thanks, too, to Rebecca Hains for sharing her work. I'd also like to thank other communication scholars whose work and friendship have inspired and energized me: Doug Kellner, Rhonda Hammer, Hanno Hardt, Bonnie Brennan, Hemant Shah, Sharon Dunwoody, Jo Ellen Fair, and many others.

Thanks are also due to those colleagues in the University of Iowa's School of Journalism and Mass Communication who were encouraging and solicitous as I worked on this manuscript. Jennifer Raghavan deserves a special mention for her assistance with finding sources and ordering materials for me—we are lucky to have a librarian of her caliber on our staff. I'm also grateful to Karla Tonella for her many contributions to this project.

The members of POROI at the University of Iowa deserve special thanks, too—not only for helping me out with a research assistant during the early stages of my writing, but for their constant encouragement, thoughtful feedback, and friendship. I'm also grateful to Prairie Lights bookstore, just because browsing the shelves has always inspired me to keep writing, and because the Java House upstairs was a place to stay warm and caffeinated as I worked on the manuscript!

I'll be forever grateful to my friends in Iowa City who have been so understanding of my insane schedule and who have helped out in all kinds of ways, from taking care of my kids on short notice to sending me news clippings and Web links that became grist for the *Lolita Effect* mill. Thanks to Paul and Julie Casella, Pam and Todd Hubbard, Jenny and Tom Brands, Satish and Sheila Rao, Deanna Johnson, and especially to David Ozolins and Cheryl Jacobsen, and to their children, for their friendship and help (Cheryl has the distinction of being the first person to order this book!).

When I set out to write this book, I didn't know that I would find an agent who believed fully in my vision, or that she would send my manuscript to an editor who would champion it just as fervently. I am still pinching myself over the fact that Jennifer de la Fuente and her associates at Venture Literary were willing to take on an unknown media scholar and work so tirelessly to find a publisher for her first non-scholarly effort. That they found Juliet Grames is even more amazing. Juliet's enthusiasm for this project, her sensitive editing of the manuscript, and her dedication to her work have been invaluable, especially as I slogged through the final chapters of the manuscript.

Finally, my lasting gratitude goes to my husband, Frank, whose partnership and love have been my mainstay for all these years. We've grown and changed together, learning and marveling as we have discovered new ways to see the world. After more than twenty years together, we know each other more deeply and passionately than I thought any two people ever could. I knew this book would take a lot of my time and energy, but it could not have happened if Frank had not risen to the occasion, parenting our two daughters while I holed up in the attic and pounded away at the keyboard. Frank has always been my first and best editor, and I owe everything to him.

Finally, I thank my two smart, exuberant, beautiful daughters, whose joy in life makes me want to keep on working to make the world a great place for girls.

Introduction
SEXY GIRLS IN THE MEDIA

⟨◦⟩

> She it was to whom ads were dedicated: the ideal consumer,
> the subject and object of every foul poster.
>
> —VLADIMIR NABOKOV, *Lolita*

LAST HALLOWEEN, a five-year-old girl showed up at my doorstep decked out in a tube top, a gauzy miniskirt, platform shoes, and glittering eye shadow. The outfit projected a rather tawdry adult sexuality. "I'm a Bratz!" the tot piped up proudly, brandishing a look-alike doll clutched in her chubby fist. I had an instant, dizzying flashback to an image of a child prostitute I had seen in Cambodia, dressed in a disturbingly similar outfit.

I was startled and put off—but perhaps I shouldn't have been. The little girl who came to my door is part of a widespread cultural shift that has become an American norm. Increasingly, very young girls are becoming involved in a sphere of fashion, images, and activities that encourage them to flirt with a decidedly grown-up eroticism and sexuality—and the girls playing with these ideas are getting younger and younger every year.

So why am I perturbed by this trend? I am a pro-sex feminist, by which I mean that I don't see sex as taboo or hush-hush; I think sex is a normal and healthy part of life, even of children's lives. I want my two young daughters—indeed, all girls—to grow up unafraid of and knowledgeable about their bodies, confident about finding and expressing sexual pleasure, able to be both responsible and adventurous in the realm of sex. I want to talk to my daughters honestly and communicate my perspectives and values about this complex aspect of human experience (and I want them to be able to have these same kinds of conversations with their dad, and with other people whose opinions matter to them). Above all, as they grow into adults, I want them to be able to think ethically about sex, just as I want them to carefully think through their ethical positions regarding everything else. These are the themes I try to emphasize when I teach classes in gender and sexuality, and when I present workshops to elementary- and middle-school children.

For years I've fought against the ways in which girls' sexuality has been denied, repressed, and moralized about. I despise the social double standards that celebrate boys' "studliness" and condemn girls' desires. I believe in girls' agency and strength, and in working to ensure that they have the space and safety to make free choices about their sex lives.

But the flip side of those proactive ideas is the cold recognition that female sexuality in our world is often exploitative, abusive, and harmful. Girls and women are battered, raped, sold, and slain, and these acts are sex crimes, motivated by gender and sexuality. An estimated two million children, most of them girls, are sexually abused every year through child prostitution and trafficking. There is such a thing as sexual harm. And there is a battle being fought against sex and ideas about sex that destroy the lives of women and girls.

All of these issues come up when I hear about three-year-olds wearing *Playboy* T-shirts to school, or grade-schoolers aspiring to be lap dancers. Many cultural critics these days see these developments as harmless, or even positive. Jennifer Baumgardner, coauthor of the feminist manual *Manifesta*, argues that when little girls sing Spice Girls songs or don stiletto heels, they are tapping into a spirit of "fierce, fun independence." It's easy to recognize how alluring these symbols of playful femininity are, and how they can be reworked ironically or campily to convey new messages about "girl power." But is it realistic to believe that young children would be aware of these subversive and liberating possibilities? How should we respond to the increasing sexualization of girlhood, especially when it begins in kindergarten or earlier?

One angry mom calls these kids "prosti-tots," and another describes them as "kinderwhores." Others declare that corporate marketing machines are turning little girls into "sex bait." It's easy to see why. While the exhibitionist antics of Paris Hilton and the Pussycat Dolls mesmerize small girls around the world, retailers like Abercrombie & Fitch create thong underwear for ten-year-olds adorned with seductive slogans like "Wink, Wink" and "Eye Candy." Wal-Mart carries junior girls' panties that read, "Who needs credit cards . . . ?" on the crotch (it's hard to see this as not implying that selling sex is a great option for teenage girls). Not to be outdone, the British chain BHS has launched a line of "Little Miss Naughty" underwear that offers push-up bras and lacy briefs to preteens. In 2007, toy manufacturer Tesco sold a pink plastic "Peekaboo Pole Dancing" kit, complete with tiny garter and toy money for stuffing into it, on its "Toys and Games" Web site, until pressure from parents' groups forced them to reclassify the product—though it's still on the market.

The turn of the new millennium has spawned an intriguing phenomenon: the sexy little girl. She's an all-too-familiar figure in today's media landscape: the baby-faced nymphet with the preternaturally voluptuous curves, the one whose scantily clad body gyrates in music videos, poses provocatively on teen magazine covers, and populates cinema and television screens around the globe. She's become a fixture in Western pop culture: we all know her various incarnations, from Britney Spears to the sex-kittenish cartoon girls of animé, from Brooke Shields's child prostitute in *Pretty Baby* to JonBenét Ramsey's beauty queen persona and the Australian preteen sex symbol Maddison Gabriel. She's been celebrated and censured, and she serves as a symbolic flashpoint for raging debates about gender, sexuality, the definition of childhood, and the criteria for social standards of acceptability.

Perhaps one reason for our fascination with the sexy little girl is her tricky double role in contemporary society—she is simultaneously a symbol of female empowerment and the embodiment of a chauvinistic "beauty myth." She invokes the specter of pedophilia while kindling the prospect of potent female sexuality. "If you've got it, flaunt it!" we urge, while at the same time we decry the absurd and capricious standards of femininity that dismantle women's lives. "Why the fascination with JonBenét?" we demand, as we scour the tabloids that blare the latest news of her case, accompanied by titillating photographs of the blonde six-year-old in showgirl plumes. The sexy girl fascinates us and repels us; she haunts our imagery and our imaginations, and we know her best by a nickname that evokes meanings far beyond their literary origin: she is Lolita.

The term has become an everyday allusion, a shorthand cultural reference to a prematurely, even inappropriately, sexual little girl—that is, a girl who is by legal definition not yet an adult and is therefore outlawed from sexual activity. Because of this legal and cultural taboo, she is also wrong—wicked, even—to deliberately provoke sexual thoughts. And the "Lolitas" of our time are defined as deliberate sexual provocateurs, turning adults' thoughts to sex and thereby luring them into wickedness, wantonly transgressing our basic moral and legal codes. Everything about this Lolita is unacceptable, and therein lie both her allure and her ignominy.

The original Lolita—the twelve-year-old Dolores Haze, protagonist of Vladimir Nabokov's 1955 novel—was a rather different girl. As the feminist scholar Alyssa Harad put it, "Lolita is the archetype of a special category of girl who seduces without knowing it, who works her charms unconsciously, even unwillingly, who attracts without necessarily being, in any of the most obvious ways, attractive." It is clear in the book that she is the powerless victim of her predatory stepfather, Humbert Humbert. Nabokov's Lolita is a nuanced character whose sexuality is complex—like many preadolescent girls, she is sexually curious—but she has no control over her relationship with Humbert, which is abusive and manipulative. Yet the care with which Nabokov presents her case, and his emphasis on Humbert's malfeasance, has been overlooked in the years since the novel's publication. It is as though the very fact of Lolita's sexuality—the public acknowledgment that a preteen girl could be sexual, the bold focus on an incestuous liaison between grown man and little girl—has made her into a fantasy figure, an image of Humbert's projection rather than the sexually abused and tragic figure of the novel.

It is this fantastical Lolita who has entered our culture as a pervasive metaphor. She is eagerly invoked in the popular media, as a sign of just how licentious little girls can be. "Bring back school uniforms for little Lolitas!" demands London's *Daily Telegraph* in an article condemning contemporary sexy schoolgirl fashions. According to a recent *New York Times* article, girls wear skin-baring and infantile costumes like babydoll dresses and high-heeled Mary Janes to "evoke male Lolita fantasies." Tokyo's *Daily Yomiuri* refers to "the Lolita-like sex appeal" of nubile preteen Japanese anime cartoon characters. The "Long Island Lolita," sixteen-year-old Amy Fisher, was the target of media vilification as a wanton home wrecker. Even in an essay about a cathedral in Barcelona, critic Will Self writes, "La Sagrada Familia wins me over with its sheer wantonness as a building—this is the Lolita of sacred architecture."

It is evident from these and many other such examples that Lolita is our favorite metaphor for a child vixen, a knowing coquette with an out-of-control libido, a baby nymphomaniac. This creature fulfills the fantasy projected by Humbert Humbert, yet she is worlds away from the original Lolita, who neither initiated nor provoked her nonconsensual sexual relationship with Humbert. She was sexual, true, as are virtually all humans, but she was not allowed to experience her sexuality in safe, ethical directions of her own choosing. Instead, her sexual appeal was an artifice imposed on her in ways that suited a molester's needs and vision. In truth, she was raped and victimized. Furthermore, she was deprived of her childhood.

Lolita may be an apt metaphor for the sexy girl in contemporary culture, but not in the ways the term "Lolita" is usually used. The Lolitas that populate our mediascapes are fabrications. They serve market needs and profit motives, and they are powerfully alluring, especially to the young girls whose vulnerability they exploit. They are framed in a clever rhetoric of empowerment and choice. But they skillfully conceal the narrow, restrictive, and ultimately disempowering definition of sexuality that is delivered by these images and their accompanying messages. Rather than offering girls—and the rest of their audiences—thoughtful, open-minded, progressive, and ethical understandings about sexuality, our media and our culture have produced a gathering of "prostitots"—hypersexualized girls whose cultural presence has become a matter of heated public controversy.

This is the Lolita Effect.

Today more than ever, the sexy girl is at the center of a storm. Sex is a battleground in contemporary society, as anyone keeping track of news headlines is well aware. As our understanding of gender and sexuality grows more complex, debate about what is "right," "normal," or "acceptable" in the once-clandestine realm of sex has become more open and more intense.

Recent medical breakthroughs, such as the introduction of a cervical cancer vaccine or FDA approval of a "morning-after" pill, have unleashed storms of resistance from conservative groups, for whom these developments signal the imminent threat of uncontained promiscuity and underage sexual activity—arguments that are just as fiercely countered by mainstream and liberal pundits. The demands of gays and lesbians for the right to marry and to legally adopt children have been denied any claim to legitimacy in some communities while gaining ground in others. In many U.S. public schools, sex education is not part of the curriculum, in large part due to intense political and theological opposition. Meanwhile, the United States has the highest rate of teen pregnancy and abortion in the industrialized world—twice that of the United Kingdom, four times that of France and Germany, and more than eight times that of Japan. Clearly, something isn't working.

Yet in this tumultuous environment, media images of sexuality are everywhere. Advertisements for such shopping-mall stalwarts as Victoria's Secret and Abercrombie & Fitch are notoriously erotic, and MTV and BET music videos routinely—indeed, almost inevitably—feature sexual themes and explicit lyrics. Currently, Shai, a French clothing company, is using an online hard-core porn video to sell high-priced T-shirts; Ivy League undergraduates are editing and posing in campus skin mags; and, according to a *Wall Street Journal* report, one-third of all video games feature sexual themes, including sexual violence. These trends are periodically critiqued and condemned, but they are nonetheless everyday features of our contemporary society.

In this cultural context, children's sexuality is fraught with controversy, and the media are often the most obvious targets in any discussion of these issues. But the media's role in kids' lives is a contested one, despite years of research and reflection on the topic. Mediated images of sexuality have been identified as perilous to teens' healthy development, especially for girls. Mary Pipher, in her best-selling critique, *Reviving Ophelia*, noted that "because of the media . . . all girls live in one big town—a sleazy, dangerous town," adding, "with puberty, girls face enormous pressure to split into false selves. The pressure comes from schools, magazines, music, television, and the movies."

Pop culture figures like Paris Hilton and Lindsay Lohan have been charged with promoting inappropriately hypersexualized clothing to grade-school girls all over the world. Media standards of beauty are implicated in a wide range of disorders affecting adolescent females, from body image to low self-esteem to poor school performance. Girls who watch sexualized media are more likely to engage in sex—and teen media contains ever-increasing levels of sexual content. We also know that teens seek out sex-related media content—not just for titillation or to defy social taboos, but to gain information about a baffling and complicated aspect of their lives. As one teenage girl explained, "You can learn a lot from what [media] have to say instead of being embarrassed to ask your parents."

In the face of these findings, "Blame the media!" becomes an appealing battle cry, but scapegoating the media as the source of all society's ills is both shortsighted and simplistic. The idea that contemporary children and teenagers are zombielike victims and dupes of a media conspiracy is equally improbable—as the research shows, and as those of us who spend a lot of time around kids will already know. Children and teens are sharp, cynical, and savvy media critics. As one fourteen-year-old girl put it, "It's television. I just kind of watch it. I don't take it as an example. I know it's just TV."

Yet if it's "just TV," and if most of us are aware, at some level, that mediated representations of not just sex but all aspects of life tend to be sensationalized and unrealistic, why is there such widespread consternation about sexy girls in the media? Isn't entertainment supposed to be fictionalized? If we care about girls' empowerment, are these media images helping to challenge puritanical constraints that disallow girls' desire and sexual development—or are they perpetuating gender roles and body images that are ultimately destructive? How do girls—and boys—see all this, and how are they dealing with it?

These questions are particularly difficult. Even for those of us who seek to be open-minded, nonjudgmental, and healthy in our approach to sexuality, media images and messages are minefields. Of course we don't want girls and young women to have to cover their bodies in shame. But is it really okay for girls (and everyone else) to idealize and strive for body types that require diet aids, unhealthy levels of exercise, bulimia, and plastic surgery to attain? We don't want sex to be a taboo topic or a scandalous secret—but aren't there drawbacks to the media motif that a girl's "hotness" matters more than almost anything else? Feminist perspectives on sexual assault have taught us never to blame the victim: what a woman wears is never a justification for rape. But at the same time, shouldn't we be troubled about the availability of thong underwear for toddlers or low-rise jeans for 'tweens?

These are real concerns in today's world. At their core, they are ethical questions. They are the kinds of questions I hear frequently from parents, teachers, and students when I conduct workshops and teach classes on gender and the media. And there are no simple answers to any of them. Kids grow up in a media-saturated environment in which sex is emphasized. Media venues are by no means the only influence on social and cultural ideas about sex and body, but they are a significant one. Some parents report feeling as if they are fighting against a tidal wave of sexual messages aimed at their young children.

And they are. Market research indicates that children and teenagers are major media consumers: a 2005 Kaiser Family Foundation study found that eight- to eighteen-year-olds spend an average of six and a half hours a day with media. According to the marketing firm Teen Research Unlimited, American teenagers spend 11.2 hours a week watching TV, 10.1 hours listening to FM radio, and 3.1 hours a week playing video games. Teens and young adults spend 16.7 hours a week online. Both boys and girls rank MTV as their favorite cable channel, spending an average of 6 hours a week watching it. These numbers hold true across racial groups, with studies showing African American youth consuming two more hours of media content per day than white or Latino youth. In addition, nearly half of all black youth, and a third of Latino youth, watch rap music programming several days a week (a quarter watch daily).

On a typical day, a young person is faced with a media environment that includes more than 200 cable television networks, 5,500 consumer magazine titles, 10,500 radio stations, 30 million or more Web sites, and 122,000 newly published books. This is a global phenomenon. In China, teenagers spend an average of $50 billion annually; like their American counterparts, they spend about a third of their free time watching television, and they also read books, newspapers, and magazines extensively, which occupies 22 percent of their free time. That adds up to eight hours a week of media use for the average Chinese teen. One survey estimated that Shanghai teens are online more than 38 hours a week.

Following these trends, the spending power of South African teens is close to $1 billion a year, and "TV is the favored way to reach them," according to an international marketing guide. *Business Week* reports that 47 percent of India's population is under the age of twenty, with a spending power of $2.8 billion annually (some estimates put it as high as $16 billion). Indian teens watch an average of twelve hours of TV a week. Eighty-five percent of teens worldwide report watching music videos regularly, and 79 percent watch TV daily. As marketing consultant Elissa Moses puts it, "From Manhattan to Madras and Milan to Melbourne, teens who speak different languages (although many speak English) all speak the same dialect of global consumption." She identifies today's youth as "mediavores."

Our world is saturated by media to such a degree that analysis of the media often seems either pointless or overwrought. It's easy to dismiss the media as "background noise" or "just entertainment." But there are real ethical issues at stake when we stop to turn our attention to media representations of life. The growing research area of media studies has shown us that television and film shape culture and society, rather than simply reflecting existing social patterns. For years, the portrayal of people of color, especially in seemingly innocent entertainment programming like *Amos 'n' Andy* or films like *Gone with the Wind*, served to reinforce racist social hierarchies and support dominant political ideologies. Currently, media portrayals of people of Arab or Middle Eastern descent as terrorists and vandals have drawn parallel criticism. Latinos are practically invisible in contemporary media, and "nerd," "gangster," or "dragon lady" stereotypes continue to plague Asian American representations. Similarly, women's rights activists have drawn our attention to different facets of media representation that have stymied women's progress. And analyses of sports coverage have demonstrated the ways in which male violence and power are glorified while other aspects of masculinity are devalued.

But sex is trickier. One problem with thinking clearly about sexual content in teen media, and especially the sexualization of girls in the media, is that it often breaks down into a good/bad dichotomy: you're either *for* sex or *against* sex. Being at all critical or analytical of sexual representation in the media instantly seems to imply that you're in favor of censorship and opposed to sex in general, that you think girls should be wearing chastity belts and taking pledges of virginity. For those of us who don't see sex as a bugaboo, that's a crazy posi-

tion to be in. But it's equally noxious to be expected to celebrate "Girls Gone Wild" as empowering role models. So why
are we forced to choose between fundamentalist Christian
Joyce Meyers and pop singer Shakira as sexual guideposts in
the media arena? Why is there no middle ground?

In the quest for an understanding of the sexual mores at
work among girls and women in contemporary society—and
impelled by a feminist interest in girls' health and well-
being—I have been studying the media, gender, and sexuality
for more than a decade. What has become clear—yet is not
widely understood—is that media images of sexuality are
quite specific, and are driven by a variety of factors, the most
important of which is the for-profit structure in which they
operate. As a consequence, the version of sexuality that pro-
liferates in the mainstream media is not aligned with progressive politics, though the rhetoric around it offers the illusion
that it is.

For example, in the 1990s, the Spice Girls adopted the
slogan "Girl Power!" to market a highly conventional version
of femininity; historian Joan Jacobs Brumberg observed that
her college-age students related bikini-waxing to self-confidence; *Cosmopolitan* magazine, a publication famous for
instructing young women to please men sexually, describes its
audience as "fun, fearless females." Because of these rhetorical strategies, the very conservative version of sex celebrated
in these arenas is strongly linked with sexual emancipation
and even feminism.

Now more than ever, it is crucial to disentangle these
ideas. This is a political climate in which "moral values" are
trumpeted as the reason for electing candidates, and abstinence
is privileged over all other forms of contraception or sex education. It is a climate in which marriage is being defined in
strictly heterosexual terms and the rights of sexual minorities

are being denied. It is a climate in which legal access to abortion is under siege. Yet this climate is also breeding an explosion of sexually explicit images, in both mainstream and alternate venues. These political realities are framed in opposition to one another—"conservative" versus "liberal"—but if one pauses to critically examine the sexual imagery that is widely available, it is in fact not at odds with the conservative politics of the day. As indie journalist Lakshmi Chaudhry has pointed out, "In effect, the logic of the raunch culture is eerily similar to that Christian ideal of femininity, the Surrendered Wife. Both preach empowerment through acquiescence, promising greater happiness through the fulfillment of archetypal female roles."

The midriff-baring seductiveness of today's pop culture stars is framed in terms of liberation and power. There are of course such possibilities inherent in the idea of girls' accepting and expressing desire and pride in their bodies and embracing femininity. But a closer look at the imagery would reveal that only certain kinds of bodies are positioned as sexual, and only certain types of sexual display count as desirable—and that desirability is still very much a matter of appealing to a traditionally defined male gaze, despite the fact that most of the audiences for these images are female.

In terms of a politics of liberation, these themes work against the utopian vision of a world in which all women—regardless of race, age, weight, physical ability, or other categorization—might freely relish, express, and experience the joys of sex in ways they actively define, and in which all women have access to accurate, comprehensive, and beneficial knowledge about sex. This diverse and emancipated version of sexuality is the opposite of what I have identified as the Lolita Effect, a construction of sexuality that both exploits and limits sexual expression and agency, and is deliberately focused on young girls.

∽

The recognition of this reality is problematic on multiple fronts. Any discussion of sexuality (and especially children's sexuality) tends to fall toward one of two polar opposites: sexuality is either bad/dangerous/criminal or healthy/unproblematic/normal.

These categorizations force the entire discussion into pro- or anti-sex camps, drawing battle lines that leave many adults and children facing a seemingly irresolvable dilemma. Is it anti-sex to want to shield your child from certain kinds of sexual portrayals, in video games or in films? Is it pro-sex to want high school students to have access to contraception? Neither may be true, yet thoughtful decision making becomes almost impossible, given these limited options.

The dichotomy, of course, is a false one. The realities of children's sexual lives and cultural contexts lies somewhere between these two polar extremes. Both "pro-sex" and "anti-sex" sides have valid arguments that are not necessarily mutually exclusive. We can examine relationships among sexuality, legitimacy, culture, representation, and politics in ways that neither demonize children's sexuality nor flippantly dismiss the real problems inherent in a cultural climate that does not put a high priority on children's well-being. This is an increasingly urgent discussion, given the worldwide spread of AIDS, the globalization of the media, and the volatility of contemporary politics.

On the one hand, children and adolescents are sexual beings whose development into adulthood depends now, more than ever, on the ability to understand and enjoy their own sexual lives and to successfully avoid the pitfalls of teen pregnancies, sexually transmitted infections, and abusive relationships. On the other, it is equally important for adults to take some responsibility for guiding children and adolescents to adulthood. We need to be able to recognize and understand the potential dangers and problems in our social and cultural environment—problems that need to be analyzed, addressed, and even, at times, policed, in the interests of children's basic well-being and safety.

Government agencies, nonprofit organizations, and private agencies working for the benefit of children and adolescents are all doing significant work on these fronts. But philosophical differences often pit these groups against each other in unproductive ways.

For example, the Bush administration's funding for anti-AIDS programs, including the $15 billion President's Emergency Plan for AIDS Relief (PEDFAR) in Africa, Asia, and the Caribbean, is constrained by prohibitions against using any of the funds in relation to prostitution or drug use—a condition that has drawn criticism from AIDS workers, principally because prostitutes and intravenous drug users are key carriers of the virus. On the other hand, the Planned Parenthood Federation of America (PPFA) offers an informative and user-friendly Web site, including an excellent site for teenagers. But the site tends to be broadly critical of religious organizations, some of which are in fact working in support of progressive causes closely aligned with those of PPFA. In the scholarly realm, Judith Levine and James Kincaid argue that the claims of child sexual abuse are overstated, but the *New York Times* reports of increased pedophilia worldwide.

This tangle of agendas and viewpoints, often working at cross-purposes, further confounds our ability to assess the broader issues or come to any clear conclusions about them.

These "ground-level" complexities are complicated even more by debates about sexuality and gender in mainstream media and popular culture aimed at children and teenagers. Much of the analysis is resoundingly negative.

Experts on the subject recognize what many parents, teachers, and kids themselves can see: that movies, TV, magazines, and other media perpetuate sexist and harmful standards of beauty. They recognize that sexual portrayals in the media are often degrading to girls and women, and unnecessarily sensational. Most alarmingly, they recognize that the audiences for sexual media are getting progressively younger and therefore more easily influenced.

"In our hyper-commercialized consumerist society, there's virtually no escaping the relentless sexualization of younger and younger children," writes Rosa Brooks in a *Los Angeles Times* opinion piece. "[T]he sexualization of childhood is big business—mainstream mega-corporations such as Disney earn billions by marketing sexy products to children too young to understand their significance."

A *Boston Globe* news story declares, "Bombarded by sexualized cultural forces, girls are growing up faster than ever." The article describes thirteen-year-olds dressed as prostitutes for Halloween, wearing "fishnet stockings, halter tops, miniskirts, and high heels," and tracks increased sexual activity among schoolchildren. It attributes these phenomena to "a tidal wave of sexual messages targeting an ever-younger set of girls" generated by advertising, music television, and the Internet.

But on the flip side of these critiques is equally compelling research that indicates that girls do try to negotiate the tyrannical messages with which they are bombarded, weighing them against information and approaches from other sources. It's important to see media representations not just as harmful propaganda, but as opportunities to discuss these topics and appropriate behaviors with children. Both girls and boys seek out sexual media content not just for titillation but for information, as it is not readily available in other places. This has its up and down sides, depending on what exactly children are absorbing from these messages, many of which are unrealistic, medically inaccurate, and sometimes violent.

There are, of course, progressive media targeted to kids that offer a more diverse, broad-minded, and empowering vision of contemporary female sexuality—examples might include *New Moon* and *Teen Voices* magazines, the Canadian TV show *Degrassi: The Next Generation*, and Web sites like adiosbarbie.com. But many of these are low-budget, with small circulations and minimal exposure; kids' awareness is slight compared with their consumption of mainstream, commercial media products. Many girls also resist these messages, seeing them as moralizing or overly serious.

Nevertheless, some girls are finding ways to challenge sexist and repressive media portrayals and to assert control over the way they choose to express their sexuality. Some become media producers and explore these issues on Web sites and blogs, in 'zines, and on film. One example is the award-winning short film *A Girl Like Me*, made by a sixteen-year-old African American girl named Kiri Davis to question standards of beauty among girls of color. Girls' activist groups like Girls For a Change tackle social issues and address community problems. A group of teen girls in Australia recently founded Girls Together to combat unhealthy body images in the media. Girls are also vociferous and intelligent media critics. The University of Chicago's Black Youth Project found that 70 percent of African American girls were critical of the representations of black femininity in rap music and videos. (Interestingly, boys were generally positive about the representations of both men and women.)

Sexual realities today are complicated, to put it mildly. Homophobia runs rampant in our schools, and gay and lesbian teenagers still attempt suicide at higher rates than others. Promiscuity is celebrated among boys but remains an easy justification for denigrating girls. There is still a great deal of resistance to publicly acknowledging preadolescent sexuality and ongoing confusion about how best to deal with it. Despite the current availability of legal contraception for minors, more female than male high school students are having unprotected sex, and 60 percent of all·rape victims are girls under eighteen.

And on the whole, the mainstream media are carriers of the Lolita Effect. Most media aimed at adolescent and preadolescent girls focus on attracting male desire—"how to get the guy." And the route to that all-important end involves acquiring a specifically contoured body featuring large breasts, flat abs, and slender thighs; facial features approximating a Caucasian ideal; and a wardrobe and cosmetic stockpile whose elements must shift constantly in order to stay au courant. These stipulations are the basis of the Lolita Effect: a webwork of widespread myths about female sexuality, myths that displace reality and interfere with girls' ability to contend with their sexual development in proactive, diverse, healthy, and progressive ways.

In media studies, we don't consider myths of this sort to be fictions, though they seldom have a basis in fact. They have real impacts and real social ramifications; they become part of a social system that creates power hierarchies, spawns industries, and shapes our lives. Because of this, myth analysis is an important and specialized field of study, and it is crucial to recognizing, understanding, and combating the Lolita Effect.

But really, myth analysis shouldn't be the exclusive purview of scholars and academics. Myth analysis is a tool that everyone needs in today's media-inundated world. We need to deconstruct these myths—to figure out their origins, motives, and implications—to make good decisions about the media messages we receive constantly. In the realm of girls' sexuality, the myths of the Lolita Effect are so powerful and pervasive that it has become difficult to identify or confront them at all. But for girls, and the adults who care about them, being able to negotiate the thicket of these Lolita myths intelligently is a crucial part of growing up in the twenty-first century.

To help with that process, this book will provide a grounded, step-by-step approach to strategies for analyzing the myths of adolescent female sexuality in the media. I've identified five core "myths of sexuality" at work in the Lolita Effect: the myth of sex as girls' exhibitionism, the myth of sex in terms of an ideal body type, the myth of sex as linked to youth, the myth of sex as violence against women, and the myth of the male gaze. Each chapter of this book explores and explains a specific myth and how it works, while offering effective ways to challenge the detrimental effects of these myths in girls' lives.

In real life, sex is at its core a relationship, and a very complex one. It involves not just bodies but emotions, ethics, power, legal issues, and many other dimensions. Yet with the Lolita Effect, these complexities are blotted out. Sexuality is instead defined in strictly limited (and constraining) terms. So for many girls, relying on the media as a sexual guide is an iffy business: media imagery can be disheartening, anxiety-producing, stressful, disorienting. And even if it is not, in the realm of sexuality, the narrow definitions and body politics of the prevailing Lolita myth are a barrier to awareness, clarity, free thought, and effective action.

It is important not to buy into the Lolita Effect. There isn't a lot of existing research on how adults deal with these messages about girls, but it's clear that some parents accept and even encourage these ideas. One high-profile example is

Patsy Ramsey, JonBenét's mother. Another is Teri Shields, mother of the actress Brooke Shields, who notoriously allowed the eleven-year-old Brooke to appear nude as a child prostitute in the Louis Malle film *Pretty Baby*. Lynne Spears, Britney and Jaime Lynn Spears's mother, has recently fallen under a great deal of criticism as a parent in the wake of her daughters' highly publicized sex lives. Other parents are disturbed but resign themselves, recognizing the uphill battles involved in taking on the juggernaut of media culture. Girls themselves wrestle constantly with these issues; studies show they are certainly not passive victims of the media. But the images are so sophisticated and expertly contrived that their underlying dangers are often hard to spot.

If we're going to help girls gain control over their lives and their decisions, we need to try to broaden our perspectives and give our daughters the resources to make good choices. We need to be able to understand the media's role in defining sex and sexuality, and then deal with it in ways that work best for us. We can't do this without the right tools.

With this in mind, this book will rigorously examine the Lolita Effect. It will unveil the myths that make up the spectacle of girls' sexuality in mainstream pop culture and then offer strategies for responding effectively to this alluring, yet precarious, landscape.

42 /

Chapter 1

HOW LONG HAS THIS
BEEN GOING ON?
GIRLS AND THE MYTHS OF SEX

∞

> "You mean," she persisted, now kneeling above
> me, "you never did it when you were a kid?"
> "Never," I answered, quite truthfully.
> "Okay," said Lolita, "here is where we start."
> . . . She saw the stark act merely as part of a
> youngster's furtive world, unknown to adults.
>
> —VLADIMIR NABOKOV, *Lolita*

I MET NYDIA at a middle school in an impoverished Texas subdivision. She was a slender, pretty twelve-year-old, with long dark curls and sparkling eyes. Her teachers had identified her as "at risk": she was gang-affiliated and had been molested by a family member. But she had spoken up about the molestation, reporting it to authorities and succeeding in getting the perpetrator arrested. I admired Nydia for her resilience, obvious intelligence, and ambition.

Nydia's school had a high dropout rate, with many eighth-grade girls leaving because they were pregnant. "That ain't gonna happen to me," Nydia confided to me. "I ain't gonna have no baby. I don't want a baby messin' up my life. I'm going to wait till after college." But a few months later I learned that Nydia had become pregnant and dropped out of school.

Here are some things I've learned from talking to girls: You can't get pregnant if you jump up and down after intercourse. You can use a plastic sandwich bag instead of a condom —it works just as well. You don't need to use contraception if you don't have sex very often. If you haven't gotten AIDS after having sex a lot, you are immune to it. Douching with Coke prevents pregnancy. Oral sex isn't real sex.

Girls I talk to tell me these things seriously; they believe them to be true. They are sure they won't get pregnant or be at any kind of risk if they are careful and follow these guidelines. In the middle schools I visit, the myths about sex are powerful. They circulate more widely than the basic facts about human growth and reproduction offered in the mandatory health class on this topic. What's even more significant is that the girls—and their partners—are making dangerous choices based on their belief in these myths.

We're becoming increasingly aware that children are engaging in sexual activities that were formerly taboo. In late 2007, a Maine middle school began making contraception available to children as young as eleven. We're hearing stories of oral sex on school buses and "rainbow" slumber parties, in which teen girls put on different colors of lipstick and perform oral sex on a favored boy. Preschool teachers even describe toddlers simulating intercourse. It's easy to dismiss much of this as rumor or "moral panic," or to see these reports as the media's sensationalizing of unusual behavior. But the evidence is contradictory. Groups that monitor teen sex recognize that sexual activity now begins at eleven or twelve in the United States. "I don't think the public is yet willing to admit that adolescent sexuality really does begin in middle school," observed John Schlitt, executive director of the National

Assembly on School-Based Health Care, in a recent interview.

Recent investigations at an elite prep school in Massachusetts reveal that sex is a routine part of life among the students: "Group sex acts were just like showering together after practice," write the authors of *Restless Virgins*. Two recent U.S. surveys indicate that one in five young adolescents (younger than fourteen) has had sex and that many more are engaging in oral sex. Overall, the rate of teen sex in the United States has remained steady (at about 46 percent) since 2001, apparently unaffected by aggressive abstinence-only campaigns in the schools. All over the world, the age of first intercourse has been dropping steadily since the 1960s; it varies from country to country and is difficult to document because of the secrecy and stigma around it, but officially it stands at about sixteen in the United States, fifteen in Niger, and fourteen in the United Kingdom. Rates of teen pregnancy are rising in the United States, and they remain the highest of all industrialized countries; and the same goes for rates of sexually transmitted diseases (STDs)—over four million U.S. teens contract a sexually transmitted disease every year. Teenage pregnancy is a leading cause of death among girls aged fifteen to nineteen in developing countries, with more than one in six girls giving birth each year in these regions. The World Health Organization estimates that two-thirds of sexually transmitted diseases worldwide occur among teenagers and young adults.

These are not negligible numbers. Sexual activity is rapidly becoming a reality of childhood and adolescence; sexual awareness and activity are occurring at earlier and earlier ages. We need to face the facts.

But in most contemporary societies, we have a tendency to be scandalized by the idea of children and sexuality, a reaction that I see as the root of our problem. Because they are human, kids are sexual, with innate sexual impulses and responses, feelings and curiosities; this is a fact that was taken for granted in earlier centuries and reestablished by the "sexological" research of Sigmund Freud, Albert Kinsey, and Havelock Ellis. Even today, developmental psychologists and pediatricians are aware that sexuality is an integral aspect of childhood. But in one study, survey data showed that while 58 percent of students at a middle school were sexually active, 98 percent of their parents thought otherwise. It appears, then, that adults' reluctance to admit that children are sexually active may lead to increased misinformation and even more frequent or dangerous sexual activity.

We've got to wake up. To imagine that childhood is a pure and innocent state, closed off from the rest of the world, is to live in a fantasy of denial—more so now, when the models of the Victoria's Secret catalogues, Viagra ads, the raunchy scenarios in music videos, and the news of politicians being caught in a compromising position in public bathrooms are part of everyday life, even for preschoolers. As the humorist Brian Unger asked after the Larry Craig fiasco, "What do you say to a child who asks, 'Mommy, Daddy, why is my senator trying to get down with a dude in an airport bathroom?'"

Being horror-stricken by children's natural curiosity about sex is a dysfunctional response to a complex reality that calls for intelligent, proactive engagement on the part of involved adults. This is not to condone early sexual activity. But instead of wringing our hands or shrugging our shoulders helplessly, we should be thinking about how best to enable kids to develop healthy, sensible, and responsible understandings of sexuality at appropriate stages of their development. Sex is unquestionably part of their lives. The challenge for all of us is to figure out how best to help children negotiate this complicated, and often treacherous, terrain.

Children are being exposed to sexual messages at increasingly early ages, and the sexual content of children's media is on the rise: a study of prime-time TV showed that references to sex are common in the programs children and adolescents watch the most. A Kaiser Foundation study reported that in the last two decades sexual references in children's media have increased both in number and in their explicitness. One in nine TV shows for teens includes a scene in which intercourse is depicted or strongly implied. From the spring dance sex scenes in *Beverly Hills 90210* in the 1990s to hot-tub threesomes in *The O.C.* to quickie sex on a bar in the top-rated CW program *Gossip Girl*, casual "hookups" unencumbered by prophylactics or forethought—or even foreplay—are standard fare in teen TV. Very occasionally, the potentially serious consequences of these encounters are mentioned, but they are inevitably dismissed as mere worrymongering. And at least one study shows that the teen audiences of these shows believe the sexual situations to be "very realistic," and that the viewers strongly identified with the main characters.

Is sexual representation itself a problem? There are valid arguments to make in favor of informing children about sex; and sexual representation, many argue, is far less problematic than the gratuitous and horrific violence that is routinely incorporated into children's popular culture. But these arguments preclude any close analysis of *how* sex is being presented in the media, and by extension in our culture and society. Media representations of sex circulate widely and shape our understandings of the issue. Kids need to be informed about sex, especially when they are certain to encounter it in their everyday life, and it should not be a taboo. Nonprofit organizations like the Media Project recognize that kids are thinking about sex, that they are curious and largely uninformed, and that the media can be a powerful tool for education about sexual health and behaviors. On the other hand, the majority of the sexual messages kids are receiving are often not in their best interests.

Kids are evidently getting the message that sexual behavior is appropriate at very early ages. As they enter the 'tween years—eight to twelve—many of them begin to engage in sexual activity. But even before that, sexualized behaviors are becoming more evident. There is a partially biological reason for this, as puberty is starting at earlier ages for reasons that are still scientifically unclear. But there are also social and cultural factors that are sexualizing the sphere of childhood in ways that need to be considered and questioned. What factors are at work? What are the effects on children's lives?

As one study puts it, "Socializing forces ranging from parents to peers, from doctors to actors, and from television to the internet, present sex alternately as something forbidden and dangerous yet irresistibly desirable and pleasurable. Sex is showcased as a rite of passage that promises entry into the adult world. However, it is a journey rife with potential perils such as unwanted pregnancies and sexually transmitted diseases, and the road maps provided by one source of information may influence how the other sources are received: whether they are followed, questioned or rejected." It is also clear from the research that although teens and children live in an increasingly sexualized environment, teenagers and children are ignorant of the information that could help them to negotiate sex more skillfully and safely. Survey data indicate that nearly half of all teenagers are unaware of how to seek confidential health care services or birth control. They are largely uninformed about both the emotional and the physical consequences of sexual activity.

This was driven home to me recently when one of my college sophomores wrote an article on "hooking up," the current buzzword for casual sex. Her narrative waxed enthusiastic about the joys of impetuous, unfettered sexual encounters. She interviewed a number of college students for the story, and they all came through with happy, bawdy anecdotes of random sex with people they'd met in bars, during spring break in places like Acapulco and Daytona Beach, and at house parties. After I read her essay, I suggested that there might be aspects to the story that she hadn't considered: perhaps she ought to interview a counselor at the student health service about the risks of STDs, or speak with someone at the Rape Victim Advocacy Program about an unwanted or coerced "hookup," or talk with a police officer about the possible dangers of going off with a stranger to have sex in an unfamiliar city. My student looked flabbergasted. It was clear that none of these possibilities had occurred to her. She is part of a generation of adolescents who seem to understand sex only in binary terms: abstinence or indulgence, with no middle ground. While today's youth may be sharp media critics, they are not always in touch with realistic alternatives that would help them negotiate their own sex lives judiciously—especially if they have never been encouraged to look critically at the images and messages everywhere around them.

The middle ground is complex. Few adolescents, let alone children, are equipped to tackle this terrain on their own—they *are* children; emotionally, psychologically, and intellectually. They are, in general, not on par with adults. If we shrink from the realities of our sexualized environment, we renege on our obligation to help our kids to handle these issues with awareness and good sense. Without any countervailing voices, they will get their information from the sphere in which sexuality is most openly and appealingly represented: the commercial mass media.

In fact, they *do* turn to the media for sexual information, privileging the media over parents, peers, and other sources.

And, in fact, studies indicate that exposure to sexual media predicts young adolescents' sexual behavior: kids who watch highly sexualized media are about twice as likely to have sex early as kids who don't. This finding holds true across class and race.

The media, by and large, encourage young people to see sex as fun, impromptu, exciting, and uncomplicated—yet accessible only through consumerism, and available only to those kids who conform to specific ideals. Despite the efforts of some advocacy groups to push for honest, accurate depictions of adolescent sexual health in the media, the victories are few and hard-won. When clear, medically accurate information is presented, outcries of indecency often result in instant censorship of the material, as when *Seventeen* magazine recently ran a column on vaginal health that was pulled from supermarket shelves after parents complained it was "too graphic." Meanwhile, subtler, less "graphic" but more inaccurate and harmful depictions of sexuality go unchallenged.

This is because the profit motives of the media's construction of sex presents an obstacle to the realistic, practical information kids need to manage their own sex lives. Of course we don't want kids to be frightened of sex; it's important for everyone to find pleasurable, fulfilling sexual activity. At the same time, we don't want kids to see sex only as a fun-filled theme park that doesn't call for responsibility or sound judgment. And we need to think about why the sexual (or sexualized) activity of very young children is rapidly becoming a social norm.

This is a difficult issue to approach. Sex is complicated: physically, psychologically, emotionally, socially, and politically. Sexuality can't be addressed without a clear recognition of its place in the human experience and an acknowledgment of all its potential pleasures and risks. But when these issues are raised with respect to young kids, all hell breaks loose.

When pediatricians, policymakers, or parents' groups take progressive steps to deal with the realities of children's sex lives, they are met with vocal opposition, most often from conservative groups that seem to object to any public discourse about children and sex. For example, in 2006, cancer researchers suggested that the HPV cervical cancer vaccine be required for girls as young as ten in order to prevent the later occurrence of sexually transmitted viruses responsible for more than two hundred thousand deaths a year. Groups such as the Family Research Council voiced objections, advocating instead an abstinence-only approach to adolescent sex. Some groups continue to oppose anything but abstinence-only programs, despite credible research indicating that comprehensive sex education in schools is an effective strategy to help kids defer sexual activity, and that abstinence-only programs can actually cause more unsafe sex among teens. Abortion laws are another hotly contested area. While most medical groups, including the American Medical Association and the American Academy of Pediatrics, are opposed to requiring parental consent for underage girls' abortions, conservative groups insist that parents be notified despite the health risks and other potentially threatening fallout for the girls, who may delay the procedure or attempt to "take care of" the problem on their own.

On the other hand, when media literacy groups or advocacy projects point to the risks inherent in the explicit sexual representations available to children, they are dismissed as killjoys, eggheads, or closet conservatives intent on censorship and moral policing.

The bottom line: We live in an increasingly sex-saturated society, while lacking the ability to talk about children and sex in measured or meaningful ways.

We've got to get past this. In the United States, attitudes toward sex, especially toward children and adolescents and sex, are characterized by a mix of prudishness and laxity that work against each other in ways that leave kids bereft of resources. So they turn to the most easily available sources—their friends and the media—for clues about how to negotiate sexuality. While kids are becoming more sexually curious, and even sexually active, at earlier and earlier ages, they are underequipped to handle their experiences in ways that are in their own best interests, swept along on a surging cultural tide without working lifelines.

Perhaps because of these attitudes, we are in a crisis of ignorance: the United States has the highest rate of teenage pregnancies, births, and abortions, and the highest incidence of adolescent STDs in the industrialized world. More sexually active American adolescents report not using contraception than do adolescents in any other industrialized country—twenty percent of teenagers in the Unites States don't use contraception, compared with 4.1 percent of teenagers in the United Kingdom, 6.5 percent in Sweden, and 12 percent in France.

It's instructive to look at how adolescent and preadolescent sex is handled in other countries and cultures with lower teen birth rates and better records of adolescent sexual health. In France, Germany, and the Netherlands, teens are having sex at about the same rates as U.S. teens (with around half of all teens sexually active), but their pregnancy, abortion, and STD rates are minuscule; at least one study chalks this up to the fact that they are given comprehensive sex education in the schools and have greater access to contraception. Finland has an almost nonexistent incidence of STDs among teens and a very low teen pregnancy rate, because of an intensive public health campaign, access to low-cost or free health care, and coordination between the medical and the education communities. In Iceland, where teen birth rates are dropping but rates of illegitimate birth are rising, the family structure is such that young couples can live with their parents in intergenerational households, where babies are taken care of by family elders while teen parents attend school; this setup stays in place until the couple achieves financial independence and can set up a household. As the sociologist Stephen Wieting argues, this arrangement in fact sustains a "pre-marriage" tradition that in fact leads to greater stability, better care of children and teenagers, and higher levels of education and gender equality. One study of European teenagers found that in the countries studied, "adolescents are valued, respected, and expected to act responsibly. Equally important, most adults trust adolescents to make responsible choices because they see young people as assets, rather than as problems. That message is conveyed in the media, in school texts, and in health care settings."

This recognition of adolescents as vital members of society who should be trusted and treated with respect is a very different cultural position from the simultaneous panic and reverence that frames adolescence in the United States. In fact, Margaret Mead showed us almost a century ago that in cultures where adolescent and childhood sexuality is accepted as normal and the whole community is involved in monitoring appropriate sexual activity, adolescence is not a time of trauma, but a period of preparation for successful adulthood and integration into the community.

Does this mean that childhood sex is okay as long as the kids don't get pregnant or contract a disease? My answer is an emphatic no, because overall, the risks of early sexual activity are greater than the benefits. Even apart from the societal and personal consequences of teen pregnancies, and the medical and economic problems of widespread STDs, sex is linked with issues of personal power, emotional involvement, psychological development, and physical well-being in ways that are much more far-ranging than these basic public health issues. Kids just aren't equipped to negotiate these risks alone. That is why it is important to focus on the problems that stem from a cultural emphasis on sex without any real consideration of these related issues.

We've either got a wink-wink, nudge-nudge, attitude toward underage sex, or a fearful repressive reaction, and perhaps because of both, we fail to see the ways in which kids are generally getting odd, inaccurate, and often harmful messages about sex. As a culture, we seem terrified of any open discussion of children and sex. Our refusal to engage thoughtfully and critically with the realities of childhood and adolescent sexuality has encouraged a kind of sexual dysfunction that has serious repercussions, both for kids and for society at large.

One clear consequence of underage sexual activity is the impact on public health, along with the related economic impact. Teen pregnancy and sexually transmitted disease pose enormous health risks and costs to any society. Babies born to teenagers are more likely to be premature or seriously underweight, and therefore at higher risk of infant death, blindness, deafness, mental retardation, and cerebral palsy. Babies of teens are more likely to suffer from congenital problems, and to be malnourished, neglected, and abused in later life. Teen mothers are more likely to have high-risk pregnancies, and teens who engage in unprotected sex are also in danger of contracting STDs while pregnant, which can affect the baby. Teen mothers are less likely to complete their educations, and are therefore less employable and less likely to earn enough to support themselves or their children in later life. The estimated financial costs of teen pregnancy are in excess of $40 billion each year in the United States alone.

But the implications of sexual misinformation and early sexual activity extend far beyond the mere financial costs. Throwing contraception at kids, as in the case of the Maine middle school, is a Band-Aid solution at best. Lectures on abstinence are ineffective and unrealistic, particularly in light of the ongoing and ever-present media glorification of sex. Kids have complicated, multilayered, and profound associations with sex that need to be explored and brought to the surface in order to develop any kind of effective intervention strategies.

Research shows that many adolescents and preadolescents are aware of the basic "facts of life" but are ill-equipped to deal with real-life sexual situations. They lack the confidence to either refuse sexual activity or to insist on the use of contraception. They are terrified of seeming naïve or inexperienced. Clearly, the highly clinical and/or moralizing sex talks they get at school aren't helping them negotiate the real world of sex.

A related—and significant—aspect of teen and "'tween" sexual activity is the regressive and oppressive gender politics at play. Most discussions of oral sex among middle-school children refer to the fact that girls are "like a service station for boys," as Liz Perle, vice president of Common Sense Media, puts it. Girls in these sexual relationships are the "pleasure providers." There is little, if any, reciprocity in the relationships. "Equal-opportunity sex and mutually respectful sex have not come about," observes Barbara Dafoe Whitehead, a social historian of teen sexuality. Girls see their sexual role as providing boys with sexual satisfaction. Some girls report feeling a sense of power from initiating and providing sexual favors, but they don't appear to experience any physical pleasure or emotional fulfillment themselves. These trends are harmful for girls and get in the way of equitable, mutually fulfilling sexual and other relationships. They may also leave girls feeling reluctant to say no. Gender roles, power, and interpersonal communication are not part of their understanding of sex. These subtleties are not included in most sex-ed programs, yet they should be crucial elements in helping kids to handle their sexual lives.

Another neglected and largely unreported aspect of adolescents' sexual relationships is violence. The American Bar Association reports that one in five high-school girls has been physically and/or sexually abused by a boyfriend. Fifty-seven percent of U.S. teens know someone who has been physically, sexually, or verbally abusive in a dating relationship. Forty-five percent of girls know a friend or peer who has been pressured into either intercourse or oral sex. One in three teens reports knowing a friend or peer who has been hit, punched, kicked, slapped, or physically hurt by her dating partner. A sad side note to these statistics is the fact that only 7 percent of these girls would consider reporting the abuse to the police. Why, we ought to be asking, are violence and coercion so prevalent in adolescent sexual relationships? Why are the victims usually girls? And why won't they report it?

I've discussed teenagers in the passages above, but sexual activity before the teen years is becoming more prevalent and is more problematic. From the Peek-a-Boo Pole Dancing Kit to the sexy French maid Halloween costumes sold in toddler sizes to the Playboy bunny motifs on children's accessories, an overtone of sexuality is shaping girlhood, and it's a specific, regressive version of sexuality—one that ties female sexuality to sex work, and establishes that connection as part of childhood. It's hard to argue that this is a healthy, progressive, or unbiased version of sex.

These cultural artifacts and images are not only engaging children in an adult performance of sexuality, they are sending a powerful message to adults: that sex, or more specifically sex work, is an acceptable part of childhood. These cute, child-sized accoutrements of sex work are potent symbols that make the idea of childhood sex—sexy little girls—culturally acceptable.

This is happening in an environment in which child pornography is on the rise—the volume of such material seized from computers is doubling annually, according to a recent *New York Times* story. In the last five years, the National Center for Missing and Exploited Children has collected over eight million images of explicit child pornography. Austrian authorities recently broke a global child porn ring involving seventy-seven countries. And there is empirical evidence that the use of child pornography is linked with actual child molestation and abuse.

These trends indicate a sexual attitude toward girls that should trouble us all. These problems are evident in every country in the world, and the data are too serious to ignore.

Forty to forty-seven percent of sexual assaults worldwide are perpetrated against girls aged fifteen or younger. UNICEF estimates that up to 21 percent of all children have been sexually abused, with girls far more likely to be abused than boys. Accurately estimating the prevalence of sexual abuse and violence in the developing world is difficult due to the limited amount of research on the subject, but adolescents and young women in many parts of the world experience abuse in the forms of domestic violence, rape and sexual assault, sexual exploitation and sex trafficking, and/or female genital cutting.

Child sex trafficking is on the rise all over the world. UNICEF estimates that 1.2 million children are trafficked every year; 90 percent of them are girls. Mexico's social service agency reports more than 16,000 children engaged in prostitution, with tourist destinations being among those areas with the highest number. In Lithuania, up to 50 percent of prostitutes are believed to be minors. Children as young as age eleven are known to work as prostitutes. The BBC reports that in South Africa, hundreds of girls have been kidnapped, gang-raped, and prostituted, due to widespread myths about girls and sex. In the Congo, the *New York Times* reports, savage rapes of girls occur daily, some so violent that the girls' reproductive and digestive systems are damaged beyond repair. "Some of these girls whose insides have been destroyed are so young that they don't understand what happened to them," says a Congolese gynecologist; the victims are as young as three years old. The International Labor Organization estimates that 15 percent of India's 2.3 million commercial sex workers are children under fourteen, most of them girls. "They are sexually exploited in brothels, massage parlors, hotels, escort services, private houses known as 'madhu charkas,' railway stations, bus stations, streets, public parks, and more recently in circuses." Worldwide, girls are the targets of sexual abuse and exploitation on a barbaric scale.

Mary Pipher, the author of the groundbreaking book *Reviving Ophelia*, and other analysts of girls' lives, have been criticized for focusing only on the negative aspects of girls' adolescence and sexuality. Their critics argue that adolescence can and should be seen as a time of promise, potential, and positive growth. And for many girls, it is true that adolescence is a period of pleasure and progress. Childhood and adolescence are vital life stages when both boys and girls experience rich and rapid change. The psychologist Jean Piaget saw childhood as a time of invention, creativity, and ceaseless learning. "That humanity which is revealed in all its intellectual splendor during the sweet and tender age of childhood should be respected with a kind of religious veneration. It is like the sun which appears at dawn or a flower just beginning to bloom," wrote the pioneering educator Maria Montessori. Children and adolescents have almost limitless capabilities of strength, intellect, resilience, and inventiveness. This holds true for children in all racial, cultural and class groups. It is clearly important *not* to frame childhood, adolescence, or sex in purely dark and dire terms. Some girls grow up in safety, loved and secure, privileged and prospering. This is what we want for all our girls—and boys.

At the same time, the problems that the research reveals are real, and it would be an ostrich-like move to focus only on the kind of adolescence that is untouched by adversity or trauma and thus to blithely ignore the cultural, political, economic, and structural realities that constrain and jeopardize many girls' lives, especially girls who live on the precarious margins of society, girls who are not of the First World, who are not privileged by class, who express non-mainstream sexual preferences, or whose bodies transgress social norms in ways that can result in abuse. The goal of this kind of recognition is not to define girls as helpless victims of an unjust world order, nor is it to blame the girls themselves. Rather, the goal is to confront the situations, define them accurately, and then devise effective counterstrategies. These strategies would foster girls' own capacity to question the status quo, resist peer pressure, and make positive choices. They would teach girls to negotiate a world that often operates at their expense. And they would create solidarity among those who want to work in kids' best interests.

There is nothing regressive, patronizing, or disempowering about such aims. Critiquing the status quo is useful, energizing, and crucial if change is to happen. My own experiences with girls, including my own daughters and their friends, have shown me that girls are keenly aware of the ways in which culture and society impact their lives: they are intelligent, thoughtful, lively, perceptive, and eager to engage in spirited discussions of any number of topics. Critical perspectives appeal to them. But often, they have had little opportunity to express their own understandings of their culture, or to give voice to critical viewpoints.

In every society, girls' sexuality is overemphasized, while other attributes take second place. This overemphasis need not result in violence—but it often does. This overemphasis need not result in severe constraints on girls' lives—but it often does. A key question is: why?

To answer that question, we need to think of sexuality not as a biological fact, but as a cultural construction. How do we think about girls' sexuality? Where do we get our ideas about it? How do we understand it—as a part of physical development, as a part of culture, as a characteristic, as an expression? How do we talk about it—with girls, as well as about them?

The rapes of girls in South Africa are linked to a myth about girls' sexuality: that AIDS can be cured or prevented by having sex with a virgin. The prostitution of young girls in Southeast Asia is linked to the myth of the "Lotus Blossom," the obedient, feminine, and servile Asian girl. In the United States, the "myth of the slut" operates to ostracize and humiliate adolescent girls, as Emily White describes in her powerful book on the topic. She calls the slut label a "horrific hallucination" fueled by myths about girls' bodies.

Myths are, by definition, untrue. But myths cannot be dismissed as fictions or fairy tales, because they have a real impact on girls' lives. When sexuality is understood only in terms of cultural and social myths that operate in ways that are counterprogressive, hidebound, and restrictive, we have a problem. It is imperative, therefore, to examine the myths.

Myths are transmitted in various ways in different cultures, societies, and historical moments. A powerful mythmaking apparatus in contemporary society is the mass media industry. As the cultural critic Douglas Kellner writes, "Radio, television, film, and the other products of media culture provide materials out of which we forge our very identities, our sense of selfhood; our notion of what it means to be male or female; our sense of class, of ethnicity and race, of nationality, of sexuality, of 'us' and 'them.' Media images help shape our view of the world and our deepest values: what we consider good or bad, positive or negative, moral or evil. Media stories provide the symbols, myths, and resources through which we constitute a common culture."

We live in a media-saturated environment. Yet most of us don't stop to think about the media as a source of myth. In the following chapters, I will examine the five core myths of the sexy girl in mainstream media and discuss their implications for girls' lives, while offering strategies to help girls analyze and challenge them. These are the myths that work to perpetuate the Lolita Effect.

Chapter 2

THE FIRST MYTH
IF YOU'VE GOT IT, FLAUNT IT!

> I had left my Lolita still sitting on the edge of the
> abysmal bed, drowsily raising her foot, fumbling at
> the shoelaces and showing as she did so the nether
> side of her thigh up to the crotch of her panties—
> she had always been singularly absent-minded, or
> shameless, or both, in matters of legshow.
> —VLADIMIR NABOKOV, *Lolita*

FOUR-YEAR-OLD Chelsea likes to compliment her best friend on looking "hot." Nine-year-old Lexi loves her Pussycat Dolls T-shirt, emblazoned with the tagline "Don'tcha wish your girlfriend was hot like me?" Middle-school girls—and boys—quickly identify "a hot body" as a marker of ideal femininity.

The goal of hotness is pervasive in girl culture: recently, the *New York Times* profiled a group of accomplished teenage girls: they were varsity athletes, academic achievers, classical musicians, and volunteer workers, all at once. In their classrooms, they wrote essays on Kierkegaard and Nietzsche; away from school, they aced piano competitions and starred in theater productions. Yet they readily admitted that it was much more important to be "hot" than smart. "Effortlessly hot," as one of them explained.

Achieving "hotness" is more complicated, in many ways, than mastering a sonata or getting a high SAT score. The term is everywhere in kid culture: teen magazines use "hot" as the adjective of choice to promote everything from new workouts to fashion to movie idols; the FOX teen choice awards include "choice hottie female" and "choice hottie male" awards; Talib Kweli's "Hot Thang" has ridden high on the music charts; the chain store Claire's advertises "what's hot 4 school!" Clearly, "hotness" is a hot commodity among youth.

To be hot is to be sexy. Of course, there's a progressive and exciting element to this—for too long, we've failed to recognize the importance of girls' sexuality. It shouldn't be shameful or scandalous for girls to acknowledge and express their desires, and it's important for girls to be conscious of themselves as sexual beings who deserve to find pleasure through sex.

But are four-year-olds, or nine-year-olds, or even middle-school girls entering their teens, in a position to think through the ways in which they are expressing their sexuality, anticipate the responses to it, and handle the implications of their decisions? Is it repressive—or patronizing—to have qualms about young girls' gleeful embrace of the "hot" body and its accoutrements? Is it best to give them free rein in the blissful belief that the pursuit of "girl power" will enable them to make all the right moves?

Of course not.

Women and girls have questioned and challenged the sexual double standard for decades now, and, perhaps because of this, we're at a moment where sexiness really matters to girls today; you'd have to be pretty oblivious not to notice the place it occupies in girl culture. The conventional scientific wisdom is that interest in sex escalates as children approach adolescence; this is a biological viewpoint that connects the hormonal shifts and physical maturation of puberty with an increased interest in sex. But now sexuality marks preadolescence and childhood, too, and for many adults, this is justifiable cause for alarm. In today's world, children as young as eight report worrying about being popular with the opposite sex; first-graders describe being sexually harassed by classmates; and by middle school, kids are steeped in sexual jargon, images, and exploration. Sex educator Deborah Roffman argues that little girls start wanting to look good for others at age four. And as the psychologist Sylvia Rimm has observed, "There's *plenty* of sex taking place among middle schoolers today."

There's a biological explanation for some of it: the age of puberty has been steadily falling since the nineteenth century; for girls, who typically mature faster than boys, the age of first menstruation has dropped by three to four months every decade since 1850. In general, girls now enter puberty between the ages of eight and thirteen. (In the United States, girls of color mature earlier than white girls, and these trends have been noted all over the world.) There is no evidence that this trend is slowing—it's likely that the age of puberty will continue to drop. Experts have no definitive explanation for this phenomenon, but in part the hormonal and physical changes that are occurring at younger and younger ages may contribute to the increasing sexualization of childhood.

Psychologists, pediatricians, and others who study child development are aware that kids' cognitive maturation is not keeping pace with these physical changes. Sex is complicated and emotionally fraught; it is intriguing; it can feel pleasurable and transgressive, but it carries consequences and risks that young children are not well prepared to recognize or handle. And socially and culturally, we don't have support systems in place that offer children the guidance they need to cope with either their rapidly changing bodies or an increasingly sexual environment.

The media aimed at girls have been quick to capitalize on all this—they work hard to ensure that sexiness is central to girls' consciousness, and they target preadolescents as well as teenagers with sexually charged messages. Teen visitors to the popular ELLEgirl Web site are alerted to the "sexiest of lingerie lines," featuring transparent bras and thong panties; they're also informed that school hallways are "a giant catwalk" that they need to "work," and that they'll turn boys' heads if they wear "sexy attire" to school. At the same time, on the Bratz.com Web site, preschoolers learn that to "look like a movie star" they'll have to don skintight spangled gowns with plunging necklines and front slits that run all the way up to the crotch. Disney's Hannah Montana videos on YouTube are followed by hundreds of fan messages that gush about how "hot" the fourteen-year-old performer looks. The Teen Choice Awards music nominees feature videos like Ne-Yo's *Because of You*, with explicit scenes of foreplay apparently inspired by a plethora of barelyclad women. And on gURL.com, a Web site that describes itself as "a leading online community and content site for teenage girls," the message boards include photographs of the adult movie actress Jenna Jameson and postings from teenage girls who say they want to be porn stars like Jenna when they grow up.

In a way, this is not surprising; the ideals of femininity in soft porn—a kittenish innocence coupled with exhibitionism—lie on a clear continuum with the ideals of femininity presented in media aimed at younger girls; the bodies on display, in particular, are almost indistinguishable. As Sharon Lamb and Lyn Mikel Brown point out, when preteen idols like Disney's Hilary Duff (and Britney Spears before her) "get repackaged into an adult form of girl, almost always soft porn, marketers are hoping your daughter won't bat an eyelid."

The messages about sex that girls are getting from these media tap into the sexual awareness and anxiety that mark the 'tween and early teen years. The girls who comprise these media audiences are already aware that sex is important; that desirability is vital to social success; that in their peer groups, sexual badinage and knowledge will give them an edge; and that "hot" is the highest accolade a girl can get. Over the past century, our culture's preoccupation with girls' bodies has intensified, and girls themselves have become evaluated in terms of their sex appeal; for young girls, sex "is something engaged in for bragging rights," as journalist Ariel Levy puts it. These messages have multiple sources—they include peers, popular culture, and sometimes even parents—but the underlying theme is clear: hotness matters. Little Chelsea in her preschool playgroup knows this as well as any teenager does.

Yet the definition of "hot" is murky, and the steps to its achievement are fraught with angst. On one hand, hotness is culturally emphasized as an important—perhaps even *the* most important—characteristic of girlhood; on the other, simultaneously, the specter of the slut or the "ho" still haunts young women. Girls are sometimes celebrated for their sexual exploits and for projecting sexual availability, but they are also isolated, tormented, and stigmatized for perceived promiscuity. There is also the very real danger of sexual violence and abuse that perpetrators may justify because of a victim's projection of sexual availability. Walking the line between acceptable hotness and unacceptable sluttiness is the almost impossible challenge presented to today's girls. Understanding female desire and female empowerment as part of that picture is even more troublesome, particularly when girls think they are expected to desire—or to pretend to desire, or be proud of having engaged in—sex, often unreciprocated or unfulfilling sex. Now that these issues have impinged upon childhood, more questions arise: preteens barely know what sex is, but the culture is coaching them to project a very adult sexuality, and they respond with justifiable glee. Grade-school girls freely use the term "hot" without fully understanding its implications; seven-year-old Jeannine translates it as "cute" and explains that wearing a cleavage-enhancing bra makes a girl look "hotter."

While "hot" is a generic term that has a variety of meanings, at its core, it's about bodies and, ultimately, about sex. It's pointless to wonder whether children who are in grade school or middle school *should* be thinking about sex: the reality is that sex pervades their world.

For children to take an interest in sex is not out-of-the ordinary or scandalous. Even toddlers "play doctor" to explore each others' bodies and mimic intercourse, though scholars are still debating what constitutes "normal" sexual behavior in young children. Sex is part of life, so it is bound to surface in different ways at different developmental stages; it is not cause for alarm unless there is harm or abuse involved. Of course, sexuality needs to be dealt with in ways that are appropriate for the age and maturity of the child, the cultural and social context, and above all, the ethical implications of the situation, but sex per se cannot reasonably be viewed as harmful to minors.

And yet, there is widespread (and well-founded) consternation about children's sexuality in current times—particularly girls' sexuality. The American Psychological Association even convened a task force in 2007 in response to public concerns about the overt and problematic sexuality in girls' culture. Importantly, the task force made a distinction between "healthy sexuality" and "sexualization"—a difference that transforms sex into myth. This difference is key to understanding and challenging the Lolita Effect.

∞

Adult concern about girls' sexuality is not generally about sex (though that is the terror that lurks beneath the feelings of panic). Rather, it's about the *projection* of sexuality—the signals that girls send out about their sexuality, often naïvely, in response to the prevailing media and marketing trends, signals that adults fear will attract harmful sexual attention. As the columnist Rosa Brooks lamented in the *Los Angeles Times*, "old-fashioned American capitalism . . . is busy serving our children up to pedophiles on a corporate platter." Jill Parkin of Australia's *Courier Mail* decries the new trend of "little girls dressed as sex bait."

These charges open up quite a can of worms. Can marketers in fact "serve" children up to pedophiles? Is there any real danger in young girls wearing low-cut, skimpy, or "trashy" clothes, or is this just a harmless fashion trend designed to raise parental hackles, like so many others in the past? Could it even be seen as a feminist move toward embracing a femininity or "girliness" scorned by previous generations and linking it to power rather than passivity?

For some social critics, it is actually possible to see the alarm over girls' fashion as a "moral panic," a furor over nothing. Kerry Howley, a columnist for the online magazine *Reason*, argues, "A sixth-grader in a short skirt could well be a sign of a sexually dysfunctional society, a pie-eyed Paris in the making. Or she could simply suggest that eleven-year-olds pick an outfit the same way they long have, hoping to find acceptance within a social group and signal mastery over a shared culture. Fashion can suggest sexual availability, or it can imply inclusion. Are they dressing for men, or for one another?" One could, Howley posits provocatively, interpret children's embrace of these sexual symbols as a form of "grrrl power" that allows girls to take control of their sexuality at an early age. The manufacturers of the controversial Bratz dolls offer the same line of reasoning, contending that Bratz "are about self-expression, self identity."

This is a seductive argument, especially for those of us who are fiercely opposed to any repression or stigmatization of girls' sexuality. Could it be that toddlers in lacy G-strings are being empowered to take charge of their own sex lives? Could it be that French-maid outfits and pole-dancing kits for preteens are helping to fight the feminist struggle for equality?

Put in these terms, the idea becomes laughable, although it is certainly the argument that is being made as these narrowly defined versions of girls' sexuality continue to proliferate and circulate in our culture. When you stop to think about it, it becomes clearer that it is not girls' sexuality in and of itself that is a problem; the problem is that the *expression* of girls' sexuality seems to be possible only within an extremely restrictive framework. Girls' sexuality, it seems, has to comply with the markers of sexuality that we recognize, and it cannot be manifested, recognized, or mobilized in other, potentially more empowering and supportive, ways.

This is a form of mythmaking. When a concept as complicated, multilayered, and diverse as sex is reduced to expression through a single channel—the one involving lacy lingerie, skintight clothing, and the rest of what Ariel Levy calls "the caricatures of female hotness"—it has to be seen as a construction or a fabrication, in which the complexities of the concept are flattened out into a single, authoritative dimension, and in which all other possibilities are erased.

So it is important to think about the ways in which girls are being coached to aspire to "hotness" by popular culture, and how the commercialized definitions of "hot" offer beguiling but problematic representations of sex that limit its vast and vital potential.

Sex and sexuality are varied, complex, and multifaceted; they have inspired poetry, music, literature, theory, philosophy, law, and theology; their nuances and manifestations are multiple and mysterious, even after centuries of study. Sex is both natural and cultural; it operates differently in different cultures, contexts, and eras. It is part of being human, and it will be a force to reckon with as children grow older; it's important for them to understand it, to come to clear conclusions about it, to have the resources and reasoning to cope with its exigencies. It would be senseless to treat "sex" as a simple concept. It is not to be feared—it's shameful that for thousands of years, girls' sexuality was treated with fear and loathing. In many ways, it's a positive development that girls' sexuality is emerging into public spaces. Now we can talk about it, and we can try to do so without shame or terror.

As a result, media sources are key to such discussions. More than we would like to admit, kids trust the media about sex. Even when children are not alert to the fact that they are getting sexual information from the media, the messages continue to come in loud and clear. Sometimes older kids will deny that they are influenced by the media, but they're quick to acknowledge that most other kids are (in media studies, we call this the "third person effect"—the media are perceived as influential, but only for nebulous "third persons"). For girls, in particular, the media are guides to successful, peer-endorsed femininity.

The clearest message to girls from virtually all contemporary media is that being hot is a social imperative, and to be hot requires a specific set of prescribed attributes. For it's also commonly understood that not everyone *is* hot—hotness is a quality reserved for the select and favored few. So hotness creates hierarchies of sexuality, a problem to begin with, as sex would function best outside of a ranking system.

How do we know who's "hot"? Teen and preteen media aren't shy about labeling hot people, in just the way products and trends are anointed with the same adjective. The "hotties" are identified as such on magazine covers, in advertisements, and on Web sites. But the slightly less blatant marketing of designated performers—actors, singers, sports stars, and models—adds to the myth of "hotness" and cements the definition of ultimate sexuality.

Sexuality, in these media constructions, is about *appearing* sexy. "Desires are the pulses of the soul," wrote the Puritan preacher Thomas Manton in the seventeenth century, but the soul has nothing to do with desire in its twenty-first-century media-generated form. It's all about looks and arousal; hot girls are "eye candy," and sexuality involves public sexual performance.

It is possible to construe sex in terms of intense intimacy and private desire; sexual attraction can be triggered by the subtlest of synergies, by chimerical connections, by mutual understanding, even by something as subtle as a glance. But this is not the version of sex preferred by the media. Hotness, in its media-driven definition, is achieved only by visibility. From the *Girls Gone Wild* franchise to the pages of teen magazines and dolls sold to preschoolers, baring the female body publicly defines sexuality in contemporary media.

∽

This process of definition is the first step in mythmaking. We tend to think of myths as stories of the past: fictions that are told to illustrate a moral, or to offer some understanding of bygone beliefs. But it's important to be aware that myths function powerfully in our lives today, though we often don't recognize them as such because they are so ingrained in our routines and our consciousness. We seldom question reality, and reality is therefore built on unquestioned assumptions.

There are societal forces—the law, religion, educational institutions, and, increasingly, the mass media—that work to construct our reality, using rhetoric and discourse to make arguments that form the basis for our social norms. Sometimes these arguments are open and transparent, as in a court decision, and sometimes they are subtle and covert. In media studies, we use myth analysis to identify the ways in which myths are constructed and reinforced by the texts and images that circulate widely in our society. We look at how ideas are conveyed through these images, and how texts and images are deliberately linked in order to ensure that viewers interpret them correctly—which is to say, in accordance with the intentions of the message's creator.

Words can subtly instruct viewers to interpret images in certain ways. In her brilliant analysis of women's magazines covers, Ellen McCracken points out that the typical cover images on *Cosmopolitan* magazine could easily be seen as trashy, unsophisticated, or even funny—but the magazine's title, *Cosmopolitan*, links the images with sophistication and glamour. In the same way, whatever picture adorns *In Style* magazine is inferred to *be* in style because of the compelling rhetorical impact of the title and the supporting cover lines.

In the same way, "hotness" or sexiness is relentlessly linked to particular images in Western popular culture. For example, in a recent issue of *Seventeen*, the top-circulating teen magazine (which is read by girls as young as ten), a photo fashion spread titled "Sexy and Seventeen" featured a series of slender Caucasian models in clothes that revealed their under-wear—sweaters unbuttoned to expose brassieres, models wearing only a top and panties or a camisole with tap pants. The "sexy" headline linked the body displays with desirability. "Dare to bare," urges a headline in *Teen Vogue* that features teen girls in minuscule mini-skirts, their body-baring bodaciousness contrasted with a little girl wearing a frumpy mid-calf-length plaid skirt. The message there is that exhibitionism is daring, while conservative clothing is childish and boring. "Viva glam!" crows an ad for M.A.C. cosmetics, in which a buxom model poses in tiny strips of cloth that barely cover her curves, again celebrating semi-nudity as the path to glamour.

Appealing to younger audiences, the Bratz line of dolls, which are marketed to preschoolers with the tagline "Girls with a passion for fashion," sport fishnet stockings, bustiers, and tiny miniskirts, prompting *New Yorker* writer Margaret Talbott to observe, "They look like pole dancers on their way to work at a gentlemen's club"—but the slogan is calculated to persuade us that their sleazy attire is the epitome of fashion. In the children's TV cartoon *Winx Club*, the brave, kind, and magical fairies whose mission is to save the world are outfitted like 1970s pole dancers, in thigh-high platform boots, hot pants, and tube tops, again linking ideal femininity with hypersexual body display. The FOX television series *The O.C.*, popular with teenagers for four seasons, featured frequent scenes of girls in their underwear or other states of undress; these are the girls designated as objects of desire for the boys in the cast.

Music videos—by both male and female artists—almost inevitably feature semi-clad women and fully clad men, and the lyrics establish these women as desirable and sexual. This pattern has been documented in a number of research studies, and at the time of this writing, the top three videos on MTV—

50 Cent's "Ayo Technology," T. I.'s "You Know What It Is," and Maroon 5's "Wake Up Call"—all contain images of female strippers performing for fully dressed male viewers; all of the representations of women in these videos conform to the porno version of sexuality that involves skimpy clothing or stripping and sexual servitude to men, while the lyrics establish the men's voracious desire for these women. The top videos on *Billboard*'s R&B/Hip-hop charts are similar in content: Plie's "Shawty" enthusiastically describes raping and beating women who appear to be prostitutes, decked out in fishnet hose and hot pants.

In these representations, sex is purely physical and based on female exhibitionism; this physicality can trigger high emotion, which is often violent (a subject discussed later in this book); but the women's sexuality never translates as anything other than a stimulus. It has nothing to do with intimacy, mutual respect, or love, ideas that have become virtually unthinkable in the arena of contemporary sexuality. The construction of the myth of female sexuality in music videos connects sex directly with female body displays and male desire, and disconnects it from "softer" emotions like tenderness or affection.

This is not to say that such emotions are essential components of a fulfilling sexual relationship (though that would be my own preference). There are other, progressive or even transgressive ways to look at all this: women are, in fact, as visually oriented as men; women and girls can and do take pleasure from viewing male bodies, but women are rarely, if ever, represented as "gazers" in music videos. The women are not independent actors; their choice of attire or profession always hinges on male viewing and male approval. Male bodies are never on display for women. Nor is there any variation from heterosexuality. Gone, too, is the notion of mutual attraction: the women are on display for the men, and the men are the arbiters of women's hotness. How, then, are women sexually empowered, when the only path to empowerment lies in attracting male lust by conforming to the conventions of the striptease?

Similarly, movies popular with teens riff on sex with scenes where boys are clothed but girls are not—even though these are often rated R, indicating that they are intended for young adults, they are routinely seen by much younger viewers. The 1999 film *American Pie*, widely lauded as a groundbreaking teen sex comedy, is an example of this pattern: throughout the film, girls' bodies are on display for male viewing pleasure, as in a notorious scene where the film's male protagonist, Jim, sets up a Webcam so that he and his friends can watch a female classmate undress. After the boys have spent considerable breathless time watching the girl, Nadia, undress and masturbate, the tables are seemingly turned: Nadia asks Jim to strip for her. But at this point, spectatorship becomes travesty: Jim's nutty striptease dance is wholly ludicrous, the sexual charge of the earlier scene is sabotaged, and things devolve into pure farce. Female sexual spectatorship or empowerment are therefore not valid concepts in this film or any other mainstream movie intended for a teen audience.

On the whole, the boys are the ones who initiate sex. Even in *American Pie*, the one female character who acts on her desire and takes control of a sexual encounter is herself portrayed as wholly undesirable—a "band geek." The truly sexy girls are the ones who are on display for men and who, themselves, cannot take the initiative sexually and are ambivalent about or unaware of their own desires. The film offers, overall, a message of female sexual passivity and male sexual agency.

Films intended for much younger audiences echo the same tropes, though less explicitly, featuring women's bodies on display for fully clothed men. Disney cartoon heroines—Ariel in *The Little Mermaid*, Jasmine in *Aladdin*, Pocahontas in the film of that name—are frequently scantily clad, and their body proportions mimic those of centerfolds (Pocahontas has been called a "buckskin Barbie" by one critic), with large breasts, wasp waists, and long legs. The corresponding male cartoon characters, of course, are fully clothed.

The core message is not hard to recognize: if you're female, your desirability is contingent on blatant body display.

∞

Girls' bodies *are* beautiful, and there is nothing shameful or shocking about them. But then again, all bodies can be seen as beautiful: there is great beauty in the range, the musculatures, the skin tones, the stunning diversity of human bodies. Bodies, too, are utterly ordinary. In many cultures, exposure of the body—mothers breastfeeding in public, or naked infants and small children—is natural and uncomplicated. Ideally, all bodies would be accepted as facts of existence. If bodies were to be celebrated, they would be celebrated in equitable and wide-ranging ways: all sorts of bodies would be on display, for all sorts of reasons; viewing pleasure might well be one of them. None of this would matter, if power and prejudice didn't enter the picture.

But they do. The display of female nudity is not a new feature of Western society. The art historian John Berger traces the history of the female nude in classical art, and he recognizes it as a patriarchal ploy: the painters and the patrons of art were traditionally men, and to bare the female body was to shore up masculine power in society. Representations of nude women added up to one key point, in Berger's analysis: "Men act and women appear." Stripping women and putting them on display in paintings turned women into submissive sexual objects. "Women are there to feed an appetite, not to have any of their own," he points out. Edouard Manet's famous painting *Dejeuner sur l'herbe*, for example, focuses on a supine nude woman surrounded by animated, fully clothed men; Eugene Delacroix's *The Death of Sardanapalus* depicts nude women being raped by clothed men, watched by their king.

Contemporary nudes—the women of pornography, of art, of advertising and marketing—are descendants of this patriarchal tradition. The argument for female beauty is a pretty flimsy one: men's bodies are beautiful, too, and could easily be displayed as widely and insistently as women's But they aren't—and the few public artistic depictions we have had of the male body have, again, been done by men in a homoerotic context (think of Michelangelo's *David* or the photography of Robert Mapplethorpe). But despite years of lore, women are as acutely visual, and as visually stimulated, as men; feminist scholarship has firmly established the existence of the female spectator, the active viewer. Any acknowledgment of women's active role in the dynamics of attraction would put sex on a more equitable footing, but this role is never acknowledged as viable in the mainstream media. Women's bodies are to be displayed, and this display is the basis for sexual attraction, according to the myth.

Representations of sex are to be expected in our society, just as other aspects of life—friendship, parenthood, religion, sports, violence, and everything else—are, and should be, represented. Censorship is not the answer: repressing or stifling free expression is an ostrich move that can only fail as a response to a problem. But it is not censorship to critique representations that may be harmful or offensive.

Publicly displaying the nude body has deep roots in power games. In 1809, a South African woman named Saartje Baartman was exhibited naked in a cage, like an animal, to audiences all over Europe and the United Kingdom. "Prancing in the nude, with her jutting posterior and extraordinary genitals, she provided the foundation for racist and pseudo-scientific theories regarding black inferiority and black female sexuality. The shows involved Saartje being 'led by her keeper and exhibited like a wild beast, being obliged to walk, stand, or sit as ordered.' " Her nudity was used to tacitly reinforce roles of racial and sexual subjugation. Early European anthropologists photographed naked natives of non-Western cultures in order to demonstrate their inferiority and reinforce the superiority of the clothed, "civilized" Western spectator. These portrayals and the power politics they supported used nudity as a strategy for establishing superiority and inferiority, with the clothed "superior" always in the position of gazing at the unclothed "lesser being."

Nowadays, the rhetoric has been reversed to mask these power relationships. Girls are told constantly that body displays are empowering. There is power, they are told, in revealing their physical assets. Attracting the male gaze elevates them in the sexual hierarchy—and indeed, it is the only recognizable way for them to express sexuality in contemporary culture. This limited and in many ways disempowering construction of female sexuality is framed as liberating, assertive, a form of self-expression that rejects old-fashioned prudery— and in the case of very young girls, and perhaps more insidiously, as routine.

No one stops to question why boys are never the objects of the gaze; why, if being on display is so empowering, males don't embrace this form of sexual expression, too. The baggy jeans and oversized T-shirts popular among boys today are designed, in fact, to conceal the body as much as possible. Boys are in the relatively comfortable position of observing and evaluating without themselves being observed or evaluated. And girls are bombarded with the myth that semi-nudity constitutes "girl power."

Girls' bodies are not just bared to indicate sexuality, they are bared by means of specific attire intended to convey "hotness"—a style of fashion commonly identified as "hooker chic." These are the clothes that have provoked strict dress codes in schools, and fury and consternation among many parents, child psychologists, and educators. "Hooker chic" is the principal reason that Bratz dolls have attracted so much negative attention, and it's the look of choice for the women of music videos, kids' cartoons, and teen TV. The therapist Charles Foster, author of the book *Parent-Teen Breakthrough*, recognizes these provocative styles as appealing to teens and preteens precisely because they infuriate elders, but observes that girls often don't understand the erotic implications of the clothing. "They understand in a general sense that dressing provocatively gives them power," he said in a *Boston Herald* interview, "but I don't think they understand they're playing with fire, or danger, or the kind of interest they're creating in the minds of the men looking at them."

Clothes convey meanings. We're all aware of that: our social codes include appropriate attire for different contexts and situations; even in America, where the boundaries are more blurred than in many other cultures, we know that blue jeans ought not be worn to black-tie events and that grimy beachwear would probably not score points at a job interview, because modes of dress convey attitudes, qualifications, social awareness, and class rank or status. Anthropologists, sociologists, psychologists, historians, and other scholars understand clothes to be a nonverbal system of communication—an expressive medium—with profound and different meanings in various cultures. One important function of clothing is to "mark the borders" between groups—clothing can signal who we are, and who we are not.

Because of this, clothing provides important visible cues about gender identity. As long ago as 1962, the sociologist Gregory Stone proposed that individuals feel validated when the identity they intend to convey through their appearance, especially their dress, is understood by others. People dress in order to transmit messages of gender and sexuality. "Gender is a pervasive aspect of how humans are socialized to use clothing in everyday life," observes the psychologist Susan Kaiser. Every society has rules about gender-appropriate clothing, though these vary widely: in some cultures, like many in Asia and the Middle East, women's bodies are traditionally more concealed than men's, whereas in others, such as the Kalabari tribe of Nigeria or certain South Pacific cultures, women's bodies are traditionally more revealed. Western attitudes toward body baring are complicated; Victorian mores deemed women's bodies scandalous and indecent, yet even in 1857, the American feminist activist Elizabeth Cady Stanton complained,

> Why is it that at balls and parties, when man comes dressed in his usual style, fashion requires woman to display her person, to bare her arms and neck? Why must she attract man's admiration? Why must she secure his physical love? . . . [T]he shortest way to a man's favor is through his passions; and woman has studied well all the little arts and mysteries by which she

can stimulate him to the pursuit. Every part of a women's dress has been faithfully conned by some French courtesan to produce this effect. Innocent girls who follow the fashion are wholly ignorant of its philosophy. Woman's attire is an ever-varying incentive to man's imagination—a direct and powerful appeal to his passional nature.

Stanton believed that women's clothing styles were designed to stimulate men's sexual interest, and it's true that because of the complex system of meanings carried by clothing, we all respond psychologically and emotionally to the way people are dressed. So it would be naïve to contend that clothing styles don't cause reactions, sometimes unwanted ones. For example, in the early days of World War II, the Mexican American teenagers ("pachucos") who adopted zoot suits as part of urban style were attacked by enraged white servicemen, for whom the suits represented a racial threat: "Gangs of marines ambushed zoot-suiters, stripped them down to their underwear, and left them helpless in the streets. In one particularly vicious incident, a gang of drunken sailors rampaged through a cinema after sighting two zoot suiters. They dragged the pachucos onto the stage, stripped them in front of the audience, and urinated on their zoot suits. During the ensuing weeks of 'rioting,' the ritualistic stripping of zoot suiters became the major means by which the servicemen established their superiority over the pachucos."

Clothing also provoked much of the brutality of the Stonewall Riots of 1969, in which police singled out cross-dressers and gender nonconformists for persecution. "The first hostile act outside the club occurred when a police officer shoved one of the transvestites, who turned and smacked the officer over the head with her purse. The cop clubbed her," reports David Carter in his history of the riots. Another early victim of police brutality during the Stonewall fracas was a lesbian who was beaten and arrested because "she was wearing pants and what one witness described as 'fancy, go-to-bar drag for a butch dyke.'" These examples are offered not to justify the attacks or to blame the victims, but to illustrate how clothing is interpreted as a justification for violence by perpetrators seeking a sign of difference that marks their targets. Clothes carry powerful messages in our society, and it would be naïve not to recognize this fact and deal realistically with it.

In the same way as zoot suits, drag, or other modes of dress, "hooker chic" clothing sends out strong signals. In our cultural understanding, specific garments are associated with women's sex work: stripping, prostitution, and pornography. We could all probably easily list these costume elements—fishnet stockings, hot pants, tube tops, platform or stiletto heels; worn together, they project sex for sale. But even clothing styles that don't adhere to this stereotype can be interpreted as provocative: soft-core porn focuses on women's nude or seminude bodies, often bedecked in clothes that have similarly sexualized connotations—lacy lingerie, garters, thongs, and so on.

When these clothes and these body displays enter the realm of children's media and marketing, it's the associations with sex work that are most troubling. The principal complaint about Bratz dolls and fashions is the way the clothing hints at "gentlemen's clubs" and "pole dancing"; and this issue is taken to the limit by Tesco's marketing of the pink plastic "Peekaboo pole dancing kit" for little girls, which comes with its own little garter belt *and* fake money to tuck into it. What could it mean when Playboy stationery is sold alongside Winnie the Pooh and Dora the Explorer letter paper? Abercrombie & Fitch's thong underwear for preteens, and La Senza Girl's push-up bras in little-girl sizes, bring up the same problematic associations.

It's not that bodies are indecent or that girls should cover themselves head to foot to fend off lecherous glances. It's not that femininity itself is a problem or that wanting to be attractive is wrong. It's that ideal girlhood in children's media is construed in terms of sex work—in terms of the commercialized, often exploitative and illegal, realm of sexual commerce. The mythmaking machines of media and marketing persistently tie ideal femininity and attractiveness to a very specific mode of sexuality, one that involves exhibitionism and a submissive appeal to the male gaze, without any consideration of the girl's own interests, ideas, or sense of well-being.

Healthy sexuality is much more than this: at its best, sex is a rich and pleasurable aspect of human experience that calls for both trust and responsibility. The possibilities of "good sex" are wide-ranging and progressive—but not when sex is delimited to sex work, which is almost exclusively defined by women on display for the arousal of male audiences, and not when sexual knowledge is transmitted mainly via the media, which effectively removes it from human experience. The airbrushed, underdressed, eroticized versions of girls that pervade the screens and toy aisles of our culture are effigies. They are not real girls, but they serve as compelling role models for real girls.

Focusing girls' attention so insistently on this aspect of sexuality—the presentation of their bodies in ways that attract boys' sexual interest—also diminishes their ability to see that other aspects of their lives are important, too. "Hotness" as an imperative belittles the value of intelligence, artistic ability, spiritual growth, political awareness, or indeed any other aspect of personality that could enrich girls' lives and translate into potent adulthood. Things are clearly out of balance when girls like Chelsea and Lexi fixate on "hotness" as their most wished-for characteristic. Sexuality is a significant part of being alive, of course, but so are other things, and our culture refuses to acknowledge that sex is no more or less important than any other aspect of social life and human development. At the same time, by being coerced to think so much about "hotness," girls begin to see themselves and each other as principally sexual beings—and really, as sexual objects on display—rather than as multidimensional people. This is a focus that impoverishes their lives.

So the first myth of the Lolita Effect is the translation of girls' sexuality into the visual metaphors of sex work.

What we can do

It seems hopeless to try to challenge the pervasive and persuasive images of the media juggernaut. But it isn't. Girls are smart, critical, and thoughtful consumers, and they are well aware of the contradictions they encounter in their daily negotiations with identity and gender. My own work with girls has demonstrated that there are effective ways to help them to recognize, respond to, and challenge the effects of this first myth. Talking things out with thoughtful and caring adults has ripple effects; kids tend to continue the conversations among themselves. They also know they can broach these topics with adults and get considered, supportive responses, even in one-on-one settings. As part of such a conversation, it's worthwhile to point out that "hotness" is only one characteristic that might describe a girl, and that accomplishments in other arenas are valuable and valued, especially in regard to personal growth and self-actualization. Such conversations may not be all it takes to challenge the juggernaut of popular culture and marketing, but they start the wheels turning.

- ### TALK ABOUT CLOTHES

Teenage girls are keenly aware of the symbolism of clothing and the politics of the body; they are exquisitely sensitive to the slightest nuances of dress and self-adornment. When I've raised some of these issues in workshops with middle-school girls, they are quick with their criticisms and acute in their perceptions. Raising critical questions about the implications of body display and "hooker chic" attire generates vociferous debate, especially in a group setting, and it's worthwhile to air out different perspectives on the subject. Clothing is a hot-button issue that divides mothers and daughters, so the subject needs to be brought up without passing direct judgments on the girls' choices; it can be broached as a more objective conversation about clothes and the messages they convey.

Casual media encounters like watching television or looking at a magazine together can offer everyday opportunities to encourage girls to think critically about what they see around them—and to make critical thinking a habit. When you're starting a conversation, let her tell you what a certain outfit says to her, and use her thoughts as a jumping-off point.

- ### ANTICIPATE COMPLEX REACTIONS

It's easy to dismiss provocative clothing trends as "just fashion," but fashion is never "just" anything, and girls know that codes of identity are bound up in clothing choices and self-presentation. They may contend that clothing can project "attitude," especially if adults see it as trashy or overly sexual.

This is a perfect opportunity to talk about real-world responses to such projections; girls are also hypersensitive to the stigma of sluttiness—another word that warrants further exploration. While adults see health, development, and well-being as of utmost importance, for adolescent girls, social identity and acceptance is an immediate—and, in a very real way, a primary—concern. Because adolescence is a time when identity issues are being worked out intensely and emotionally, discussions like these can be highly productive, especially if the tone is friendly, open, and supportive.

• REIN IN YOUR OPINIONS UNTIL SHE INTRODUCES THEM HERSELF

A great challenge for concerned, well-meaning adults is not "setting the record straight" in the terms I have been using throughout this book. These are terms that appeal to an adult perspective, which focus on media influences and personal consumption of media, and which don't look closely at the immense social and personal pressures girls perceive themselves to be (and often are) under. But as you talk these things through, patient adults will find that girls arrive at similar conclusions about "hotness" on their own terms. If, however, they don't, you should be clear about what you think. Your ideas will stay with them, perhaps to emerge when they are older and more able to process them.

• HAVE READY EXAMPLES

Using examples from the media and examining the connections that magazines, videos, and TV shows are making between attractiveness and body displays will help girls to recognize the pervasive patterns in media definitions of "hotness." Ask the girls to examine the pictures and the texts and to think about the implications of what they see:

Is the language coaxing us to see the image in a particular way? Could there be other ways of interpreting the picture?

Is it "hot" or "sexy" just because the text tells us it is?

Because the myth of exhibitionism has become taken for granted in our culture, questions need to be raised about other alternatives.

Is it possible to express sexuality in other ways?

Is "hooker chic" the only avenue?

Do the media formulas actually allow girls to think about how they perceive and experience sex and attraction?

From whose point of view are the videos presented?

What about the movies and the magazines?

Are girls' perspectives and voices heard?

Is there a difference between the ways boys and girls are represented?

If so, what are the differences the girls notice and what are the reasons for the differences?

If they had a chance to control the representations, would they be different from those in the mainstream media?

If so, how?

• TALK ABOUT "HOTNESS"

Girls will have strong feelings on how significant "hotness" is, and the relative marginalization of other aspects of girls' lives. These discussions should always stay "sex-positive," in the sense of validating the importance of feeling attractive and of maintaining control over their own sexuality. There is no need to demonize sex, or to focus on it as something scary and negative, because the goal is girls' healthy sexual development. Some topics you might talk about:

Do they think hotness is as important as everyone else seems to think?

What do they (and their friends) pride themselves on?

What do they excel at?

Do they perceive these abilities and talents as having greater, lesser, or equal immediate worth as hotness?

Greater, lesser, or equal future worth?

What about for men? Does hotness have greater, lesser, or equal short- and long-term value than other attributes?

• Talk about what's unfair

Girls are quick to recognize inequalities based on their gender. For many, this discussion represents the first time girls' pleasure, girls' feelings of self-worth, and girls' ideas about expressing sexuality and femininity outside of cultural norms have been highlighted. These discussions are important in order to overcome what Michele Fine described as "the missing discourse" of girls' desire.

• Set up a peer discussion

Discussion groups are effective because they build on the importance and intensity of peer group relationships in girls' lives. Social connections and peer relationships are central to their development, as numerous studies have indicated; and these peer connections can be a force for positive change, serving to combat threats to their well-being and consolidate their identities. Girls express an overwhelming preference for group versus individual counseling sessions. A number of programs geared to helping girls negotiate the challenges of adolescence depend on group processes for successful interventions. After-school girls' groups, mother-daughter groups, and other supportive social networks are all effective ways to build trust and air out problems.

• Talk about boys

You can't have this kind of discussion without bringing up boys. Media messages about sex go out to boys as well as girls, shaping boys' expectations and views of girls, defining both femininity and masculinity. Is it possible for girls to attract male attention in ways that are not geared to the myth of "hotness"? Girls need to discuss this possibility as they explore a variety of mutually satisfactory ways of connecting with boys. Because it is unrealistic to think that most teenage girls will be able to entirely rid themselves of the idea that they want to invite male attention, any critical media analysis is meaningless if girls, in despair, still think "hotness" is the only way to get male attention. But they need to know that boys can, and do, value other qualities in girls.

• HEAR BOYS' SIDE OF THINGS

Co-ed discussion groups can be very effective, though these are best launched after girls have had a chance to talk about these issues without boys present. It can be eye-opening for boys to hear critical discussions of these representations and to think about the impact of these images on girls' lives and on their own relationships with girls. In my own presentations, I have found that some boys are open to such ideas, while others are highly resistant. Nonetheless, the discussions are important ways to begin to unravel the myths, to offer a different perspective.

One compelling co-ed exercise for high school students is to have boys and girls separate by gender to make two lists. The girls should make a list of characteristics they believe an ideal guy should have, and another they believe an ideal girl should have. Boys should make two corresponding lists. Then, the boys and girls should be brought back together into one group to discuss the lists. This tends to foster empowered and provocative group conversation.

Another exercise: Have boys and girls physically imitate the ways in which men and women are positioned in fashion advertisements and ask them to describe how the poses make them feel (for example, awkward, strong, silly, vulnerable, sad, angry, passive). Then discuss how the poses help or hinder the persuasive messages. Who is being targeted? Are there consistent differences between male and female poses? If so, why? What messages are women and men likely or supposed to get from these differences?

A third exercise: Have girls and boys separate to discuss the kinds of media they consume (television shows, videos, video games, magazines, movies and so on) and then identify how the "ideal" males and females are portrayed (this can include physical characteristics, like hair and eye color, body size, and so on, attributes like marital status and wealth, and behaviors). Then bring the groups back together to share perspectives: how do they differ in terms of the kinds of media consumed and nature of the images described. Are male and female ideals similar? If not, why not? Discuss the implications of the stereotypic ideals: To what extent do these reinforce and perpetuate less than ideal attitudes and behavior patterns? How do students experience these? Do they notice their younger siblings being affected?

• Talk with younger children

Grade-school and preschool children are far less aware than teenagers of the implications of the clothing they wear, and they're usually oblivious to the sexual messages they may be sending. But simple questions can help young children start to think about the issues. Asking, "Why do you think she's hardly wearing any clothing?" can begin a useful conversation about body exposure; even a preschooler can recognize that the clothes adorning dolls and models are not the same ones that the women in their lives are wearing. "Why do you think I (or your teacher or favorite aunt) don't dress that way?" is a good starting point for talking about appropriate clothes for different situations and about the media figures as fictions (or myths) whose activities and choices are not the same as real women's.

• REINFORCE NON-APPEARANCE BASED COMPLIMENTS

Make sure to compliment young girls and encourage them on things besides their appearance, since most of the compliments they receive will tend to be from well-meaning people who focus on the way they look. One little girl I know pipes up, "And I'm smart, too!" when people tell her she's pretty. I make it a point to applaud my own young daughters for their artistry, academic achievements, generosity, and original ideas. We need to work to make sure they know that we value them for more than their looks, and that their other attributes are equally, or perhaps even more, important.

• DRAW THE LINE ON WHAT'S OKAY

It's also okay to draw the line, but to explain why. Young children may not understand why you don't want to buy them the Peekaboo Pole-Dancing Kit, but saying you don't think it's appropriate is good enough. Providing simple explanations that convey your own values and perspectives is an effective way to talk about these issues with kids.

• RESPOND CONSTRUCTIVELY AND CREATIVELY

What do you do when your seven-year-old wants to roll her skirt up to micro-mini shortness, or when your fifteen-year-old wants to go out in a bustier and thong-revealing jeans? You probably can't pull the old switcheroo that you could when she was a toddler, distracting her with an appealing substitute. Instead, with both the grade-schooler and the teenager, you can talk about why you think the clothing is inappropriate or doesn't work well.

Young children can understand that clothes tell a story about them, and that the story told by the minuscule skirt isn't a helpful one. On the other hand, it probably doesn't hurt to let her play around with clothing experiments at home, in a safe environment, if you explain that just as you would not go out with matted hair or a mud-pack on, you wouldn't go out inappropriately dressed. My own kids come up with all kinds of outlandish outfits that they know they shouldn't wear outside the house.

With an older girl, you'll need to figure out your own limits. Speak with her privately—not in front of her friends or yours—about how clothing sends signals, and the differences between what's in the media and what works in real life. A lot depends on your relationship with each other here. You can explain why you don't think the clothing reflects well on her; she'll know you are not having an unreasonable knee-jerk reaction to current fashions, that you have put thought into your opinions, and that you really care about her. You should talk about why she wants to wear a particular outfit and have her explain what she thinks it projects. With older teens, the least productive thing to do is put your foot down, as that is a move that may only cause resistance and rebellion. (Nonetheless, it may be necessary at times.) Pick your battles: a bizarre hairstyle or accessory probably isn't cause for alarm. Really sleazy clothing is another issue, and one that merits serious discussion. The earlier you begin talking about these issues, the better.

One conversation won't be enough, but recognizing media myths and comparing them to real life is the first step toward resistance. Myth analysis is a strategy that enhances media literacy, a valuable skill in coping with a media-saturated environment that targets girls by way of sex.

Chapter 3

THE SECOND MYTH
ANATOMY OF A SEX GODDESS

∞

With her brown bobbed hair, luminous gray eyes
and pale skin, she looked perfectly charming. Her
hips were no bigger than those of a squatting lad.
—VLADIMIR NABOKOV, *Lolita*

I'M IN AN elementary school classroom in Iowa, standing
in front of a roomful of lively and diverse sixth-graders. I ask
them what a "perfect girl" looks like. The answers tumble
out: "Young!" "Thin!" "Blonde!" "Long hair!" "Long legs!"
Finally, twelve-year-old Katie earnestly sums it up: "She would
look like Barbie."

I get the same answer every time I ask this question: in
my college-level classes on gender and sexuality, in casual conversations with colleagues, when I talk to my friends' preschool children. Over and over again, "Barbie" is what they
come up with, despite all the years of critique, the debates,
and the derision; despite the incursion of the newer, more popular dolls; despite Fat Pride and the butch mystique. "Perfect
girls" in the new millennium, apparently, still look like Barbie.

Barbie has been recast as a feminist these days; in the

progressive *New Moon* magazine, twelve-year-old Abby Jones writes, "One of Barbie's slogans is 'Be who you wanna be.' You can buy Teacher Barbie, California Girl Surfer Barbie, Pet Doctor Barbie, and many others. In the Barbie movies, Barbie is smart, strong, and courageous." Like Abby, I'm all in favor of Barbie's dizzying array of career trajectories, of the way she has overcome her mathphobia, and of her recent forays into tattoos and piercings. But it's also clear that Barbie's body stays the same throughout all her incarnations: translated to human scale, in a now-infamous formulation, she would be a 5-foot 9-inch woman with an 18-inch waist, 36-inch breasts, and 33-inch hips, and she would weigh 110 pounds. That's too skinny to menstruate, according one medical analysis of the doll. She may even be too skinny to stand upright. And it's still the ideal girl's body, the exemplar for all races, classes, and nations. Recent studies have shown that preteen girls still longingly described Barbie's body as "perfect."

Of course, many of us are aware of the tyranny of the Barbie body, which is why the Dove company's "real beauty" campaign has excited so much interest, and why we're all quick to disparage the pro-anorexia movements, and the thinness of runway models. But the models are still out there, and their images pervade fashion magazines, TV shows, movies, and music videos: it doesn't take a rocket scientist to see that America's Next Top Model, the Pussycat Dolls, and the girls of *Sábado Gigante* are all living Barbies. Media executives are casual and upfront about this: Kim Todd, the executive producer of the teen TV show *Falcon Beach*, admitted in an interview, "The way we cast the show is, we held this dynamite audition and then started asking, 'What do they look like in a bathing suit?'"

So it's not surprising that on MySpace and Facebook, young girls are asking each other about diet pills and laxative treatments that will help them lose drastic amounts of weight, or that the number of girls under eighteen getting breast implants has tripled in the last five years. In fact, the Barbie body is pretty much unattainable for most girls without borderline starvation and plastic surgery, yet studies show that adolescent girls see media bodies as realistic ideals to strive toward; as the media scholar Renee Botta found in her research on high school students, girls "look toward people they see on television to define what their own bodies should look like."

"Love your body!" commands a cover line on *Shape* magazine—and every teen magazine follows suit, with regular stories that purport to debunk the media myths of perfect bodies. But while these articles piously declare that all body sizes are beautiful, and trot out Queen Latifah, Beyoncé, and J-Lo as bodacious examples of nonconforming bodies, there are no visual examples of truly large or large-boned girls. This is not to endorse obesity, which is quickly becoming a global health crisis, but to recognize the improbability and equally unhealthy characteristics of the media's contrasting ideal. Neither Beyoncé nor J-Lo is heavy, by any stretch, and both are aerobicized and muscular, with tiny waists, taut abdomens, and trim thighs. Queen Latifah is an anomaly in a media landscape populated by the svelte young women in music videos, yet she too is noted for undergoing weight loss and breast reduction; she works out with a trainer and kickboxes. She may be "plus size," but her body is muscular and taut. The enemy for girls and women is "the soft, the loose, unsolid, excess flesh. . . . Simply to be slim is not enough—the flesh must not 'wiggle.'"

There is no realistic alternative presented in these magazines' pages—no one with a soft belly or a jiggle anywhere is presented as sexy or sexual. In addition, the articles are flanked—surrounded, really—by advertisements and photographs that feature only girls with digitally manipulated, buns-o'-steel Barbie bodies. For example, in the February 2006 issue of *Cosmo Girl*, a story called "Global Body Image Survey" admonishes girls, "If you're obsessed with your outer appearance, it's harder to focus on the more important things, and you can end up missing out on a lot." But the article is preceded by a story about Jennifer Aniston, a curvy actress who reportedly wears a size 2 dress, and the cover story and photo are about another actress, Sophia Bush, whose body is unquestionably in the Barbie mold. Two pages later comes a photo spread featuring the famously thin Olsen twins—one of whom has been rehabilitated for an eating disorder. So the potentially progressive message of body acceptance and healthy diversity in the "Love your body!" stories is immediately overwhelmed and undercut by the visual celebration of the slender-yet-curvy body that is invariably defined as *the* desirable female body in today's media culture.

This holds true across all media. In television shows for teens, from *Laguna Beach* to *Gossip Girls*, the main girl characters are simultaneously both slender and voluptuous. This is a body rarely found in nature. Thinness tends to work against curviness; buxom bodies tend toward plumpness. As the communication scholar Kristen Harrison points out in her article "The case of the curvaceously thin woman," the media ideal of a woman's body would require size 4 hips, a size 2 waist, and a size 10 bust—practically a physical impossibility. Maintaining these discrepant proportions, she goes on, takes dieting to whittle down the lower body and "creative means" of upholding the large breast size. So the media have seized on a body type that can be achieved only through artificial techniques and painstaking devotion to artificially creating a certain body image.

One notable exception to the 36-18-33 body is Disney's "That's So Raven," whose protagonist does not conform to the "Barbie" body type; indeed, several episodes of this show have focused on body image and resistance to stereotyped and fantastical body ideals. In one notable episode, Raven wins a teen magazine fashion design contest, then challenges the magazine's editors, who want to digitally alter her body to conform to Barbie-like proportions for the magazine cover. The show's ultimately progressive message is that Raven's natural, healthy, larger body size wins accolades from the fashion show's audience.

But Raven is a rarity in a media landscape populated with living Barbie dolls—and Raven is African American. Raven's race undoubtedly has something do with the fact that "That's So Raven" is the only mainstream show for kids featuring—and even celebrating—an alternative body size, and its lasting popularity is testament to the fact that body conformity is not essential to commercial success. (The show is popular with 'tween audiences across racial demographic groups.) But even among African American girls, and other girls of color, the thin/voluptuous body has become an ideal. Contrary to earlier findings, African American girls report increasing pressures to be thin, both because of peer and media influences and because of men's preferences.

But being thin is not enough: thinness must be coupled with lush curves in the "right" places—the breasts—in order for the ideal to be achieved. And these body characteristics don't normally tend to coincide: when weight loss occurs, breast size tends to decrease. Most fashion models stand 5 feet 10 or taller and weigh less—often much less—than 140 pounds. They are expected to fit into a dress size between 2 and 4. Men argue that stick-thin fashion models are not sexy or attractive, but *Playboy* centerfolds are similarly atypical in their physical characteristics—with vital statistics of 34-23-34 and weights significantly less than those of other women in their age group.

In addition, almost all photographs in fashion and beauty publications and, increasingly, almost all video images of models are technical wonders of the digital age. The models themselves are pale shadows of their media images, which are airbrushed, edited, and altered so as to create flawless facsimiles of femininity. They are a far cry from the real world: according to the National Center for Health Statistics, the average American woman is about 5 feet 4 inches tall and weighs 163 pounds. The model—the adored ideal—is both a genetic anomaly and a fabrication of technology, constructing a physical type that is unattainable for almost all girls and women.

So why do the media, the fashion industry, and the marketing moguls choose to glorify the most unrealistic body possible? Why is a body so filled with contradictions—narrow hips, tiny waist, tightly muscled, and topped by large breasts—the one held up as the ultimate goal?

At the same time that this body is, in reality, virtually nonexistent, the message to its viewers is that it can, in fact, be achieved, if only the girls who want it try hard enough. If they diet enough, if they exercise enough, if they buy the clothes that minimize bulges and maximize cleavage, if they consume the right low-calorie foods, if they follow the dictates of the magazines whose siren calls offer the allure of "Lose 10 pounds fast!"—if they just want it badly enough, it will happen.

It probably won't, but the ongoing pursuit of the ideal body is an expensive proposition. Diet pills and products, gym memberships, stylish clothes to flatter the figure (and become instantly outmoded), high heels to make legs look longer, plastic surgery to inflate the bust and suction the fat, anticellulite creams and potions—the products required to attain the Barbie body are myriad and costly. Multiple industries depend on girls' yearning for the Barbie body: the fashion, diet, exercise, cosmetic, and plastic surgery industries all generate multibillion-dollar annual profits. These are the very industries that advertise in the media that promote this ideal body.

And advertising is the lifeblood of the media, its major source of revenues. It is advertising, not subscriptions, that generate profits for the media. *Seventeen* magazine earned $101.9 million in advertising in 2006, while the Web site *Teen People* had advertising revenues of almost $77 million. The Coty cosmetics corporation spent $19 million in 2005 to advertise products targeted to fifteen- to twenty-one-year-olds. To post a single ad for four weeks on MySpace costs between $80,000 to $300,000—and the site's annual advertising revenues are estimated at $250 million, primarily because of the high proportion of young users. Health and beauty products contributed $1.63 billion to prime-time TV in 2006.

Corporations from food manufacturers to lingerie retailers spend literally billions of dollars every year advertising to the youth market. This extensive network of interrelated corporations would collapse if girls and women stopped their pursuit of the "curvaceously thin" body. The media must promote the Barbie body in order to attract advertisers; advertisers must promote the Barbie body in order to sell the products needed for its attainment. The media and the fashion and beauty industries work hand in glove, driven by a common profit motive. The relationship is symbiotic; if one of these components were to fail, it would have a negative impact on all the others. So the relentless glorification of the Barbie body persists.

Because the Barbie body is a doll's body, molded in plastic and manufactured in a factory, its achievement can be reached only through the purchase and consumption of non-human products, products that are supposed to induce the human body to approximate plastic, or in some cases to substitute or insert plastic into human tissue. The latter processes involve surgeries, performed at enormous expense, physical pain, and sometimes serious risk. The Barbie body is emphatically not found in nature.

The chieftains of media and marketing take full advantage of this reality to peddle the necessary equipment for achieving such a body to girls of all ages. This is why the lingerie chain La Senza Girl offers push-up bras to preteens and the toy company Boutique in a Box sells fake nails for toddlers. This is why eighteen-year-olds are saving their money for $300 Botox injections and eleven-year-olds are badgering their parents for spray-on tans and weekly spa appointments. This is why girls in China are undergoing excruciating leg-lengthening operations, and girls in India and Africa are slathering on carcinogenic skin-bleaching creams. The consumerism needed to pursue the Barbie body is high-dollar and never-ending, and the patterns of consumption established in childhood remain with women for the rest of their lives.

There are other, more insidious factors at play in the Barbie ideal. The Barbie body is not just slender, fat-free, and busty; it is also white. Despite the existence of "multicultural" Barbies in various skin tones, and despite the fact that divas of apparently different racial backgrounds are celebrated as beautiful and desirable, they are all very close to a Caucasian ideal of beauty, with small straight noses, large eyes, and long, straight hair. For the most part, the skin tones are light; the occasional dark-skinned girl or woman is an anomaly, tossed in to make a politically correct point or highlight a contrast. For girls of color, the sexy ideals are Tyra Banks and Alicia Keyes, Vanessa Anne Hudgens and Jessica Alba, Brenda Song and Rihanna. They all have Barbie bodies and close-to-Caucasian features. For every larger-boned, full-lipped, or curly-haired icon, there are fifty who reestablish the dominance of the Caucasian archetype.

In the year 2006, eleven of the twelve covers of *Seventeen* magazine featured a Caucasian model; nine of these were blondes; and seven of the nine had blue eyes. In 2007, ten of twelve *Seventeen* covers featured Caucasian models, of whom seven were blue-eyed blondes. That these physical traits were accorded privileged status by this publication was also evident from accompanying text. Cover lines like "885 ways to look hot" (September 2006), "875 ways to look beautiful" (March 2006), and "The best ways to get gorgeous" (October 2006) cued readers to interpret these characteristics as highly desirable and inherently linked with beauty. As the sociologist Laurel Davis has pointed out, "there is a racial hierarchy among women in terms of appearance. Women with white skin, blonde and straight hair, blue eyes, and small noses are at the top, and women with dark skin, black and curly hair, and big noses are at the bottom. . . . Women who conform to the ideal, or come close to conforming, can feel superior to other women simply because of their racial characteristics." *Seventeen*'s choice of cover models reinforces this racial hierarchy.

So the Barbie body is even more unreachable for girls of color—for most nonwhite girls, long blonde hair, blue eyes, and light skin must be acquired artificially, and the means are available for those who have the money: hair highlights and bleaches, professional relaxing treatments, hair weaves, skin-lightening creams, and colored contact lenses are all on the market and reaping profits for their manufacturers and distributors.

One might ask, is there anything wrong with this? Girls just want to look pretty, and they get both pleasure and self-esteem from enhancing their appearance.

In fact, the concepts of pleasure and self-esteem are double-edged swords. The purchase of beauty products is a pretty questionable way to get a confidence boost: hair color fades, weaves fall out, breast implants need replacement. The artificial supplements have built-in shelf lives that guarantee the frequent outlay of money. And the temporary buzz they bring is built on insecurity, the constant anxiety that one's body is not good enough without these aids. The media teach us to find pleasure in approximating the unreachable ideal, but because the Barbie body is a myth, we can never fully acquire it, and the anxieties it creates remain with us. The pleasure of pursuing a beauty regime is always linked with the pain of self-doubt.

The Barbie body functions to exclude and deny entire groups of girls from sexuality. Beyond being racialized, this body is also supremely physically able. The Barbies that we admire—from the lifeguards and surfers in every TV show set on a California beach, to the dancers in music videos, to the models of the Victoria's Secret fashion show—are poetry in motion. For a girl with a physical or visible disability, the message is clear: You can't be sexy if your body is differently abled. If you have crutches, a birthmark, a prosthesis, or a hearing aid, your desirability instantly plummets, at least by media standards. Girls with disabilities describe how boys flirt with them before realizing that they are disabled; once the realization sets in, "the switch on the sexual circuit breaker often pops off—the connection is broken. 'Chemistry' is over." The ecofeminist writer Ynestra King describes seeing a woman in a wheelchair wearing stiletto heels and fishnet hose, and the horror and ridicule she provokes in bystanders: "That she could 'flaunt' her sexual being violates the code of acceptable appearance for a disabled woman." An able-bodied woman wearing these markers of sexuality would have garnered approval or leers; but the disabled woman was viewed as offensive. Medically speaking, this is nonsense: people with disabilities have varying levels of sexual desire and functioning, just as nondisabled people do. Many people with disabilities are fully capable of developing warm and satisfying sex and love lives. But you'd never know this from the sexy girl ideal.

Class is another category that the Barbie ideal exploits to exclude entire categories of girls from sexuality. The high monetary cost of the beauty products and treatments needed to acquire the Barbie body adds a class dimension to the definition of the sexy girl. For poor girls, these products are out of reach or attained only through the sacrifice of other consumer needs, ones that may be more pressing or useful, like nutritious food in the short term, or college savings in the long term. American women spend more each year on beauty than on education, according to the *Economist*. The average British woman spends more than £182,000 on beauty products and treatments in a lifetime; in New Zealand, that figure is estimated at NZ$200,000, the average cost of a house. (Cosmetic sales in the UK hit £1 billion in 2006.) The *Singapore Times* reports that teen girls in Singapore spend thousands of dollars a month on beauty and clothing. The worldwide beauty industry generates profits of about US$160 billion a year. In the United States, women are much more likely to be poor than men, and while this statistic is due to a variety of factors, the fact that women outspend men despite earning less may be a contributing factor. A recent survey by *Barron's* showed that women's savings stand at negative 1.4 percent, while men have a collective savings rate of 12 percent. These trends may be linked: if large proportions of girls' and women's incomes are being spent on cosmetics, grooming, and fashion, then little is left to put away for education, retirement, or medical catastrophes.

Overseas, cosmetics and beauty corporations are aggressively marketing in impoverished and Third World countries. In India, for example, makeup sales rose from $2.3 million in 1997 to $14 million in 2005, and sales of hair-care products generate $19.3 million, according to the market research firm Euromonitor. The beauty industry reports double-digit growth in Asian markets in the last year. In China, cosmetics sales reached approximately 5 million euros in 2004. In Bulgaria, women's spending on cosmetics and beauty aids grew by 130 percent between 1997 and 2002, because of Western marketing campaigns aimed at women. But these are countries where many people live on less than $1 a day.

While of course women (and men) should not be denied the pleasures of self-adornment and the feelings of attractiveness that come with them, the economics of beauty do raise questions about the ethics of imposing expensive First World products and standards of beauty on girls and women with severely limited incomes and little hope of achieving the ideals. The massive expenditures on these products would not be necessary if "global" standards of beauty were not as improbable, and if their attainment were not so expensive.

One concern is the marketing rhetoric that forces Western, Caucasian standards of beauty on non-Western girls and women, e.g. the bleaching cream campaigns that stress "whitening" and "brightening" as beauty goals that improve on dark skin. "Darkening of skin has always been viewed as a sign of ageing," reads one Estée Lauder press release, advertising WhiteLight Brightening Essence, one of many skin-bleaching creams that are not sold in the First World. L'Oreal's upscale Vichy line of skin lighteners is advertised with a photo of a dark-skinned Indian woman's face being "unzipped" to reveal a (tacitly more beautiful) lighter-skinned selk. The product's slogan is "Skin bright, perfect white."

Elizabeth Arden's "Sheer White" skincare line is advertised in Asia with the face of Catherine Zeta-Jones, a Caucasian woman, and Olay's line of whitening creams are promoted overseas with taglines like "You're always searching for perfection. Occasionally you find it: flawless, fair skin." Not only are these cosmetics marketed globally on the racist premise that light skin is preferable to dark skin, but they are prohibitively expensive, as much as $70 an ounce.

Plastic surgeries to achieve Caucasian facial and physical features are similarly racist, expensive, and dangerous. South Korean (and other Asian) teenagers routinely have blepharoplasties, or eyelid surgeries, to get "rounder, prettier" more Caucasian-looking eyes, at a minimum cost of $800 for the procedure. An ABC news report points out that in China, where the average annual household income is $4,300, the cost of a popular leg-lengthening surgery is $12,000—yet hospitals have waiting lists for the procedure. "Parents make their kids get plastic surgery," says South Korean surgeon Dr. Shim Hyung Bo, "just like they make them study. They realize looks are important for success." So the pressures on non-Western girls are even more intense, for reasons that stem from, and reinforce, an underlying racism in our conception of beauty.

There's an argument out there that cosmetics, plastic surgeries, and dieting make girls feel good about themselves. That may be true on some level, yet the "feel-good" is often the result of initial feelings of inadequacy and body dissatisfaction that are appeased only by consuming these products. Plastic surgeries like breast implantation actually reduce feeling in the erogenous zones, so girls' sexual pleasure is in fact impaired by such surgeries. The feel-good may be psychological and not physical: is that a worthwhile trade-off?

Our myths of sexuality are linked to body types that are not only unrealistic and unhealthy, but also clearly racialized.

They encourage girls to scrutinize their own bodies critically and to overvalue girls whose bodies come close to the ideal. They encourage girls of color to internalize and embrace racism. They encourage girls with physical disabilities to see themselves as asexual and undesirable. The ultimate message is one that negates the idea of diversity and inclusiveness: the sexy girl is defined so narrowly that true diversity is set apart from sexuality. Sexiness, desirability, and ultimately *worth* is tied firmly in our mainstream media to the achievement of the slender, taut, bosomy, and ultimately Caucasian Barbie body. Media myths of sexiness thus influence girls' relationships with themselves and their own bodies, their relationships with other girls on the basis of their bodies, and their perceptions of human sexuality, which in fact is *not* dependent on body contours. Sex is a gift available to every human being.

For economically privileged girls whose lives are not complicated by racism, poverty, or national origin, pursuing media ideals of sexiness may be fun and entertaining; it may gain them some social power and peer acceptance. But the fallout for other girls, the vast majority of girls who do not fit into that privileged group of elites, is serious, in that the feelings of exclusions and oppressions that mark their lives are intensified by the second myth of the sexy girl.

And the bottom line is the bottom line. The industries that foster this myth are multibillion-dollar transnational enterprises whose success depends on the myth of the anatomy of the sex goddess, regardless of its impact on girls' lives.

What we can do

Most girls are, by now, aware of body image as a social problem. They know about anorexia and bulimia (though many of them secretly starve themselves, and binge and purge, anyway). They know that the media perpetuate unrealistic body types.

But they often aren't aware of just how unrealistic the images are, how much they have been digitally manipulated before they are published or aired on television. They don't know that the models and actresses themselves don't look like their media-generated images—that, in fact, no one can look as perfectly sculpted and blemish-free as the carefully edited pictures that are held up as achievable ideals.

• SHOW HOW AIRBRUSHING LIES

A great way to begin a discussion about this is to show Dove's wonderful video "Evolution," which in sixty amazing seconds shows how an average-looking young woman is converted into a flawless beauty to appear on a billboard makeup ad. The video is easily available on YouTube. A very effective follow-up to this video is the first part of Jean Kilbourne's documentary "Slim Hopes," which can be purchased from the Media Education Foundation at www.mediaed.org/videos /MediaAndHealth/SlimHopes (there are special prices for high schools that make it an affordable investment). The film, like the Dove video, also demonstrates the technical manipulations that go into creating media images of beauty and desirability.

Showing girls visual evidence of the basic falseness of media images can generate a conversation about why artificial images are held up to us as ideals to pursue.

• CALL BARBIE OUT

This is a good time to point out that even when apparently progressive, prodiversity messages like "Love your body!" appear in magazines or on TV specials, they are off-

set by the vast numbers of images of Barbie bodies that surround and neutralize them. A realistic range of body types is
not regularly seen in the mainstream media. Some questions
to ask:

> *Do people really prefer looking at these artificial girls?*
> *If so, why?*
> *Does it make it different to know that the images aren't real?*
> *And if no one, not even the models, looks like that, why are we*
> *supposed to try so hard?*

- ## DISSECT THE BIG-BUSINESS SIDE OF THINGS

For girls, the discussion of economics comes as a surprise
most of the time. They have not thought about the connections between the advertising and marketing of beauty products and the content of the media; they've never realized that
the liquid foundation recommended in the advice column of a
magazine is also advertised on the back cover, and that the
magazine profits from making the recommendation. But once
the facts are provided, girls are quick to realize that they are
being manipulated into supporting gigantic industry profits
that often come at their expense. This starting point can grow
into the realization that it's up to all of us, as consumers, to
make informed and wise decisions about how much to pursue
the "Barbie" ideal. Some questions to ask:

> *How much money do we want to invest in that goal?*
> *How does it make us feel?*
> *Are there more rewarding ways to spend our time and money?*
> *What about the long-term?*

• Talk about why we want to be Barbie

It's not that anyone needs to completely reject social definitions of beauty; rather, it's important to think about where they come from and what they represent. It's important to know the motivations behind them, and to look at their relationships to class, race, and physical ability, among other things. Discussions of the major plastic surgeries being undergone by girls in other countries to attain Western beauty ideals is also a good way to examine global media flows and the many inequities between Third World countries and the world's wealthier nations. It's important to use this information in deciding how to respond to the media images and manipulations that are aimed at stimulating consumerism and creating new global markets for products, some of which are banned in First World countries because of their medical implications.

• Define "sexy"

It's also important to think about these issues in relation to sex. Some things to talk about together:

Is sexiness really about the Barbie body?

Is a girl or woman with a Barbie body really sexier than someone without one?

What constitutes sexual desire and sexual appeal, anyway?

Whose sexuality are we talking about—for whose sexual pleasure are these body issues created?

Would someone who is unhappy about their looks, constantly dieting and exercising, and obsessed with purchasing creams and potions, be a better sex partner than someone who is relaxed, interested in other things in life, and well nourished?

If people are thinking about long-term relationships, what are the elements that could sustain such a partnership?

How do they intersect with sexiness?

These are important questions to ask boys as well as girls, because their implications affect everyone.

⚭

After I talked about these issues at one elementary school, a little boy wrote me a note: "Now I know my girlfriend does not need to look like a model. Girls can be pretty and nice in real life, in lots of different ways." If that message could get out to kids everywhere, we would go a long way toward challenging the second myth of the sexy girl and making sex into a more ethical and positive experience that everyone should be able to enjoy.

Chapter 4

THE THIRD MYTH
PRETTY BABIES

Ah, leave me alone in my pubescent park . . .
—VLADIMIR NABOKOV, *Lolita*

IN 2007, A twelve-year-old girl named Maddison Gabriel created a sensation at Australia's Gold Coast Fashion Week. Named the "official face" of the event, she walked the runways, her preteen body provocatively on display in revealing couture outfits and skimpy swimwear. This public performance unleashed storms of controversy. An ABC news report called her "Lolita-inspired," and the *New York Daily News* dubbed her "The kitten of the catwalk." One Web blogger noted sardonically, "Kids can be hot, too!" She reignited the ongoing public debates about girls' sexuality, debates that have been raging ever since a sixteen-year-old Britney Spears pranced around in a Catholic school uniform and babyish pigtails in her first music video.

Britney's school uniform and pigtails were, of course, deliberate choices. She wore her uniform to maximum seductive effect, with the shirt tied high above her midriff and the skirt shortened to micro-mini brevity. The same uniform appeared in a book of erotica in 2007, when the celebrated fashion photographer Santé D'Orazio chronicled the sexual awakening of Kat Fonseca, a "beautiful Latina schoolgirl." In the book *Katlick School*, Kat, like Britney, starts off clad in the classic Catholic school uniform: a microscopic pleated skirt, white blouse, and sneakers. "There is something powerfully erotic about Catholic schoolgirl uniforms," writes D'Orazio's coauthor. "It's a charming fetish, as psychosexually resonant as the black motorcycle jacket or the nurse's uniform." D'Orazio's photographs in *Katlick School* become increasingly explicit, first offering glimpses of the girl's Snoopy underwear, and eventually portraying Kat completely out of the uniform, posing in nothing but a pair of thigh-high boots. "I was experimenting with a symbol of virginity, the untouched, the ideal, the romantic notion of the pure," explained D'Orazio in *Maclean's* magazine. "That is what the uniform signifies." It also, of course, signifies childhood. The schoolgirl uniform is easily recognizable as the classic "Lolita" garment—it's a favorite motif in child pornography.

The idea of the sexy little girl is a potent one in the adult imagination, and in recent years it has become insistently present in mainstream, as well as alternative, media.

Back in 1998, that "fetish" school uniform worked to elevate the underage Britney Spears to instant sex symbol status. Photographed shortly thereafter for the cover of *Rolling Stone* magazine, she posed, even more scantily clad, with dolls and stuffed animals in a child's bedroom, further reinforcing a "jail-bait" innuendo. "The world wasn't prepared for the incendiary combination of girlish purity and sex-kitten naughtiness she would come to embody," wrote Jenny Eliscu in *Rolling Stone*. "According to [photographer David] LaChapelle, he didn't have to do any coaxing to get Spears to flaunt her sex appeal. 'We wanted a very Lolita-ish picture,' he says. 'I distinctly remember her manager walking into her bedroom where we were photographing her with her shirt open and her boobs popping out. He was like, 'What are you guys doing!' And Britney said, 'Yeah, I don't feel comfortable.' But as soon as he walked out of the room, she completely unbuttoned the sweater and we continued."

Britney's allure was that of a "Lolita"—very young and very provocative. She quickly became an icon, followed by Christina Aguilera, whose image was more sexually charged and whose song lyrics were more overtly sexual than Spears's. These performers had tremendous appeal, not only among audiences their own age but among adult men *and* very young—'tween and even toddler—girls, who imitated their provocative dress styles. In a parallel move, African American elementary-school girls were adopting the sexy clothing styles—the transparent tops, hot pants, and stripper-style pasties—of rappers like Li'l Kim. All of this provoked a great deal of public debate and a range of responses, from defenses of girls' right to sexual expression to policing in the form of school dress codes and television specials devoted to these performers' influence on young children.

It's readily apparent that these representations have become a feature of everyday life. Arguably because of the popularity of these media representations, little girls' shirts feature slogans like, "so many boys, so little time" or "hottie." The 9x Games Web site has a "Sexy Schoolgirl" dress-up game, and health clubs offer pole-dancing classes for girls as young as seven. Increasingly, adult sexual motifs are overlapping with childhood—specifically girlhood, shaping an environment in which young girls are increasingly seen as valid participants in a public culture of sex.

In some ways, this is not a new idea: in the 1932 short

film *Polly Tix in Washington*, a four-year-old Shirley Temple played a pint-sized prostitute. Sashaying around in lacy lingerie and ropes of pearls, she announced, "Boss Flint Eye sent me over to entertain you . . . but I'm expensive!" Critics have commented on the overt lewdness of this and other films the toddler was cast in as part of the "Baby Burlesk" series, which were designed for adult viewers and included frequent scenes of little girls in diapers aping the sexual behaviors and attitudes of much older women. In her later films, too, Temple projected an "oddly precocious" sensuality, as the film historian Marianne Sinclair has observed—in fact, the acclaimed novelist Graham Greene was sued for commenting on it in a film review.

Our sex goddesses have often been very young, and it's striking that the role of child prostitute was the springboard for the careers of many of them: not just Temple, but the fourteen-year-old Jodie Foster in *Taxi Driver*, twelve-year-old Brooke Shields in *Pretty Baby*, and thirteen-year-old Penelope Cruz in the French soap opera *Série Rose*. While all of these media vehicles were commentaries on child sexual exploitation, they were at the same time titillating representations of a "nymphet" sexuality that instantly positioned these child actresses as sex symbols while they were emphatically underage. The roles also reinforced the inevitable link between girls' sexuality and sex work.

This issue was still alive in May 2004, when the film critic Richard Roeper pointed out the "stripper-schoolgirl fantasy" projected by the teenage screen stars Britney Spears and Lindsay Lohan in movies like *Crossroads* and *Confessions of a Teenage Drama Queen*. Commenting on the "stylized, sexualized" roles these then-teenagers played, he acknowledges that they inspire "pure lust" in male viewers, though middle-aged men are disallowed from admitting that they are aroused by these young girls. "We generally ignore, or at least pretend to ignore, the sexual electricity of the young actresses," he writes, but ends his article by arguing that they are "objects of fantasy" and are intended to be seen as sexually desirable by adult men, despite their tender years.

Or perhaps because of them.

The American media ideal of female sexuality has been getting progressively younger over the years. In the middle part of the last century, our icons of female sexuality were downright elderly by today's standards: Marilyn Monroe was twenty-seven when she immortalized the seductress Lorelei Lee in *Gentlemen Prefer Blondes*; Elizabeth Taylor was twenty-four when she sizzled onscreen in *Cat on a Hot Tin Roof*; Sophia Loren was twenty-three as the sensuous Abbie Cabot in *Desire Under the Elms*. These film sirens were legally and physically adults; their much-admired bodies were women's bodies— voluptuous and fully developed. Their bodies would not meet today's standards of sculpted muscularity and narrow-hipped leanness. They looked too much like mature women to have present-day appeal in an era of the Lolita Effect.

The British model Twiggy Lawson is often cited for introducing the slender, boyish, adolescent body type as a Western feminine ideal. She was only sixteen when she started modeling in 1966: she was five feet six inches tall and weighed a mere ninety pounds, prompting the media scholar Marshall McLuhan to remark, "Twiggy is an X-ray, not a picture." By the late 1980s the slender adolescent body had come to epitomize female beauty. "A girl at the edge of puberty has a naturally hairless body that demands no shaving, waxing or chemicals to feel smooth. She has the soft, wrinkle-free skin of childhood older women can only regain with surgery and careful application of creams and cosmetics. . . . Her body is naturally small, supple and nothing if not youthful," observes the sociologist Wendy Chapkis. The Western ideal of female beauty, she writes, is defined by "eternal youth."

This emphasis on youthfulness as the mark of beauty and desirability has led to the increasing use of very young girls as models in fashion and advertising, often in very sexually suggestive contexts. Most catwalk models today are between fourteen and nineteen years of age, and some are as young as twelve—like Maddison Gabriel, and Gerren Taylor, who was not yet in her teens when she began modeling for such haute couture houses as Betsey Johnson and Tommy Hilfiger. Victoria's Secret model Adriana Lima began modeling at twelve, and Sports Illustrated swimsuit model Laetitia Casta started at fifteen. The American designer Calvin Klein is infamous for his use of young models in sexually provocative advertising. In 1995, he launched a series of blue-jeans ads that featured very young-looking teenage models in situations that had overtones of child pornography. Klein withdrew the ads and offered a public apology in the face of growing media criticism of these depictions, although some media scholars saw the criticism of these ads as a conservative and moralizing attempt to deny the political and sexual efficacy of youth. There's a difference, though, between sexual agency and sexualization: sexualization is a version of sex that is disempowering and objectifying. The Klein ads showed the models being coerced by adults to remove their clothing in situations that (inevitably, it seems) suggested sex work. There's a real problem here: children cannot and should not be seen as willing participants in sex work.

But the clothing trends and media portrayals of sexy children are, in fact, promoting that very idea, and young girls in particular are increasingly posed in commercial photography and other media as sexual objects of the adult gaze. A series of Louis Vuitton print ads featuring seductive topless photographs of preteen girls appeared in major mainstream magazines a couple of years ago: they went wholly unremarked. A recent *Newsweek* article described Halloween costumes in little girls' sizes that include fishnet stockings, corsets and "Chamber Maid" outfits marketed as "sexy" and "hot." And an Australian billboard for Lee jeans featured a teenage model wearing hotpants, exposing a breast, and sucking on a lollipop.

Actually, in this last example, the model was eighteen, but posed and made up to look at least five years younger. This is a different twist on the same idea: that ideal female sexuality is youthful, or even childlike. A notorious ad for Akademiks clothing featured a woman in panties and pigtails (it was withdrawn from New York public transit for its implications of oral sex). Numerous clothing ads feature grown women dressed as little girls, sucking on lollipops, with tiny barrettes or bows in their hair, kneeling, crouching or lying flat in positions of utter helplessness and subordination. The model Kat Fonseca in *Katlick School* was eighteen when the photographs were shot, but styled to look younger, posed in Snoopy underwear and sucking her thumb. Childishness is sexy, these messages imply. Ergo, children—especially little girls—are sexy.

These depictions, and their ultimate conclusion, do nothing to foster a healthy, balanced understanding of sex as a normal part of human life that is best experienced in adulthood. This idea alone is still being publicly debated. Sex as an adult activity is a feature of advanced civilizations. In the Dark Ages, children were seen as fair sexual game for adults: "The practice of playing with children's privy [*sic*] parts formed part of a widespread tradition," as the medieval historian Philippe Aries has noted. In most ancient cultures, both

Eastern and Western, incest, adult-child sex, and pedophilia were commonplace. "The history of childhood is a nightmare from which we have only recently begun to awaken," wrote the psychohistorian Lloyd deMause. "The further back in history one goes, the lower the level of child care, and the more likely children are to be killed, abandoned, beaten, terrorized and sexually abused." In a recent speech, he observed, "A childhood more or less free from adult sexual use is in fact a very late historical achievement, limited to a few fortunate children in a few modern nations."

In *The History of Philosophy*, the philosopher Michel Foucault traces the "ponderous silence on the sex of children and adolescents" to the sixteenth century, when childhood, as a separate developmental phase, is generally believed to have been invented. Child sexual abuse as a concept and a crime was unknown until the 1700s. The recognition of childhood as a separate developmental stage that needs special nurture, attention, and tending is a humane development, one that gave rise to specialized fields such as pediatrics, developmental psychology, and early childhood education. There were downsides to these outcomes—when they were misapplied, these practices became tools for repressing and policing children—but on the whole, their intentions were to support and cherish children so that they could grow up in safe, healthy, and stimulating environments.

But today, there are challenges to the strict social taboos on adult-child sex. The essayist and journalist Judith Levine points out that among teenagers, at any rate, there is widespread consensus that early sexual experiences can be both pleasurable and harmless. She argues for lowering the legal age of consent to twelve. There are multiple complications to this position, of course: in addition to the need to ensure that there is no coercion involved in such encounters, the health risks of early sex are significant. Are twelve-year-olds really capable of distinguishing between coercive and noncoercive sex? Do they have the judgment to take precautions that will prevent pregnancy, sexually transmitted disease, and serious emotional aftermath? In most cases, probably not.

The media's sexual objectification of girls includes girls much younger than twelve these days, anyway. Even Levine could not argue that a child of ten or younger could, with clarity, initiate, participate in, and control a sexual encounter with an adult. Yet the numerous media representations of very young girls in highly sexual situations and poses implies that they are classic "Lolitas"—knowledgeable, wanton, and seductive. It sends a powerful message to adults that little girls should be viewed as sexy—that is, as objects of a sexual gaze—because of the symbolism of the clothes, poses, and situations in which they are presented.

This is not to advocate the censorship of such representations—for, after all, censorship would disallow the novel *Lolita* or Shakespeare's *Romeo and Juliet* from publication, and perhaps even ban this book (!)—but to point out once again the pervasive representation of children's sexuality in relation to sex work. As a culture, we have very few other ways to represent or acknowledge children's sexuality, and we seem incapable of dealing with it in ways that might be in the best interests of the children themselves—that is, *outside* of the realm of sexual commodification and commerce, in non-exploitative and supportive ways. Judith Levine may have a point that noncoercive sex among teenagers is not automatically harmful, but that is not the kind of sexuality generally depicted in the mainstream media.

Sexual curiosity and even some experimentation—playing "doctor," playing "house," and noticing physical differences—are ordinary features of childhood, and sex as a topic of interest will unquestionably become more salient as children enter and progress through adolescence. But most contemporary societies are in agreement that sexual intercourse is best delayed until physical and psychological maturity is reached. There is widespread legal consensus that it is necessary to establish an "age of consent" as to when a person can voluntarily engage in sexual conduct. Statutory rape laws and marriage laws are attempts to recognize the maturation and psychological development that are necessary to voluntarily consent to sex; so are the laws regarding mental retardation and sexual intercourse.

But there is also much debate about what that "age of consent" should be, and it varies from country to country; it's also often different for boys and girls, with the legal age often inexplicably lower for boys than girls. The legal age is as young as twelve in Zimbabwe and thirteen in Japan; as high as eighteen in many other countries, but even then there is considerable variation. Within the United States, the legal age is as low as fourteen in some states, and there is ongoing debate about whether close-in-age sex should count as statutory rape.

All of these ambiguities affect the definitions of child exploitation, pornography, and prostitution, which continue to be legal minefields for courts and law enforcement agencies. The line between artistic expression and child exploitation is judicially unclear; as of this writing, the U.S. Supreme Court is weighing this problem in *United States v. Williams*, as they consider whether the promotion of child pornography is protected by the First Amendment. Currently, in Japan, the practice of "enjo kosai," in which older men pay teenage girls with money or expensive presents for sex as well as other kinds of companionship, is a culturally sanctioned form of child prostitution, and in Kenya child prostitution is "accepted as normal," according to an article in the British medical journal *Lancet*.

In general, we seem to lack clarity about child sexuality. We're not clear about what constitutes child pornography, and we're equally unclear in establishing the point where mainstream representations cross over that line. We seem to be reverting to a time when childhood was indistinct from adulthood, when the concept of "child abuse" was unknown. In our justifiable fear of censorship, and the insidious push of a commercial culture intent on sexualizing girlhood, we are terrified of talking about what constitutes appropriate boundaries of sexuality, especially in relation to children.

So, what does constitute a permissible representation of children's sexuality? What doesn't? Is *Pretty Baby* okay? Is *Taxi Driver*? What about the 2003 film *Thirteen*, in which adolescent girls act out promiscuous sex as well as drug use? And just how young is "too young"?

My answer has to be firmly against censorship, because the vast array of human experience needs to be represented, in art and in literature, as well as in other forms. Child prostitution exists. Middle-school students are engaging in high-risk sex and substance abuse. These are realities that should be acknowledged and represented. Art, film, and literature should spark widespread debates and discussions of these issues.

While recognizing the value of realistic representations, as a society we have a concurrent obligation to examine the realities and beliefs underlying these representations. We are also obliged to examine the representations themselves. What are their goals? How were they made? Is there a social benefit or harm in such representation? What are the social costs and benefits at stake? What are the social implications of such representations?

For many Americans, sex at puberty—and the representation of such sex—is acceptable and unproblematic. An extended discussion on the popular "Movie Forums" Web site, for example, indicates that many viewers of the award-winning film *American Beauty* did not see the middle-aged Kevin Spacey's sexual interest in a high-school cheerleader as pedophilic or debauched. "Pedophilia is having sex with children, not highly sexed high school girls!" wrote one person on the site's discussion board; and the quickly posted response from another reader was, "I agree. To me pedophilia is more about abusing kids (like in 'Happiness'), and with kids, I mean those who haven't reached puberty yet. I don't think 'American Beauty' is about that kind of pedophilia. It's more about 'forbidden fruit.'" Yet even this response indicates some confusion about sexual standards: Why is this fruit "forbidden" if puberty indicates sexual readiness? And if puberty is the marker of the ability to consent to sex, what should we make of the recent incidence of eight- and even six-year-olds attaining puberty? Can physical maturation predict the ability to make a consensual decision about sex? Of course not: this is why the legal age of consent is not, and should not be, tied to the physiological onset of puberty.

Why is girls' sexual desirability so culturally linked to youth—and increasingly, to extreme youth? Why is this link so strongly emphasized in the mainstream media, when child pornography is repudiated just as strongly in almost all societies? What's the line between child pornography and the sexualization of children in the mainstream media—or is there one? This is the troubling question that underlies the consternation and vocal public debate surrounding these issues. The depiction of actual intercourse would seem to be a determining factor, yet the conventions of soft-core pornography don't require that sex acts be depicted. The gray areas of sexualization, objectification, and eroticization are hotly contested. In the meantime, the highly sexualized representation of little girls has become acceptable, even routine, in mainstream popular culture. A pointed allusion to this is conveyed in the Academy Award–nominated film *Little Miss Sunshine*, when seven-year-old Olive performs a striptease routine set to the Rick James tune "Superfreak." The film makes the point that there is a hypocritical double standard at work in our attitudes toward girls' sexuality, for Olive's bump-and-grind dance is on a clear continuum with the other little girls' "acceptable" beauty pageant performances.

∞

In line with all this, the Lolita Effect in contemporary society hinges on a third myth: the idea that female sexuality is the province of youth. Because of this, it has come to seem almost natural that very young girls should be groomed to project sexual desirability. "My 26-month-old daughter didn't emerge from the womb clamoring for a seashell bikini like Princess Ariel's," lamented *Los Angeles Times* columnist Rosa Brooks in an editorial about the provocative preschool girls' fashions inspired by Disney and other children's media corporations. Girls in the pre-tween set are now buying clothes in sizes 4 to 9 that are described as "candidly provocative" in a *New York Times* article, where children's magazine editor Pilar Guzman observes, "The gap is diminishing between what's meant

for children and what's intended for their elders."
Marketers call this "age compression," or "KGOY"—
"Kids Getting Older Younger"—and this marketing construct is blurring the line between adults and children,
especially with regard to sexuality. As consumer psychologist Kit Yarrow observed in a *USA Today* interview, "Sexy
is the ubiquitous look for the entire generation." But, of
course, "sexy" is actually not the look for "the entire generation" but rather for an entire generation of *girls*. (Boys'
clothing has changed very little in recent decades.) The
sexy "look" is now marketed to girls as young as four, and
the "look" carries with it the implication that little girls are
to be regarded as sexual; it also implies that they are sexually aware, experienced, and in control.

Studies have suggested that little girls enjoy emulating
popular fashion trends, using makeup, and attracting boys'
attention by wearing skimpy clothes. In social settings where
girls are not going to be penalized or targeted for these
behaviors, it's easy to see how these things could be completely harmless, fun, or even empowering. Clothing and
makeup aren't problematic. It's the corollary assumption—
that youth is sexy, that little girls are sexy, and that because
of that they can be seen as having the same sexual awareness
as adults—that's of real concern. The problem is not with
children, but with adults: with marketers who knowingly sell
products and images with powerful sexual overtones to
young girls, and with adults who then interpret girls' bodies
as sexually available. And there's a larger, social problem,
too, in that because of the increased sexualization of girlhood, children are engaging in sexual activity at younger and
younger ages. This has fallout that's expensive both to the
kids and to society as a whole.

The third myth of the Lolita Effect implies that the younger a girl is, the sexier she is. Ideal sexiness, according to this myth, is about being young—very, very young, it seems, keeping in mind the preteen models in mainstream advertising, and the iconic place that JonBenét Ramsey occupies in our culture (many little girls follow in her beauty queen footsteps in pageants all over the country each year). This myth frames female sexuality in terms of appealing to others, but it simultaneously implies that the girls themselves are sexual participants in this cultural construction. That's a highly unlikely assumption, on the whole, when it comes to girls who are pre-tween or even younger. And as we've seen from the research, even adolescents are only just learning to negotiate their sex lives, in an environment that offers them very little information, support, or guidance, while bombarding them with unrealistic and risky sexual messages.

"The process of achieving sexual maturity begins at conception and ends at death," write the sociologists John Delamater and William Friedrich in the *Journal of Sex Research*. Female sexuality is a complex, nuanced concept that's influenced by biology and by society. But experts usually draw a line between sexual desire and other aspects of sexuality, such as sexual response or arousal or even sexual activity. Sexual desire is about a person's motivation to engage in sex; it's about acting on sexual feelings; it's about self-will. This is different from sexual arousal, which is fairly reflexive; even infants have been observed to be aroused, but we can't attribute any knowledge about sex to them. But desire is different. Biologically, sexual desire is tied to the onset of pubertal hormones, especially androgens, so girls usually don't experience sexual desire until adolescence. After that, desire can wax and wane. It is experienced at different life stages; it differs from individual to individual; and it differs across cultures. Women report that their relationships with their partners, their moods, their body image, and a variety of other factors influence their desire as well as their sexual arousal. But one study has suggested that sexual desire increases in women during the prime childbearing years. Some evidence indicates that desire tapers off when women reach menopause—but then again, other studies show that women experience a *heightened* sexual drive during the "change of life." There is clear evidence that postmenopausal women enjoy satisfying sex lives.

By contrast, the research indicates that prior to puberty, children do not experience sexual desire. In addition, they are not in control of their lives or decisions, especially their sexual decision making, and they don't have the knowledge or judgment to make such decisions anyway. It would be preposterous to agree with the judge who, in 1982, accused a five-year-old rape victim of being "unusually sexually promiscuous" (the little girl jumped on her mother's boyfriend while he was sleeping in the nude, and he raped her; the judge interpreted this act as provocation and gave the rapist a mere ninety-day sentence, saying, "I do believe she [the child] was the aggressor"). So, the hypersexual representations of very young girls forces us to confront series of uncomfortable questions. The first is: why? Why have we moved from an admiration of adult women—the Ava Gardners, the Sophia Lorens, the Pam Griers, and the Raquel Welches of previous decades—to a societal lust for grade-school girls, or even tykes barely out of diapers? If these little girls can't feel sexual desire or understand very much about it, then why are we so obsessed with fetishizing them as sexual paragons?

A possible answer is that it is a patriarchal backlash against feminism. Society has been forced to confront women as contenders in the social arena (though in fact gender equity is still not a reality of life in the twenty-first century). Nonetheless, since the sexual revolution and the legislative reforms of the 1970s, from reproductive rights to sexual harassment laws, women continue to assert themselves to seek pleasure, independence, and control in their sex lives. These gains, though fairly minimal, have generated resentment and backlash from men, as in Michael Noer's infamous 2006 column in *Forbes*, "Don't marry a career woman," in which he claimed that working women are more likely to cheat on their husbands. Little girls fit more easily into a conventional mold of female sexuality: a perspective in which she lacks authority over her own body and is therefore less threatening than any adult woman today. Because of this, little girls epitomize a patriarchal society's ideal of compliant, docile sexuality.

These images also work to overemphasize girls as primarily sexual, and it undermines them as multidimensional human beings with other characteristics and attributes. For after all, girls are also smart and thoughtful; many are artistic, musical, or athletic; most are spiritual. To grow into fully fledged human beings, these aspects of their lives need to be nurtured and valued, too. But in the media, especially media aimed at adults, girls are only sexual. They are reduced to one-dimensional, wholly limited figurines. In this way, their potential and complexity is negated. They are regarded as sex dolls, and nothing more.

But I think there's more to it than that, and once again, the motivation is commercial. For starters, getting consumers hooked on brands early is a goal of most manufacturers, so cosmetics and fashion designers are finding ways to peddle their products to preschoolers, capturing loyal consumers almost from day one. The implications of a six-year-old wearing a thong is irrelevant compared to the long-term economic gains realized by the thong manufacturers. Moreover, on the flip side, emphasizing girlishness as desirable facilitates the multibillion-dollar sales of anti-aging cosmetics, creams, plastic surgeries, and medications worldwide. In truth, nothing can reverse the aging process: no amount of Botox is going to make a fifty-year-old suddenly acquire a five-year-old's skin, and it would take a tremendous amount of money and effort for a middle-aged woman's body to even begin to resemble a twelve-year-old model's. But the emphasis on youth as sexy is an ideological manipulation that fuels the sale of such products and treatments, estimated at $57 billion a year.

Finally, there's the underground economy of little girls' sexuality: child sex trafficking and prostitution. According to the United Nations, sex trafficking is the fastest-growing area of organized crime, and it reaps about $7 billion dollars a year in profits. In some Asian countries—such as Malaysia, Thailand, and the Philippines—sex trafficking accounts for as much as 14 percent of the Gross Domestic Product. In Thailand, the yearly estimated income from prostitution from 1993 to 1995 was over $20 billion. In the Czech Republic, it is estimated at $100 million annually. As one report points out, children sold into prostitution earn profits year after year for their pimps and exploiters—unlike drugs, which are consumed immediately. There is no question that this is a thriving industry that spans the globe. Child sex trafficking and prostitution are closely linked to the robust child pornography industry, where profits also run into billions of dollars annually.

Children may be forced into prostitution and pornography to escape from extreme poverty or simply as a reflection of local sexual mores, but the media contribute to a cultural landscape in which the sexual objectification of girls is acceptable and even normal. Realistic, strong, and nonexploitative representations of girls' sexuality would be a progressive social step, but images of girls posed, styled, and framed as objects of the erotic adult gaze can't be considered the same way. They literally strip little girls of an empowered sexuality. They often employ the conventions of sex work, thus legitimizing the use of young girls for prostitution and pornography.

So two tough questions remain: Are such representations simply a playful and harmless recognition that girls are sexual? Or are they targeting girls as sex objects?

The problem here is that we have no cultural metaphors for girls' sexuality outside of objectification and sex work. I wish we could answer firmly that Halloween costumes for little girls that involve vinyl boots and corsets are just silly and fun. They may be, in contexts where girls are totally protected, safe, and secure from any misreading or violation of this intention. But I am not convinced that such contexts exist, especially for girls outside of the First World, especially for girls who live in poverty, especially for girls whose lives have rendered them vulnerable to sexual exploitation and attack. As the journalist Ariel Levy has pointed out, today, we depend on the sex industry "to mark us as an erotic and uninhibited culture," but this is an ultimately repressive idea of sex, one that works against more emancipated and diverse possibilities. "We need to make room for a range of options as wide as the variety of human desire. We need to allow ourselves the freedom to figure out what we internally want from sex instead of mimicking whatever popular culture holds up to us as sexy. *That* would be sexual liberation," she argues.

I agree. And it is important to liberate children, too: to free them from the constraining, exploitative, and commercially motivated construction of sex that seems to be our only

way of defining female sexuality. The risks of such representations are much greater than the benefits. It's imperative to
unyoke sex work from childhood: to create safe and supportive spaces in which girls can come to understand their
sexuality *on their own terms* and in their own time.

What we can do

This is a juggernaut for anyone to take on: with billions
of dollars at stake, neither the mainstream media nor the child
sex traffickers will easily relinquish their positions.

But open discussion of these issues is certainly a start:
consciousness-raising is always the first step toward change.
We need to ask ourselves if we can live with the widespread
sexualization of girls—and whether the media's insistence on
presenting girlhood as primarily sexual creates an environment in which girls can grow up with healthy, secure, and
informed perspectives on their bodies and their sex lives. Can
it be to girls' advantage if they are almost unvaryingly presented as sexual in wholly regressive and fixed ways? What about
the other aspects of their lives—their intellectual growth, their
artistic talents, their activism and community spirit, their spirituality? Does it help them in any way to be constructed as
one-dimensional dolls?

• TALK ABOUT PIGEON-HOLING

Teens and 'tweens can understand this kind of discussion;
they are often uncomfortable with mainstream cultural views
of girls' bodies as primarily sexual. They, too, want the option
to explore various aspects of their personalities and interests,
and they often resent being pigeonholed. They are acutely
aware of the hierarchies of beauty and sexuality at work in

their peer groups, and they can talk about these issues critically and thoughtfully. Having an outlet in which such ideas can be discussed is often tremendously liberating and empowering for girls, who have been cowed by the tyranny of this imagery and dissuaded from talking about it critically in peer contexts.

It's best to begin the discussions without showing any images, as the images are often confusing to girls: they are beguiled by the aesthetics of the images, which makes critical analysis harder. But beginning with a discussion of what people think of girls can elicit eager responses and well-defined examples of gendered stereotypes. You might begin with a very simple question, like, "How do you think people see girls?" or "What do people think girls ought to be like?" Let the girls talk about this until they have identified the main problems with social and cultural constructions of girlhood. These will probably include the emphasis on cookie-cutter prettiness, the expectations that girls should behave flirtatiously and never appear serious or smart, the emphasis on body ideals, and the imperative of "hotness." Then ask about the reasons they think these stereotypes exist. The media will, without a doubt, come up. This is the starting point for a critique of the one-dimensionality and restrictiveness of media representations of girls' sexuality.

• LOOK AT THE MEDIA PROJECT

The nonprofit organization the Media Project works to improve media depictions of adolescent sexuality, with the goal of educating teens about sexual health. They have consulted with the writers and producers of shows such as *Grey's Anatomy* and *My Wife and Kids* to ensure that the representations and discussions of sex are factual, responsible, and still entertaining. Checking out their Web site at www.themediaproject.com can be an enjoyable and informative exercise for adults and older teens. After looking at the site, ask girls about TV shows or movies they have seen in which sex was represented in unrealistic or disturbing ways. Brainstorm about how it could be improved.

• CREATE POSITIVE MEDIA

Encourage girls to create their own media—Webzines, films, magazines, and blogs—that grapple with these issues. With the proliferation of blogs and Internet media, it's very easy to be an active part of the solution instead of the problem. A starting place could be the New Moon magazine Web site, which features the "Luna Vida" club for eight- to twelve-year-olds and the "Orb 28" site for thirteen- to fifteen-year-olds, where girls can blog, chat, and post artwork; the print version of the magazine accepts contributions from girls. It's easy to make a homemade magazine: paper and a stapler is all you need, along with a disposable camera to shoot pictures and paste them in. Some schools offer summer camps in digital media, video production, and filmmaking; these are often inexpensive and lots of fun. Many girls create MySpace or Facebook sites that are spaces in which to express and explore ideas and issues. Applaud girls' creative efforts. Above all, encourage them to trust their own judgments.

• MOBILIZE OLDER KIDS AS ACTIVISTS

Older teens—fifteen or sixteen and up—are also often socially conscious, and when they learn about child prostitution and sex work, they are usually outraged and eager to work on behalf of girls being exploited and abused in these industries. The development of a social consciousness and real efforts to combat this problem can be the positive, humanitarian outcome of such discussions. There are a number of organizations that work to combat child sex trafficking and prostitution, from UNICEF to smaller groups that offer shelters and foster care for children in these situations. A list of some of these is provided at the end of this book.

• FIGHT BACK AGAINST THE MERCENARIES

There are steps that adults (and kids) can take to show retailers that their advertising and media strategies are losing them business and respect. Letters and feedback to corporations can help. Some companies are sensitive to consumer pressure, and many are interested in socially conscious, progressive marketing. It's worth a try, especially if corporations get the message that their customers think differently and may spend their money accordingly.

THE FOURTH MYTH
VIOLENCE IS SEXY

∞

> She sat right in the focus of my incandescent anger.
>
> —VLADIMIR NABOKOV, *Lolita*

"SEX EQUALS DEATH, OKAY?" explains Randy, a character in Wes Craven's tongue-in-cheek slasher film *Scream*. With intended irony, his prediction holds true in that film, as it does in most others in this genre. But the familiar theme of sexualized violence has intensified and changed in the new millennium: it is more savage, more graphic, and less farcical than ever before.

For example, at the start of the 2007 remake of the classic horror movie *Halloween*, a ten-year-old boy broods between intercut scenes of his nubile mother pole-dancing in a strip club. Apparently driven by conflicted Oedipal desires (the soundtrack pointedly features heavy-metal band Nazareth's version of "Love Hurts"), the boy hacks up his family in a gory killing spree. In this first section of the film, where the maniacal killer Michael Meyers' motivations are explored, his mother's sex work and his sister's promiscuity are offered as justifications for his massacres. And throughout the film (which broke box office records), sex is linked to brutal violence: almost every time lovemaking is depicted, featuring extended shots of seminude teenage girls, the masked killer furiously attacks.

This is a recurrent theme in horror movies, one that can be traced back to 1960, when an apparently nude Janet Leigh was stabbed in the shower in Alfred Hitchcock's *Psycho*. The sexualization of violence in horror/slasher films is a topic that has been debated intensely by film scholars and critics; in 1980, Gene Siskel and Roger Ebert dedicated an entire episode of their popular PBS TV show *Sneak Previews* to it, sharply criticizing the misogyny (or antifemale aspect) of these movies. In his book on the genre, journalist Adam Rockoff writes, "[I]n the slasher film, both 'good' girls and 'bad' girls are killed with equal gusto. The fact that this usually occurs after sex is less a comment on morality than a simple exploitation technique used to titillate the audience by giving them a liberal, and much appreciated, dose of nudity." But exploitation is never "simple"—it's gendered, it's political, it's motivated, and it deserves to be analyzed more closely.

Rockoff's casual presumption is that heterosexual males are the main target audience for these scenes, as the nudity is always female nudity. "Titillation" means that the scenes are intended to arouse straight male viewers—and that "much appreciated" titillation almost inevitably precedes violence against the girls. As the cultural critic Jackson Katz observes, in slasher films "you often have scenes, for example, of girls undressing, taking a shower or wearing sexy low-cut dresses, sometimes even removing clothing at opportune moments or being positioned in sexually provocative camera angles designed to sexually arouse straight boys, and then, at the moment the boys are aroused, is when the girls are assaulted." "There's something inherently sexual in every slasher movie," says *Slumber Party Massacre* director Amy Holden Jones. "What is wrong with being inherently sexual?" But the question cleverly slips the point: it isn't really the sex that's a problem, it's the persistent linkage of violence and girls' sexual objectification. Boys, though victims, are not *sexualized* victims in these films. And because of those portrayals of girls, straight boys are very likely sexually aroused when the violence occurs. So male sexual pleasure becomes identified with violence—a really disturbing connection.

Whether these scenes are intended to condone sexual violence against girls and women is controversial. In her analysis of 1980s slasher films, the film scholar Carol Clover argued that the films are "victim-identified"—that is, they allow male as well as female viewers to empathize with the girl victims, and especially with another conventional figure in such movies, the "Final Girl," a potential victim who always ends up vanquishing the killer. Clover asserts that the slasher film "gives us a clearer picture of current sexual attitudes . . . than do the legitimate products of the better studios." For Clover, as well as other critics, these films are not "simple": like other artistic products, they reflect the politics and sexual mores of their times, expressing collective fears and anxieties. For example, in the neoconservatism of Reagan's America, the *Friday the 13th* movies featured sexual violence that reinforced the moral panics of the era. As Rockoff noted, they capitalized on "the idea of these kids having this unprotected sex, setting themselves up for God knows what, and the idea of Jason as the fist of God, punishing these kids for their drinking, their drugs and their sexuality."

Interestingly, the girls targeted for violence were often negligent babysitters, who abandoned their responsibilities to drink and have sex; so by departing from traditional gender roles involving quasi-maternal caregiving duties, they were committing, it seemed, capital offenses—apparently *earning* the killer's vicious punishment. The films were conservative moral tales, with the killer wreaking a puritanical society's revenge on licentious teens. And they inevitably opened with the gory murders of sexy teenage girls.

In the twenty years since, slasher films have become legitimate studio products that are in wide distribution, and a new genre has emerged: the "horror porn" film, featuring more graphic sexual violence than the self-referential spin-offs of 1980s movies. In *Hostel*, for example, the seductive bodies of young women are lures that trap men in torture chambers: explicit sex leads to horrific violence in the film, which vividly depicts dismemberment and murder. Again, it's the young men's sexual desires and the young women's promiscuity that sets up the violence. The film was hailed as a brilliant critique of American imperialism, but its gendered connotations went unexplored in the reviews.

Hostel: Part II, released in 2007, was even more focused on sexual violence against young women, luridly portraying the sexualized torture of American college girls. Violence against women was turned into an acceptable metaphor for the excesses of American capitalism. In *See No Evil*, directed in 2006 by Gregory Dark, whose former credits include both porno films and Britney Spears videos, the eye-gouging killer fondles and partially disrobes a former teen prostitute; when bell sensors alert the murderer to sexual activity, the audience witnesses the slow and agonizing death of the beautiful young woman who "erred" (in an equal-opportunity move, her handsome young male partner is attacked, too, but his death is less graphically portrayed). In *Captivity* (2007), after unremitting scenes of the violent torture and terrorizing of young women, a lingerie-clad woman is stabbed to death and then photographed by her young son, after a presumably incestuous encounter. Sex scenes are again framed by intense violence as the victim's lover turns out to be her tormentor and a serial killer. Throughout the film, the incidental presence of teddy bears and dolls provide a sinister overtone of childhood.

These films are screened in mainstream theaters and are widely advertised; they have studio budgets and backing. Most of these films are rated R, a rating intended to convey the adult content of these films (interestingly, movies featuring nonviolent consensual sex get rated NC-17, an even more restrictive rating). But in fact, eleven- to fifteen-year-olds are the "prime market" for violent films, according to a recent *Time* magazine report, which notes that the new movies "have moved beyond the manufacture of fright (which can be therapeutic for kids) to the lovingly detailed depiction of sadism." And even movies aimed directly at teenagers follow these patterns: *Freddy vs. Jason* (2003), which won a Teen Choice award, begins with a scene of a pretty teenage girl playfully stripping to go skinny-dipping in a lake, running almost naked through dark woods, and then being savagely and bloodily impaled with a dagger.

The violent content of even PG-13 films has been steadily increasing since the year 2000, and surveys show that parents are concerned about this—more concerned, to their credit, about violence than about sexual content. In all of these films, which are enormously popular with even young teenagers, male sexuality is linked with sadism, while girls' sexuality is victimized. These films have been celebrated by film critics as slyly postmodern, technically sophisticated, and even politically progressive. But there's nothing progressive, healthy, or humane about the repeated instances of sexual violence against women; at their core, these movies carry really repugnant sexual themes.

Some film critics theorize that both male and female viewers "oscillate" between sympathy with the victims and pleasure in the violence; the well-known film scholar Linda Williams, for example, has suggested that these films appeal to both boys and girls and break down gender barriers. Other scholars claim that movies featuring explicit violence against women are "a complex study of power—in this case, the 'regime' of violent male authority wielded against the female form." The gleeful, repeated assaults on sexually provocative girls in slasher films don't come across as profound reflections on a social problem, though. If gender barriers were really being dismantled, boys' sexuality would occasionally operate the same way in these movies, if only to make a point. But it never does.

Boys tend to enjoy slasher films more than girls, as audience research shows; and viewers with the lowest empathy levels—the least capacity to sympathize with others—enjoy them the most. And studies with teen audiences indicate that films play an important role in their lives: "Teens look to movies . . . to understand reality, to understand the world they have inherited," writes the media researcher Jeanne Steele, who has done focus group research with teenagers. A survey by *Variety* showed that teenagers rank movie-watching as their number one pastime. This is key, because movies are significant forms of entertainment in the lives of young people: they offer scripts, particularly scripts of sexuality, that help to shape the way teenagers and children see the world. Younger children tend to be more influenced by media representations, but even older teens—though they see the media as "cool, but not real"—still depend on the media for information about the adult world. "They respond—viscerally, emotionally," observes Steele. Psychologists have recently suggested that teenagers' need for increasingly graphic violence in entertainment is related to higher incidences of adolescent psychiatric problems, including self-mutilation and emotional withdrawal. In short, the research indicates that the messages kids are getting about sex have real-world implications.

This is not to say that the media alone cause kids [and adults, for that matter] to link sex and violence. In fact, it seems to be the other way around: we should think of slasher films as distorted versions of sexuality that help to perpetuate an environment in which sexual violence against women is already prevalent. They exaggerate reality, presenting it as worse than it already is. They draw attention to the myth of female sexuality as a logical target for violence—and in doing so, they reinforce it.

Slasher films aren't the only media featuring sexual violence against girls and women. Video games have long been criticized for scenarios such as those in the *Grand Theft Auto* series, in which players have the opportunity to rape, beat, and murder prostitutes. In one description of the game, "You can pick up a hooker, take her out in the woods, have sex with her many times, then let her out of the car. Then you can shoot her, pull over, beat her with a bat, then you can get into the car and run her over." A recent study found that adolescent boys who played the game inferred that "prostitutes expected to be raped." Parents' groups, child psychologists, and even sex workers have protested the game, but its defenders point out that any character in the game can be treated this way—minus the sex. The *GTA* games are a "global smash hit," and have sold over sixty-five million copies in the United States alone.

Indeed, violence is coupled with sex in many of the most popular video games on the market: *Manhunt 2* offers a torture chamber in the basement of a sex club. In the *Conan the Barbarian* game, which features blood-spattered mayhem throughout, women are depicted in various states of undress. The wildly popular *Halo* series star the character Cortana, a voluptuous female creature who appears to be nude, and again her body is juxtaposed with extremely violent action throughout the game. Many violent video games feature women as strippers, streetwalkers, and sluts. In these ways, hypersexualized young women are framed by violence, even if the violence is not specifically directed against them. But the premise is similar to that of the slasher movies: sexy female bodies, and male arousal, are connected to violence.

These games are usually rated M in the United States, a designation that means they are intended for adult users; they carry similar ratings in other countries. However, as with audiences for R-rated movies, 60 percent of all thirteen- to seventeen-year-olds in the United States have played violent video games. Early adolescent boys, in particular, regularly play M-rated/violent video games. During adolescent identity formation, at a stage when sexuality and gender roles are beginning to be established, the connection between female sexuality and violence is being set up in these game scenarios.

This is not to argue that such a connection is necessarily causal: it is impossible to demonstrate that exposure to sexually violent media causes real-life sexual violence. Sexual violence was around long before these media were invented. But it is also undeniable that most published research on the topic reports long-term and cumulative negative effects of video game violence. One study of sixth- through eighth-grade boys found that previous experience playing *Mortal Kombat* resulted in significantly more aggressive behavior. A large-scale study in 2004 found that eighth- and ninth-graders who played violent video games "were more hostile . . . [and] were more likely to be involved in physical fights." Another recent study found that first-person shooter games increased hostility and aggression. In 2005, the American Psychological Association passed a resolution recommending that violence be reduced in video games and interactive media marketed to children and youth. The resolution was based on a substantial body of scholarly research indicating that exposure to violence in video games increases aggressive feelings and behavior among youth. So it is reasonable to conclude that these games contribute to children's and teens' association of female sexuality with violence.

Music videos are even more complicated, in many ways. A number of music videos objectify women in a hypersexual way, depicting them primarily as sex workers—the legendary "bitches and ho's" (as in 50 Cent's "P.I.M.P." and Ludacris's "Money Maker," for example). One study showed that 90 percent of the videos on MTV had sexually suggestive content. But there are also many progressive and politically powerful representations of women in these media. For example, Wyclef Jean's "Sweetest Girl" is about a prostitute, but the video is a powerful statement on the injustice of refugee asylum policies, and there is no sexualized violence or visual hypersexualization of women in it. Many videos by female artists have directly challenged and criticized violence against women —Eve's "Love is Blind," Ashanti's "Rain on Me," Pink's "Family Portrait," Martina McBride's "Independence Day." Other videos do sexualize women, conforming to the "if you've got it, flaunt it" mode of representation, but there is no overt violence, as in Chris Brown and T-Pain's "Kiss Kiss."

Still, violence against women does appear in music videos; for example, 2007 Video Music Award nominee Justin Timberlake's video "What goes around . . ." features a violent altercation between Timberlake and a cheating girlfriend, and ends with the girl's fiery death. Maroon 5's "Wake Up Call" features bikini-clad young women inexplicably bound and gagged; it also celebrates violent masculinity. Eminem's "Superman" depicted him shoving a voluptuous blonde woman violently against a wall and flinging her clothes after her, while he rapped, "Don't put out? I'll put you out." (Yet Eminem's later song, "Stan," was critical of violence against women.) Ludacris's "Move Bitch" is specifically about beating up a woman: "I been thinkin' a' bustin' you upside ya motherfuckin' forehead." It remains an anthem at college bars and house parties years after it debuted.

The filmmaker Byron Hurt believes that the sexualized violence and misogyny in rap music is a factor in the high levels of sexual assault and domestic violence experienced by African American women. Young black men, he believes, act out the gender relations portrayed in rap: they "try to conform to the script," he argues. A study of African American girls showed that when they were exposed to rap videos, they were more accepting of teen dating violence. Studies of music videos in general indicate that attractive perpetrators of violence in music videos model these behaviors, making real-life violence seem more acceptable. Research has also found that exposure to stereotyped gender roles in music videos has a significant effect on viewers' attitudes: middle-class young white women who are exposed to these videos are more accepting of interpersonal violence.

Television is a virtual minefield in this area. Years of content analysis show, unquestionably, that violence is rampant on television. Two out of three U.S. television shows contain violence, adding up to six violent acts every hour. The research over the last forty years is conclusive that television violence affects children's and teens' attitudes toward violence as well as their tendencies toward violent behaviors. The solution is simple: medical organizations, psychologists, research institutions, and parenting groups are united in the position that children's and teens' television viewing should be limited and monitored.

Children's programming features a great deal of violence, though it is not sexual— in fact, a Kaiser Foundation study showed that violence is more prevalent in children's TV programming than in any other category. But *sexual* violence on television is the focus of shows like *Law and Order—Special Victims Unit* and *Nip/Tuck*, both popular with older teenagers. Sexual violence is a plot device on many teen television shows: the popular *Gossip Girl* and *One Tree Hill* series have depicted attempted rapes; the latter has also featured a stalker who beats up a prostitute and attempts to kill two young girls.

Sexual violence is a feature of professional wrestling, as well, and World Wrestling Entertainment (WWE) has high viewership among teens. A study published recently in the journal *Pediatrics* found that high-school students who watched professional wrestling engaged in more fighting behaviors. The authors of the study point out, "It should not be a surprise that youth who are exposed more often to TV programs that portray a barrage of severe violence without the expected consequences, the degrading of women, sexuality connected with violence, and extreme verbal intimidation and abuse between wrestlers and their female escorts, are influenced by what they see and hear." Another study in the same journal showed that preschool boys (ages two to five) who watched violent TV developed antisocial, aggressive behaviors in the long term (nonviolent and educational television had no such effects, and, interestingly, there were no such effects on girls). But violence and television are practically synonymous, and despite the inroads on viewership made by the Internet, television watching is on the rise among all children, especially twelve- to seventeen-year-old girls.

All of this adds up to the fourth myth of the Lolita Effect: that violence against women is sexy. Images of violence against women are pervasive: on billboards, in magazines, on television. A magazine ad for the upscale Dolce and Gabbana clothing line features a man having sex with a woman, while other men stand around watching. The scene implies a gang rape. The models in the ad are beautiful, and they look intense and turned on. The woman does not appear to be afraid. The gang rape is implicitly justified.

An ad for Cesare Paciotti shoes shows a man stepping on a beautiful, red-lipsticked woman's face.

An ad for Radeon gaming software depicts a topless young woman with the product's name branded on her back: the brand is red and raw.

When I show these images in my classes, the students say they are "sexy." I ask them to imagine a puppy, or a little boy, in these situations: they are shocked. The images of violence are arousing only when the violence is aimed at girls.

The debates about sex and violence in the media have always hinged on the issue of causality: the media, it is widely argued, don't *cause* people to go out and perpetrate violence.

That's true. Audiences don't watch something in the media and then run out and imitate it immediately. Media influences are far more subtle and gradual than any simplistic "imitation theory" could explain.

While the media may not cause our behaviors, they are culture mythmakers: they supply us, socially, with ideas and scripts that seep into our consciousness over time, especially when the myths are constantly recirculated in various forms. They accentuate certain aspects of social life and underplay others. They are a part of a larger culture in which these myths are already at work, making it possible for the myths to find fertile ground in which to take root and flourish. They can reinforce certain social patterns and trends, and invalidate others. They can gradually and insidiously shape our ways of thinking, our notions of what is normal and what is deviant, and our acceptance of behaviors and ideas that we see normalized on television, in films, and in other forms of popular culture. The myths are sugarcoated: they are aesthetically appealing, emotionally addictive, and framed as cutting-edge and subversive. But violence against women is neither edgy nor subversive: the violent abuse of women has been around for a long time. It's important to recognize that media-generated sexual violence against girls highlights and perpetuates a well-established system of brutalization.

Here are a few of the assaults on teenage girls that occurred in 2007: Sixteen-year-old Tiffany Howard of Colorado Springs was shot and killed by her jealous seventeen-year-old boyfriend. In Chicago, seventeen-year-old Chavanna was strangled, shot, and stabbed by her teenage boyfriend. Sixteen-year-old Demi Cuccia was stabbed to death by her boyfriend in Monroeville, Pennsylvania. A fifteen-year-old girl in Davis, California, sustained serious brain injuries when she was pushed down a flight of stairs by her boyfriend. Eleven-year-old Cindy was gang-raped by five teenage boys in her neighborhood. And in a scene right out of a slasher movie, two teenage girls in Iowa were forced to strip and take showers by their nineteen-year-old neighbor, who then stabbed them with knives and bludgeoned them with a hammer.

The new millennium has brought advances in many areas, but violence against girls and women is not one of them.

Teenage girls report being beaten, burned, choked, and shoved by their boyfriends; they also report verbal and emotional abuse. Many have been raped, or coerced into having sex. Women are as likely to be killed by their partners today as they were thirty years ago. In the United States, 85 percent of "intimate partner violence" is perpetrated by men against women, and adolescent girls and younger men are most likely to be the victims in these cases. Approximately one in five girls experiences physical or sexual dating violence. In Japan, 50 percent of girls and women have experienced violence in a relationship. Sixty percent of girls in Croatia have suffered violence in a romantic relationship. Some recent studies indicate that most violent relationships involve both partners as perpetrators, but these findings are controversial—and, in any case, domestic violence can't be counted as progress! While both boys and girls can perpetrate violence in dating, girls are more likely to be seriously injured because of it. And sexual violence is much more often directed against girls and women than against boys or men. One Chicago high-school teacher reported that his male students believed violence against their girlfriends was acceptable: "If she does something to provoke you, then you have to put her in her place," one of his students claimed. But girls, too, increasingly believe that violence is normal and justifiable in the context of a dating relationship, which makes them more accepting of it and less likely to report it.

According to the human rights group Amnesty International, one in three women—or one *billion* women worldwide—have been "beaten, coerced into sex, or otherwise abused in their lifetimes. Usually, the abuser is a member of her own family or someone known to her." The World Health Organization estimates that one in five women will be a victim of rape or attempted rape in her lifetime. Most women never report these abuses, so the statistics fall far short of the realities of violence against women. Very few countries even have legal definitions of sexual assault, or penalties for it.

It's significant that sex workers experience disproportionately high levels of violence; reports show that 80 percent of sex workers have experienced violence in their jobs. The World Health Organization reports that sex workers in a variety of countries, including Namibia, India, and Bangladesh, are frequently "beaten, threatened with a weapon, slashed, choked, raped and coerced into sex." But research with sex workers also shows that they are reluctant to report these incidents for a variety of reasons—fear of the police, fear of losing their livelihoods, the belief that violence is part of their job, and cultural attitudes that encourage their victimization—cultural attitudes that unquestioningly accept the linkage between women, sex, and violence.

These examples and statistics barely scratch the surface of the problem. Violence, especially sexual violence, against girls and women happens everywhere, all the time. The scale of it is horrifying, bleak, and real.

Knowing this, it's important to ask why we need, and (judging by the numbers) savor, media fantasies that link violence with female sexuality. Real-world violence against women and girls is widespread and brutal. So, what's the irresistible appeal of its graphic on-screen representation? In many ways, such representations of violence and depravity speak to our anxieties about the world; they directly address our darkest dreads and our subconscious terrors, and they may even dispel them in the safety of a movie theater or living room. The scholar Stephen Prince writes,

To the extent that we inhabit today a culture of fear, which finds threats of decay and destruction at every turn, the horror film offers confirmation of this zeitgeist. It tells us that our belief in security is a delusion, that the monsters are all around us, and that we, the inhabitants of this collective nightmare, are just so much meat awaiting the slaughter. While this yields a dark portrait, indeed, the great paradox of the genre is that all of this is converted into a pleasurable experience for viewers, or at least for those who regularly patronize the films. This paradox, the nature of horror's appeal and the pleasure that negative emotions can provide, is not easily explained.

These representations—slasher films, music videos, violent video games—are brilliantly stylized replications of real-world patterns. They make sexual violence exciting and appealing, and they also make it seem routine. They highlight the existence of such violence, and they may help us to confront and resolve it, but in focusing on it, they energize the myth.

Because violence against girls, especially sexual violence, is so rampant, we must deal with the issue of media representations that seem to celebrate it. And again, we can't just go into a hysterical moral panic about it. We have to take a hard look at these media and think about what they mean. We need to understand the role they play in an increasingly violent world. They are not going away anytime soon—but we can use them as teaching tools in antiviolence activism.

What we can do

Most teenagers are familiar with these media manifestations of violence, given their immense popularity among their target audience. But it's important not to ignore or trivialize violent media content. Girls, in particular, report being disturbed by these representations, but they rarely have a chance to voice those feelings and talk about the reasons for them.

• ENCOURAGE GROUP DISCUSSION

Group discussions are an excellent place for girls to raise these issues. In my experience, many girls initially declare themselves to be unaffected by the violence, describing it as funny or unrealistic. These are socially acceptable ways to respond—and while they may be legitimate reactions, they may also be defense mechanisms. Flippant reactions can effectively silence others who may think differently, and they tend to deflect the problem. So it is important for an adult moderator to bring up the gender issues, by a series of questions:

> *Why are the girls so often sexual right before the violence occurs?*
> *What's the message there?*
> *Why aren't boys shown in the same way?*
> *Are girls being "punished" for being sexual?*

Girls tend not to notice these patterns, though once the discussion turns serious, some will often acknowledge being frightened, angered, or saddened by the representations. It's important to reassure them that these responses are not silly or unsophisticated: they are understandable, caring human reactions to representations of a real social problem. Engaging in a thoughtful critique of the media representations in the context of real-world violence against women can then raise the issue of sexual violence as a social fact. Girls need to talk about these issues: they need to examine closely their own beliefs, positions, and understanding of gendered violence.

• SEEK OUT AN EXPERT

It can be very helpful to invite a speaker from a domestic violence shelter or sexual assault recovery service to talk to the girls about real-world violence, its causes, and its solutions. These centers usually train volunteers to educate and mentor the public about these issues, so the presentations are well researched, well organized, and thought-provoking. They are also geared to individual and community action—and girls are often motivated to participate in antiviolence activism as a result of these talks.

• USE VISUAL AND INTERNET TOOLS

Using ads and music videos that depict violence against women is another helpful way to draw attention to the issue. A productive exercise involves asking the girls to think about another type of person, or even an animal, in the same situations depicted in the ads. Imagining a kitten, or an elderly woman, in the same scenario reframes it as violent, whereas it may have been seen as merely sexy before. (In media studies, we call this the "commutation test.") Then the question can be raised:

Is violence against women sexy?
Should it be thought of that way in real life?
So why are the ads glamorizing it?

There are a number of Web sites with examples and analyses of violence against women in advertising. One is Gender Ads (www.genderads.com/), which has links with specific, frequently updated examples of a variety of misogynist advertisements. Jean Kilbourne's excellent video presentations on this topic, the *Killing Us Softly* series, are available from the Media Education Foundation. These videotapes are a staple of many university libraries and should be required viewing for anyone interested in this subject.

Many human rights groups—Amnesty International, Human Rights Watch, Women's Human Rights Net, and many others—document violence against women worldwide and mobilize action against it. In the United States, "Break the Cycle" is a teen organization aimed at helping young people achieve healthy, nonviolent relationships and home lives (www.breakthecycle.org/). Visiting any of these groups' Web sites and looking at the data will bring home the scope of the problem. Teen groups can then be challenged to engage in antiviolence activism and education.

There are many excellent educational films available that can further the discussion of real-life violence against girls and women. The PBS short film *In the Mix—Twisted Love* is a powerful and cogent discussion of teen dating violence, and its Web site offers resources, discussion questions, and other useful links (www.pbs.org/inthemix/shows/show_dating_violence.html).

Another topical and thought-provoking video is Byron Hurt's *Beyond Beats and Rhymes*, which looks at misogyny in rap music. Information about the film is at www.pbs.org/independentlens/hiphop/. Accompanying modules on media literacy, gender violence, and masculinity are available online, as are educational materials, including discussion guides and issue briefs.

• REACH OUT TO BOYS AS ACTIVISTS

Hurt's video is aimed at boys and men—especially in the African American community. He is one of several men who are working actively against gendered violence. Another is Jackson Katz, whose Web site (www.jacksonkatz.com) is devoted to the ways in which boys and men can help in the struggle to eliminate violence against women. Katz's books, videos, and lectures are invaluable in bringing boys into the discussion. His "Ten things men can do to prevent gender violence" amounts to a call to arms for boys who see this as a social problem.

A number of positive steps have been taken in response to the problem of violence against women in the media and in the real world. These are human rights and public health issues, and it's imperative that we address them—it's literally a matter of life and death. There are innumerable resources, teaching aids, and real-world media examples of the ongoing brutality that women and girls suffer every day. Creating a safe world for girls and women begins with our taking action by using these resources to raise teenagers' awareness of this issue, to help them to analyze these media in their real-world contexts, and to take action against the problems. A list of relevant resources is provided at the end of this book.

Chapter 6

THE FIFTH MYTH
WHAT BOYS LIKE

Maybe it is a bit hard for you to realize that now
the boys are finding her attractive.
—VLADIMIR NABOKOV, *Lolita*

IN HER BOOK *The Birth of Pleasure*, the Harvard psychologist Carol Gilligan draws a distinction between "relationship"—which she defines as "being in sync with another person"—and "a relationship." For Gilligan, love depends on
being *in relationship* with another person: connected by a
bond of equality and mutuality. "Both love and democracy
depend on voice," she writes, "having a voice and also the
resonance that makes it possible to speak and be heard."
Likening love to rain, she describes how it can flow between
people, fluid and refreshing.

But that's not what the media tell us.

Seventeen magazine, for example, informs us that boys
know a lot about girls. It tells us that boys know just how to
make a "fling" last: apparently, a boy would be most likely to
stay with a girl who would "rub on his sunscreen," "plan fun

stuff," and "support him," according to the handsome lads interviewed in *Seventeen*'s November 2006 issue. Girls would be well advised to plan their activities, clothes, and behaviors with boys' tastes in mind. "Try out these girl-tested, guy-approved looks!" urges one headline on a fashion feature, and "Get his attention! Inspired by the best new fragrances, five hot musicians envision the girls who wear them. Which one are you?" In a column called "My secret weapon," girls confide how they have held boys' interest by "cooking him a meal," "writing love notes and poems to him," "making a mix CD of his favorite songs," or "wearing a perfume he likes."

The articles never point the other way: that is, there are never articles on what boys can do, or should do, to please girls, and such articles are not to be found in the magazines boys tend to read, whether that's *Playboy* or *Maxim* or *Sports Illustrated*. In the realm of love and sex, it's girls who are in the position of working hard to adapt themselves to the needs and fantasies of the mercurial males whose approval and attention they seek. And, as we know, this trend is carried over to the media aimed at older girls and women; *Cosmo*'s infamous sex tips are usually on the general theme of "how to please a man in bed" —like "The Sex Position He Craves" on the December 2007 cover, or "His Secret Pleasure Zone" on the January 2008 one. Their purported reader is a "fun, fearless female," but in the realm of sexuality, the burden is entirely on her to cater to her male partner's caprices—and the magazine is there to offer tips, advice, and (of course) products that will help in this aim.

Magazines for younger girls, too, offer one constant message: that it's imperative for girls to learn how to please boys in order to get their attention. *Seventeen* is a notable example in this area—with a circulation of 13 million, it is highly influential in the lives of girls, read by kids as young as twelve. In an analysis of all the 2006 and 2007 issues of *Seventeen*, I found that although the magazines are targeted to girls, boys' voices wielded a great deal of authority. For example, the December 2007/January 2008 issue contained a cover story titled "Kissing secrets guys wish you knew"; the story was illustrated with a full-page photo of a couple kissing, overlaid with a boy's assessment: "I like a girl who follows the 90/10 rule—where she leans in almost all the way but lets me go the last 10 percent." In August 2006, a *Seventeen* feature titled "I love girls who . . ." highlighted "ten cute international guys'" thoughts on what they found sexy in girls. In July 2006, the feature "What makes a girl stand out?" told readers "Cute guys reveal what would make them pick you out of a crowd." Quotes from boys included, "If I walk past a girl and I can just smell a tiny hint of the perfume she's wearing—that's sexy" (A.J., 19, of Tempe, Arizona). Throughout the magazine, boys were the arbiters of girls' sexuality, and their desires and preferences were of paramount importance. A girl's job, it seems, is to focus on figuring out how best to appeal to the whims of these godlike beings. The magazine is the sympathetic and knowledgeable advisor in this quest.

Many girls *are* interested in romances with boys and *do* want guidance on how to negotiate this complicated terrain, and the magazines offer quick and sympathetic solutions. Research with adolescent girls shows that they rely on these magazines for practical advice in these matters. For girls, the magazines are girl-centered spaces where their lives and longings are understood and taken seriously.

In the pages of teen fashion and beauty magazines like *Seventeen* and *CosmoGirl*, tips on getting boys to notice and "crush" on girls are skillfully intermixed with the product placement that characterizes girls' magazines, so that the advice on buying jeans, accessories, and cosmetics is seamlessly linked to the relationship guidance that purports to help girls negotiate the complexities of love and sex. "Girls are empowered to be informed consumers of boys," as one analysis of these magazines concluded. The pleasures of self-adornment and consumerism are yoked to the central goal of achieving happy heterosexual couplehood. These magazines are oddly anachronistic: they offer a prefeminist vision of a girl's life, where girls require male admiration and attention and can gain it by learning to fulfill male pleasure in very traditional ways: by paying breathless attention to boys' needs and then offering services that provide for them. These services are often highly traditional ones: primping, cooking, and supplying limitless emotional support without expecting any in return. These kinds of activities seem hopelessly retrogressive when you stop to think about them, yet, as the sociologist Dawn Currie observes, girls insist "that the sexualized representations and expressions of femininity in contemporary magazines embody a new wave of women's emancipation."

It's difficult to see where the emancipation comes in. The concept of a mutually pleasing relationship, in which both partners work to understand the needs of the other, is conspicuously absent from these media. And there are no corresponding magazines or other media for men or boys that exhort them, month after month, to learn how to please girls and women. Love and attraction are one-way streets, in the scenarios offered by these popular magazines.

The sexual advice and information in the magazines, in particular, offer a very restrictive and outdated version of girls' sexuality. In the articles on sex, "man is depicted as animal (not self-conscious), and woman is depicted as animal trainer," as one study of these magazines found. The magazines continually urge girls to at once attract and fend off male advances, which implies both that boys are uncontrollable lechers and that girls have no sexual desires of their own. In this study, which appeared in the scholarly *Journal of Communication*, the analysis showed that the sexual attitudes and advice in teen magazines have not changed in twenty years. The magazines emphasize the idea that "the sexual community belongs to men, and women survive by containing themselves and by adapting and subjugating themselves to male desires." Most problematically, in these sex texts there were "no gay men or lesbian women, no men interested in learning how to love women, no women who thought as highly of themselves as they did of men." Girls don't have the option of initiating sex or taking control of the sexual encounter, according to these magazines' prescriptions.

So a prevailing myth in girls' magazines is what the psychologist Deborah Tolman called a "dilemma of desire"—the idea that girls have no sexual authority; that sexuality, for girls, is principally a matter of resisting boys' advances rather than expressing their own desires. *Seventeen* magazine abounds with examples of this, as a look at the 2006 issues shows. In August 2006, for example, the story "Are you ready for sex?" focused on girls' sexual experience in uniformly negative terms: "81% of girls have been kissed but almost 1 in 5 regrets her first time; 35% of girls have had oral sex but almost 1 in 3 regrets her first time; 29% of girls have had vaginal sex but almost 1 in 3 regrets her first time." Regret seems to be an appropriate reaction to sexual activity. The article goes on to say, "42% of girls have had guys pressure them for sex and 51% have given in to the pressure even though they *didn't* want to" (emphasis in original). In one sense, the article recognizes girls' lack of control in sexual relationships in the real world, but in another, it denies the possibility that girls may have initiated and even enjoyed their first sexual experiences. The November 2006 issue contained a story called "I had sex too soon," quoting girls who lamented that their sexual encounters with boys had "changed our relationship" so that it ended; "hurt my friendship" because the girl developed a reputation as a slut; and "destroyed my self-esteem." Again, no positive counterstory balanced these negative accounts of girls' sex lives. It is as though sex for girls has to be unhappy, negative, and beyond their control.

Throughout the year, a regular department in *Seventeen* called "Real Life" offers first-person (usually ghostwritten) accounts of girls' experiences, most of which are sexual horror stories. One such episode, "My boyfriend was a sex offender," repeated the motif of girls' lack of desire or control: in this story, the protagonist was "strung along" by a criminal boyfriend; the pulled quote declared, "I had made a huge mistake by sleeping with him."

Through these rhetorical constructions, girls are coached to see sex as scary and problematic. These are cautionary tales, and they do serve a purpose, in that girls reading them might be emboldened to report on incidents of incest, rape, or sexual abuse.

But it would be better for girls if there were also some acknowledgment of the perfectly healthy desire and sexual interest they might actually feel, and if the advice was directed at helping them to understand how to make reasoned, proactive, and thoughtful decisions about their sex lives. If sex is always represented in negative terms, then girls who are thinking about engaging in sexual activity or who want to understand more about their desires may feel they have no place in the discussion. If girls' sexual feelings are always cast in a negative light, there is no way for girls to be able to express such feelings without embarrassment or shame. Interviews with girls show that there is active social censure against girls who display an interest in sex: they become "sluts" or "skanks." As twelve-year-old Melissa put it, "They call all the girls sluts . . . that is, if they're interested." On the other hand, girls are supposed to attract boys' sexual attention through their dress and by giving the appearance of sexual availability. The cultural messages about girls and sex are wildly contradictory. As the writer Ariel Levy points out, "We are doing little to help [girls] differentiate their sexual desire from their desire for attention."

Girls need to have a sexual voice—a way to make their needs known, to feel that they can assert themselves in sexual situations, and to express their comfort levels. That would be a first step toward preventing unwanted pregnancies, STDs, and perhaps even acquaintance rapes. Girls can't understand or explore the options they might have in sexual situations if their desires are always framed as dangerous and harmful (while they're simultaneously being encouraged to attract boys' sexual attention). Perhaps fewer girls would feel coerced, taken by surprise, or ineffective if their sexuality was, instead, framed as proactive, natural, and manageable.

Seventeen does conscientiously include a "Health" column in every issue, which is usually subtitled "Sex Ed." Here, medically accurate and straightforward information about sexuality is provided, in a rare progressive element in the magazine's construction of sexuality. Articles about birth control options, sexually transmitted diseases, and adolescent development deal with these issues in clear and direct terms. The information provided is apparently vetted by experts in the field, including professors of obstetrics and gynecology from Columbia University, Texas A&M, and other research institutions. Interestingly, each of these columns in 2006 was accompanied by a banner across the page that read, "The only 100% way not to get pregnant is not to have sex!" in an apparent endorsement of the Bush Administration's "abstinence only" regimen—the magazine's politically safe way to neutralize the apparent threat of the factual sexual information offered in the column.

But these columns are not enough to offset the many problematic sexual messages that suffuse the rest of the magazine. The health information doesn't really have a context in which it could be useful. Studies with adolescents show that they are often at a loss in real-world situations: they want more information about handling sexual situations, they are aware that they carry many misconceptions about sex, and they want to talk more about sexual feelings as well as the clinical facts of sex. The magazines' portrait of a sad, scary, and taboo sexual landscape effectively shuts down any opportunity to learn about sex in useful and thoughtful ways.

Many aspects of sex are missing from teen magazines, including an acknowledgment of different sexual orientations. In teen magazines, gay and lesbian kids almost don't exist. Sex is framed as heterosexual, with little room for alternative sexualities as viable possibilities. One "Real Life" story in *Seventeen*, "My nanny molested me" was a cautionary tale that demonized lesbianism. Only one story in 2006, "In love with a girl," celebrated a lesbian relationship. However, it was immediately followed by a two-page layout featuring a semiclad heterosexual couple in soft focus, embracing and kissing on a beach, accompanied by the text "Summer perfection: Endless sunny days at the beach, hanging out with your guy, wearing your favorite bikini and the cutest cover-up." In this way, the moment of sexual openness offered by the article on lesbian love was instantly countered by the heterosexual follow-up, which was much more powerful in terms of the size of the photograph, the brilliant colors used, and the large type conveying the message of dominant heterosexuality. For lesbian teenagers already marginalized socially, the magazines reinforce the "abnormality" and invisibility of same-sex desire.

Studies of girls and the way they read teen magazines show that they see the content of the magazines as knowledge; they rely on the suggestions, advice, and injunctions in the magazines, particularly the advice columns and "how to" features, for guidance on how to manage their lives. The magazines are written in a way that implies they are offering girls personal solutions to real-world problems, and the girls reading them tend to accept them in that light—yet they often find themselves to be unhappy and dissatisfied with themselves once they have accepted them. The sociologist Dawn Currie, who has studied "teenzine" audiences extensively, refers to this as the simultaneous "doing and undoing of the reading Subject."

The unhappiness stems not only from the contradictions of trying to "be yourself" while complying with the magazines' dictates to embrace ideal femininity, but also from the constant awareness of the critical male gaze. Girls' magazines, in particular, regularly remind girls of an invisible, phantom boy who is watching their every move. "Learn the secret signs that he's into you!" urges *CosmoGirl*. "Make your crush want you!" exhorts *Seventeen*. "Talk to him!" cajoles *Teen*. "You're, like, totally into this guy. The problem? You don't know how to approach him. Try these tricks!"

The magazines are, for the most part, staffed by women, written by women, and targeted to girls—but the phantom male's influence is unmistakable and oppressive. "Why do men's magazines and women's magazines both have pictures of half-naked women in them?" my students ask me, marveling at the similarities between *Maxim* and *Cosmopolitan*. "What's that about?" The answer is that the imaginary male viewer is present in both genres. He surveys girls' every move and every action.

This is not a new phenomenon. The art critic John Berger, in a classic essay, illustrates how women's bodies have traditionally been displayed for men's scrutiny. He argues convincingly that this is the premise of most Western works of art, from the Renaissance on. "The 'ideal' spectator is always assumed to be male and the image of the woman is designed to flatter him," he writes, using examples from Tintoretto, Mabuse, Ingres, and others. And, tellingly, he points out:

> Men look at women. Women watch themselves being looked at. This determines not only most relations between men and women but also the relation of women to themselves. The surveyor of woman *in herself* is male: the surveyed female. Thus she turns herself into an object—and most particularly, an object of vision: a sight. [italics added]

Girls and women internalize this imaginary male gaze: they learn to see themselves as they think men would see them. The irony of this is that men and boys seldom scrutinize girls or women as minutely as females do. Sometimes girls admit this—"We dress for each other," they say; and only girls notice the half-inch of a hemline or a shape of a heel that distinguishes the hip from the uncool. But this intense self-scrutiny is motivated by the imaginary male surveillance that the magazines conjure up, in the same tradition as the nude in Western art. Berger's argues that this relationship of gazing, where men gaze at women, is a power relationship: the gazer is ultimately the one who gets to judge, reject, or approve the object of his gaze. The power lies with the gazer, and culturally, men are given this privilege. Things are changing a little, and men and boys are becoming increasingly conscious of women's appraisal of their bodies, but the female gaze is still not the pervasive cultural norm. The imaginary male gaze—adopted by women—is what lurks beneath many of our cultural images, messages, and institutions.

"Do women have to be naked to get into U.S. museums?" demands a poster by the rebel art group Guerilla Girls. The answer, of course, is yes: their point is that most of the nude figures in major art museums are female, painted by men, while hardly any women artists can get their work shown. And in fact, the mass media work the same way. In media targeted to teens and children, girls' bodies are constantly on display, ostensibly for the viewing pleasure of boys. Even in shows enjoyed by young children, like Disney's *The Suite Life of Zack and Cody*, which is popular with grade-schoolers, the male gaze is evident: a running gag on the show is that the twin boys unsuccessfully hit on attractive older women. But on the show and others like it, girls don't notice men with the same casual aplomb.

And, of course, girls never notice other girls; boys never notice other boys. Let's consider the experiences that are erased by the ubiquity of the phantom hetero male. Gay and lesbian kids are conspicuously absent from Disney's youth programming, and although there is evidence of homosexuality in other media outlets, these representations are still problematic: for example, MTV's long-running *The Real World* has regularly featured openly gay characters, but the representations have been criticized for perpetuating negative stereotypes. "The token 'gay guy' on *The Real World [RW]* either has AIDS or is involved in a sex scandal. Pedro from *RW San Francisco* died of AIDS shortly after filming wrapped, while *RW Miami* cast member Danny made headlines last year when he was arrested for exposing himself while cruising a porn theater in Kansas City," observes Michael Amico in *The*

Gay and Lesbian Review Worldwide. These salacious representations contribute to the silencing and shaming of gay youth; they continue a long history of demonizing homosexuality in the media.

A show that's very highly rated among twelve- to seventeen-year-olds, MTV's *A Shot At Love With Tila Tequila*, appears to reject the heterosexual norm by featuring an openly bisexual protagonist, the Vietnamese American model born Tila Nguyen. On this reality show, both men and women compete for Tila's affections. Tila is open about her attraction to both men and women, explaining the appeal of both sexes. The show also features a "female gaze," as the lesbian contestants parade in skimpy outfits before Tila's appraising look.

"It's the first show about lesbians in love," gushes Ashli, a female contestant, on the first episode. "Just to be part of something so groundbreaking like this is an honor!"

The superficial subversions of the show, though, don't hold up under analysis. The contestants all conform, physically, to traditional gender norms: the men are uniformly well-muscled and tall, while the women are slender and large-breasted, adhering to the "voluptuously thin" ideal discussed earlier in the book. In addition, their sexual performances, including the sexually provocative outfits, are securely in the sex work vein. Women who depart from the norm are rejected: "I think butchy girls are just so creepy," shudders Tila. She insists that she needs to feel "a connection" with the contestants, but her criteria for evaluating them are based on their gendered performances. "I wish she could have seen who I really am," complains one after another of her rejected suitors.

There's a switch of gender roles in that Tila is the arbiter whom the contestants are seeking to please by offering gifts, flaunting their bodies, and displaying loverlike eagerness. Nonetheless, Tila Tequila herself rose to fame because of her appeal to the male gaze: she has modeled in the popular men's magazines *Playboy*, *Stuff*, and *Maxim*, and she has appeared on *Maxim UK*'s "Hot 100" list.

Finally, on the show, her early revelation of bisexuality is met with initial shock and horror on the part of the contestants, though, inexplicably, they stay in the game. The show pivots on intense antagonism between the men and the women, perpetuating the notion that lesbian women are man-haters and hetero men are intrinsically hostile and homophobic. The women are continually asked if they would "do" any of the men, and although they reject the notion, their lesbianism is continually questioned and challenged. Overall, gender stereotypes remain unshaken by this seemingly revolutionary program.

On the other hand, the N, the teen-targeted TV channel that is the nighttime version of Noggin, has aired truly groundbreaking shows featuring gay and lesbian teenagers, with story lines that have been praised by GLBT (gay, lesbian, bisexual, transgender) organizations as progressive and thoughtful. *Degrassi: The Next Generation*, a show that is wildly popular with teenagers, has regularly featured gay characters, and the more recent *South of Nowhere* follows a romance between two high-school girls.

"These characters on television are giving LGBT youth visible, tangible evidence that they are not alone, and that what they are feeling is not unusual or wrong," says Damon Romine, the entertainment media director of the Gay & Lesbian Alliance Against Defamation (GLAAD). "These characters can provide a lifeline for queer youth." But the organization points out that representations of gay and lesbian people of color are virtually nonexistent on television.

There's evidence that American society is gradually becoming more accepting of gay teenagers. Surveys indicate that growing numbers of Americans consider homosexuality acceptable. According to a recent *Time* magazine cover story, gay/lesbian student associations are becoming more common in high schools, and the average gay teen comes out in high school. Young adult literature frequently features gay teenagers. And a new magazine for teens called YGA (for Young Gay America) is now available. The recent book *The New Gay Teenager* presents growing evidence that gay and lesbian teens are confident of their sexuality, and that the line between "straight" and "gay" is becoming blurred and even irrelevant.

Despite these advances, there is still evidence that the lives of gay and lesbian teens are marred by stigma, sadness, and violence. The greatest rise in hate crimes is against the gay and lesbian community. Studies of school environments show that kids who don't conform to gender norms are less accepted by their peers. More than 40 percent of gay and lesbian youth report feeling unsafe in their schools, and they are more likely than other young people to be sexually harassed and victimized. Human Rights Watch has documented countless cases of brutal harassment and violence against gay and lesbian teens in schools; one gay student in Wisconsin was mocked, spat at, subjected to mock rapes, and urinated on in the school bathroom—he consequently attempted suicide. Overall, gay and lesbian adolescents are two to three times more likely to attempt suicide than other young people. They are also more likely to suffer from depression. Hostile school environments have been shown to be major factors in gay teen suicide and depression. In my own work with teenagers, it's clear that homophobia runs rampant among young adolescents—"fag" and "queer" are the epithets of choice in middle-school hallways. Significantly, while teachers would intervene if they heard racist or sexist language being used, homophobic language often goes unchecked.

The media environment could offer countervailing images and messages about homosexuality that might help to change kids'—and adults'—perceptions and treatment of gay youth. Rich Savin-Williams, the author of *The New Gay Teenager*, believes that increased positive media representation has in fact changed the social landscape for gay youth. "The success of the entertainment industry in presenting and hence normalizing same-sex desire has had an incalculable impact on the ability of adolescents to understand their own emerging sexual desires," he writes. Given this, it's important that media producers recognize a social responsibility in presenting fair, inclusive, and realistic portraits of gay and lesbian youth. It's heartening that there is growing evidence of this, but there is a lot of work yet to be done to make sure youth of all persuasions find supportive recognition. If the media are our mythmakers, then we need stories that can help kids make courageous and enlightened choices.

The myth of traditional heterosexuality is the fifth myth of the Lolita Effect. The myth casts girls in roles that are geared to fulfilling male fantasies and paying obsessive attention to male needs. These roles render girls subservient to boys. The notion of a mutual, reciprocal, and equitable heterosexual relationship is not part of this myth. The myth does not acknowledge that boys have responsibilities toward girls. It does not recognize the idea that boys can be caring, respectful, and sensitive beings. Rather, boys are constructed as sexual aggressors whose goal is to coerce girls into physical relationships, while girls are positioned as defenders of their virtue.

A secondary myth at work is that girls don't feel desire or have an interest in sex. The myth effectively prevents girls from taking charge of their own sex lives. In this fifth myth, girls have no voice in creating relationships that work according to their needs, ethics, and desires. In these constructions of sexuality, open dialogue between girls and boys about these issues is not an option, yet frank discussion and mutual respect would be the basis for the best sexual outcomes—which could include delaying or abstaining from intercourse, or of practicing safe sex in consensual encounters. Our rising rates of teen pregnancy and STDs indicate that most teens are unable (or unwilling) to engage in this kind of forthright communication.

The third dimension of this myth of retrograde heterosexuality is that alternative sexual orientations don't exist, or if they do, they are odd and deviant. When they are portrayed more humanely, they are still mired in stereotypes and represented as the exclusive preserve of white, upper-class youth. A broader range of representations would offer kids more varied scripts and more flexible options for negotiating the complexities of real-world sexuality. GLBT youth are gradually finding a presence in contemporary society, and the mainstream media could help them negotiate this emergence from the shadows by validating their positions.

What we can do

Adolescents want more information about sex—this has been confirmed in interviews, research reports, and surveys. And there are too few opportunities for them to gain helpful and supportive information about it. If they take their cues from the media, they are bombarded by a mythology that tells girls their only power is in conforming to beauty standards and behaviors that are supposed to attract male attention: they are treated as bait, not as living, thinking sexual beings.

So girls need to become conscious of "the male gaze," that phantom boy who is everywhere and nowhere.

- TALK ABOUT THE IDENTITY OF
  GIRLS IN THE MEDIA

Encourage girls to analyze the glamorous world of female adolescence constructed in these texts and think about them in real-world terms. Page through any teen magazine with a girl and ask directed questions.

Are there any indications that girls might be interested in anything besides self-adornment and boys?

> *What sort of picture of girls' lives do they represent?*
> *Are they realistic?*
> *If so, how?*
> *If not, why not?*
> *Is there any sign in the magazines that girls think about art, the environment, science, or music? (Almost every magazine does include some content of this nature.)*

Ask about how the magazines make girls feel after reading them. Do they feel good about themselves? Jealous? Or do they have mixed emotions? Talk about what might be behind their reactions, making sure to be supportive and to validate their feelings.

- IDENTIFY THE MALE GAZE

Then point to the omnipresent "he" of the texts. Ask, "Who is this guy?" Point out how his tastes, fantasies of femininity, and ideas about relationships dominate the magazines. Together, try to find examples of girls' views, where girls' perspectives are presented. You probably won't.

• TALK FRANKLY ABOUT SEX REALITIES

Look at the sex and relationship advice in these magazines with the girls. Talk about which questions and answers seem realistic.

Do all boys pressure girls?

Do girls always need to be in the position of reacting to boys' actions?

Would it be a good idea for boys and girls to talk these things over in some ethical way?

Could a girl ever call the shots?

Would that be better or worse?

Let girls know you are in their corner, and that sex is not a taboo, and that many people—including adults—have trouble understanding and negotiating their sex lives in satisfactory ways. Talk about the pitfalls as well as the potentially positive perspectives on sex and relationships. Allow girls to be media critics, evaluating and analyzing the messages as they relate to their own lives.

This is a great discussion to bring boys in on. Boys, too, may be puzzled and critical of the gender roles played out in the media. Things you can talk about:

What do they think of the "Paris Hilton" or "Tila Tequila" models of female sexuality?

What about girls who don't want to act or think like that?

Should sexual partners consider each other?

What are the costs and the benefits of mutual consideration in a romantic or sexual relationship?

Should girls be able to speak up about what they're comfortable with?

These questions speak to girls' sexual rights and responsibilities, as well as to their need to negotiate safe sexual environments for themselves. In this area, knowledge becomes power—the power to exert agency over one's sex life.

- ## SUGGEST OUTSIDE SOURCES FOR MORE INFORMATION

There are a number of ways in which girls—and boys—can gain more information and understanding of the issues at stake.

For example, the American Academy of Pediatrics recommends that pediatricians offer adolescents risk-reduction counseling about sex. During girls' checkups, a doctor or pediatric nurse can offer confidential information about the risks and responsibilities of sexual activity. It is possible that your pediatrician would also be willing to speak to an after-school group or a women-and-girls group about these topics.

The nonprofit organization Advocacy for Youth is focused on adolescents' sexual rights and responsibilities. Their Web site (www.advocatesforyouth.org/) has links, publications, and other resources where adults and kids can get information on a variety of topics, from contraception to peer communication. These issues can also be brought up in groups, both single-sex or co-ed, as even early adolescents can think about them.

- ## TALK WITH YOUNGER GIRLS ABOUT EMPOWERING THEMSELVES IN THEIR ENCOUNTERS WITH BOYS

With preadolescents, sex doesn't need to be foregrounded in the discussion, but relationships with boys can be. Teen magazines are read by girls as young as ten, and they are a fixture in middle school and public libraries. Learning to critique the gender roles and challenge the "male gaze" is a first step toward proactive female sexuality. Some of the same questions as the ones above can be explored with younger girls. In addition, you can watch her favorite cartoons and TV shows with her and ask the same kinds of questions:

> *Why does she worry about what the prince thinks?*
> *Do you think it matters a lot?*
> *Why doesn't the prince worry about what she thinks?*
> *Does he like her because she's pretty or because she's smart and kind?*

• CHALLENGE HOMOPHOBIA

Nonheterosexual relationships can also be discussed in groups or individually. Many boys and girls today are aware of homosexuality: they know that same-sex attraction exists. They may have family members who are gay, or friends with same-sex parents (at my daughters' school, several children have two moms or two dads). You can engender open and accepting attitudes among kids by acknowledging these family structures, without remarking on them as unusual or problematic. In small, everyday ways, you can challenge homophobia. With my young children, I ask frequently about arbitrary distinctions: for instance, why is "pink" a girl color? What if a boy likes pink? In response to their squeamishness, I point out that it's a beautiful color, so boys ought to be able to enjoy it, as well. Lots of men have long hair; lots of girls have short hair; and it doesn't mean anything bad, I point out—it just means they like it. Girls can be construction workers, and boys can be ballet dancers, and it's all good.

If you believe, as I do, that a diverse and hate-free society is a worthwhile social goal, then breaking down prejudices based on gender and sexuality is an essential move. And awareness is the first step. Accepting sexual differences and challenging gender stereotypes offer new ways to live in a changing, diverse world. The Southern Poverty Law Center's "Ten Ways to Fight Hate" is a helpful resource for discussing proactive ways to create hate-free communities; it can be found at the organization's Web site, www.tolerance.org /10_ways/index.html. For schools, the SPLC's "Teaching Tolerance" curriculum provides wonderful classroom activities and resources for developing antibias school environments (www.tolerance.org/teach/index.jsp).

The American Psychological Association's new Girls, Women + Media Project is another good resource for acquiring materials and ideas for opening up these discussions. Their suggestions include learning about media literacy and beginning a media literacy and action group in your area. Their Web site is at www.mediaandwomen.org/index.html.

The goal of opening up discussions with kids about the sexist, rigid, and intolerant messages often found in the media is to help them learn to take charge of their own lives. In an ideal world, sex would be free of coercion: it would be consensual, intentional, and safe for all participants. In the realm of sex, people should be able to make decisions that are good for them. This may sound utopian, but I believe it to be a realistic social goal. If girls and boys could reject the messages of inequality and exclusion that are fostered by the mainstream media, they could learn more about the notion of relationship—that mutual, resonant connection described by Carol Gilligan.

These are complicated issues, but by getting kids to talk about them, you can offer hope and support as they negotiate this intricate, intimate terrain.

Chapter 7

THE SEDUCERS
UNDERSTANDING MYTH AND SPECTACLE IN THE MEDIA

∽

*T*HE GIRL SUPERSTARS of the twenty-first century are notorious for their flashiness and trashiness. Paris Hilton's sex tapes, Britney Spears's pantyless partying, and Lindsay Lohan's drunken escapades made headlines in the first years of the millennium, and the *Girls Gone Wild* franchise reaped millions of dollars in direct-mail sales. Female sexuality became a spectacle, a performance for mass voyeurism. Toned-down versions of these performances appeared in media from teen magazines to Disney music videos (it's worth noting that Paris Hilton was a 2006 *Seventeen* cover model, and Britney Spears got her start on *The New Mickey Mouse Club*).

Girls' sexuality is defined, in our media-saturated environment, as a spectacle. The spectacle is driven by the five myths of the Lolita Effect: if you've got it, flaunt it—but don't dare flaunt it unless you have the anatomy of a sex goddess; the younger you are, the better; make sure you're flaunting it so boys like it; and if you spice it up with a soupçon of violence, so much the better. Using the concept of the spectacle to think about girls' sexuality gives us a helpful way to understand it in its social context.

In media studies, we think about such "spectacles" quite specifically. A spectacle refers to the media's representations of the world through the wild mix of images and messages that are transmitted simultaneously and circulate globally. These spectacles are constructed by the media: they are exciting, colorful, glossy, slick, and professionally executed. Many billions of dollars are spent on creating and distributing them. (It's no accident that Paris Hilton's every move is endlessly replayed on television and the Web, or that Tila Tequila pops up in various rap videos and soap operas.) Most important, spectacles are created specifically to generate profits for the media and the industries that support them: advertising, marketing, public relations, and manufacturing. All of these industries are interdependent transnational operations that reap even more billions of dollars a year. Media spectacles are created not only to entertain and divert audiences, but to urge us to eagerly consume products. All of these industries would collapse if they weren't constantly hustling to generate the needs, cravings, and anxieties that fuel consumer spending. So the question "Do you think I'm sexy?" becomes a reason to shop.

It's not that all audience members want to emulate the Paris Hiltons and Lindsay Lohans of media notoriety—yet their appearances in films, videos, and magazines do boost sales, and the products they use and endorse become instantly trendy. Even very young children are aware of them. "Well before they experience puberty, children today are deeply immersed in the dirty laundry of celebrities—their eating disorders, bouts with drinking and drugs, and run-ins with the law (and each other). The gritty details are all around them," writes Stephanie Rosenbloom in the *New York Times*. Her interviews show that while preteens are critical of the behavior of these celebrities, many teenagers actually do see them as role models. "Every kid is trying to have a Paris Hilton kind of night at their prom," notes *CosmoGirl* editor Susan Schulz in the same article. For kids, this media-driven spectacle of female sexuality is inescapable, and they contend with it constantly. It's the pivot around which their beliefs, their criticisms, their negotiations, and their debates about sexuality take place. Thus, the spectacle of the Lolita Effect occupies a central place in contemporary society.

Again, this doesn't mean that all kids—or adults—unthinkingly buy into it. But it is the baseline: the assumed norm that calls for a response. The spectacle of the Lolita Effect represents not only female sexual behavior, but the ideally sexy female body, ideally sexy clothing styles, and ideally sexy entertainment. "Paris Hilton is a skank," a girl might say, but she would also admit that Hilton's slender, busty body, blonde hair, and long legs epitomize female desirability today. Moreover, because this type of body is endlessly mirrored in all forms of media, it becomes the standard against which all others are judged—and found lacking.

The spectacle of the Lolita Effect influences girls' relationships with each other, and their relationships with themselves. The best-selling author of *Queen Bees and Wannabees*, Rosalind Wiseman, points out, "Girls know they're manipulated by the media to hold themselves to an impossible standard of beauty, but that doesn't stop them from holding themselves to it anyway." They are acutely judgmental of other girls' clothing choices, bodies, and deportment, as well as their own. They starve themselves to attain the ideal body; they teeter on high-heeled shoes that hurt their feet; they spend their money on skin treatments, cosmetics and, increasingly, plastic surgeries to look more like the spectacle. The spectacle affects how they see each other, how they see themselves, and how others see them. More than 80 percent of all girls are dissatisfied with their bodies: "Even in grade 1, girls think the culture is telling them that they should model themselves after celebrities who are svelte, beautiful and sexy," reports the body image researcher Sarah Murnen, in a recent *USA Today* story. Both boys and girls taunt girls whose bodies develop early. Most girls have been teased about their appearance during their early teen years, and research shows it affects their body image in later life. The spectacle affects how girls are treated by adults; significantly, girls between sixteen and nineteen are four times more likely to be victims of rape than the general population, and 75 percent of child sexual abuse cases involve young girls as victims.

In 1967, the French scholar Guy Debord wrote, "The spectacle is not a collection of images, but a social relation among people, mediated by images." The Lolita Effect shapes the world's relation to girls, and girls' psychic relationships to themselves. Girls are often acutely aware of these things: they know they are being held up to impossible and coercive standards of beauty and sexuality, they know it affects their self-esteem and self-confidence, and they know it matters in their lives. And many girls don't feel in control of any of it: the media, the judgments of their peers, and the relentless consumer culture in which they live allow little room for negotiation.

But negotiation *is* possible. The Lolita Effect *can* be tamed and controlled, when used in ways that feel right to the user. By educating girls in media literacy, we can encourage the development of their critical instincts and help them gain mastery over the spectacle of Lolita.

Because we live in a media-saturated environment, it's important for everyone to learn how to understand and take control of their relationships with the media. This does not mean shutting the media out, which would be virtually impossible anyway, and perhaps not even desirable: the media offer entertainment, excitement, diversion, and even information. We are avid media consumers.

But it's getting increasingly important to be smart, proactive, and critical media consumers, as well. Studies indicate that most people believe they are not influenced by the media—but they think other people are. (Here is that "the third person effect" again.) Many people are vocal, perceptive media critics, making active decisions about what they watch and read, but they have never been given the tools to analyze the media rigorously and clearly.

Now more than ever, we need these tools. To negotiate the real world of the twenty-first century, we need to understand how the media operate, how their messages are structured and determined, and what motivates them. This kind of knowledge will help us make discerning decisions about how we handle media messages in our everyday lives. Media literacy of this kind empowers us to use the media, rather than allowing the media to use us—and to recognize and reject manipulations when we see them. And it's never too early to start acquiring this knowledge.

In the previous chapters, we've seen the way the media concoct a carefully calculated definition of girls' sexuality through the Lolita Effect. The Lolita Effect operates by means of a series of powerful myths about female sexuality. These myths pervade contemporary society, and it is easy to mistake them for realities: they are seldom examined, tested, or questioned, because they are part of our social belief system.

I have referred to them as myths because they are not based on "truth" in any recognizable way: for example, it is not categorically true that only slender woman are sexual, or that younger women are more sexual than older women. These are powerful narratives that are repeatedly circulated in various ways in our culture, to the point that they seem natural and not constructed by outside forces.

But they *are* constructed: one way to see that is to recognize that over time, these narratives have changed. So they are not universal truths: rather, they are specific to their historical period, their cultural contexts, and their political and economic alignments. Think about the ideal feminine body in sixteenth-century paintings: the women portrayed were heavy and pale, often with sagging skin and double chins. Titian's *Venus of Urbino* has a puffy stomach and rolls of flesh at her knees. Rubens's *Leda and the Swan* depicts a flabby woman with heavy thighs and visible cellulite—the love interest of the god Jupiter. These were beauty ideals at the time, and they would be viewed as repulsive today. The historian Peter Stearns points out that in Western culture, large women were considered fashionable and beautiful even as late as the 1830s: "Mature women were supposed to be fat," he writes. "Leanness might be a virtue in the young, but it was a positive vice in the mature." Another historian, Roberta Seid, confirms this: "Plumpness was deemed a sign of emotional well-being: it was identified with a good temperament . . . with temperate and disciplined habits, and above all with good health." In general, prior to the twentieth century, large, fleshy women were seen as attractive and erotic.

The ideal female figure has changed over time; the introduction of the corset in the eighteenth century idealized the tiny waist; the bustle in the nineteenth century emphasized the buttocks; and an S-shaped body became popular at the turn of the twentieth century in imitation of Art Nouveau aesthetics. In the 1940s and '50s, the voluptuous "sweater girl" set the standard of female beauty, exemplified by film stars like Marilyn Monroe and Jayne Mansfield: by no means under-weight, they were curvaceous and buxom.

The size of the ideal female body has waxed and waned over the years, but since the middle of the last century it has grown thinner and thinner. One study of Miss America con-testants found that their weight has declined significantly every year since1959. Similar studies of *Playboy* centerfolds, film stars, and women's magazine models indicate similar decreases in body size over time. Recognizing these shifts reveals that beauty standards are historically and socially determined; they are not innate or instinctive, and they have for many centuries required artificial methods to attain.

Myths of sexuality are not just historically determined— they are culturally and regionally specific, as well. In Brazil, for example, "the contours of a guitar, not an hourglass" have traditionally described the ideal female figure. Brazilian cul-ture encouraged men to be attracted to plump women with large buttocks. But due to international media influences, Brazilian sociologists and psychologists agree that the tradi-tional notions of beauty have been displaced by the Barbie ideal. "'Those huge breasts you see in the United States, like in *Playboy*, were always considered ridiculous in Brazil," said Ivo Pitanguy, one of the country's most renowned plastic sur-geons, in a *New York Times* interview; but now, he adds, because of North American media images, Brazilian women are actively trying to acquire the Barbie body by means of sur-geries and appetite suppressants.

In the era before mass communication, different world cultures pursued vastly different beauty ideals. In most of East Asia, willowy women with small breasts were traditionally considered graceful and attractive. In China, for most of the last millennium, the practice of foot-binding focused the admiring male gaze on feet that would now be considered deformed; in Japan, before the emperor's decision for the nation to pursue Western beauty ideals in the 1860s, a beautiful woman bound her torso so that it was as narrow, cylindrical, and curveless as possible, and blackened out her unsightly white teeth. In India, plump bodies with wide hips and full thighs were depicted in ancient carvings of goddesses and great beauties. But, "In today's world, there is so much persuasive advertising of the Western ideals of beauty that in Asia we have begun to forget the Asian aesthetic values," observes to Gauri Parimoo Krishnan, the curator of an art exhibit on centuries of Asian beauty at Singapore's Asian Civilisations Museum.

Among the Maori of New Zealand, facial scarring called "ta moko," done with chisels and permanent pigments, was practiced to increase women's attractiveness to the opposite sex (men did it, too, though not usually on the face). The Padaung and Kayan women of Myanmar and Thailand wore neck rings to stretch their necks, as elongated necks were a sign of great beauty in these cultures, as they were among the Ndebele of South Africa. And in many African cultures, "beauty has long been defined as having a curvaceous figure, plump lips, a flat nose and a full behind," but again, an entirely different standard has emerged in recent years, and beauty pageant judges in Africa cite Western ideals of beauty as the new standard.

Examples like this abound, and they indicate that local cultures set the standards for beauty in radically different ways—that is, until the mass media became a global phenomenon with the power to define beauty according to rather narrow Western criteria. Such trends demonstrate clearly that a universal, instinctive recognition of beauty or sexual desirability is a myth—one that has been created relatively recently via a media system that adheres to North American and European ideals of beauty.

We can see, then, that myths are historically specific—that is, they are situated in the time period in which they emerge and become dominant—as well as context-driven; they depend on cultural norms and values. They are the stories we tell about ourselves, and they seem to be "true" in the time and place in which they act.

Because a homogenized, Western beauty ideal is so pervasive nowadays, we have no way of seeing it as a construction or story, as one of many possible constructions: we see it as a fact.

We tend to interpret myths as facts because they have real-life social repercussions. For example, innumerable studies show that people (both men and women) who conform to current standards of beauty are more successful in their jobs: they are more likely to be recommended, hired, promoted, perceived as intelligent, and paid higher salaries. Research also shows that people seen as attractive are less lonely, less anxious, and happier than unattractive people; they're also assumed by others to have higher status, a better sense of humor, more perceptiveness, more flexibility, and more assertiveness than unattractive people. So the concept of attractiveness that holds true at any particular moment can actually increase the quality of life for the lucky people who conform to that concept.

Another real effect of a myth can be seen in the millions of women who diet, consume appetite suppressants, and undergo plastic surgeries to achieve the "thin-yet-voluptuous" body ideal: billions of dollars are generated for various beauty industries because of women's real desires to conform to this myth. Yet another fact tied to the myth is the high incidence of eating disorders among women, which have real impacts on women's bodies and lives, causing malnutrition, anemia, dysfunctions of the gastrointestinal tract, cognitive impairment, abnormal menstruation, and sometimes death.

So, we can't dismiss the myths as false, because of their forceful real-world impacts. Myths, as we understand them in media and cultural studies, hover between fact and fiction: they are fabrications of time, place, and culture, but they play out in reality.

And in media studies, myths are not just texts: that is, they aren't just about words. They are the stories we tell about ourselves, but these stories are disseminated throughout society in a myriad ways, most significantly through images that are transmitted by the media. Images swiftly and powerfully invoke ideas, and they are everywhere in our exceedingly visual culture: on billboards, Web sites, TV and moviescreens, in magazines and newspapers, books and art. In this swirling maelstrom of images, it's clear that not all of them can possibly carry the same myths or convey the same ideas: books like this one wouldn't exist if there were not a diversity of viewpoints, perspectives, and goals being debated in our cultures.

But myths, as we define them in media studies, are the *dominant* ideas at a particular point in time—the ideas that are in the best interests of the most powerful groups in society. They tend to be produced and disseminated by the people with the means to create and widely circulate them, and who will also benefit the most from them. Today, in an era of global neoliberal capitalism, myths need to shore up the financial interests of the superrich: they need to keep the machinery of capital moving. So the myths of the Lolita Effect are rooted in commodity culture and consumerism. They are geared only to fostering high levels of consumption and spending. Nothing that the myths promise can be had, except for the products. So they are, at the most basic level, marketing devices—but

along with their call to consumption they circulate certain ideologies of femininity and masculinity and sexuality. These ideologies need to be accepted by the public in order to motivate
us to consume the products that promise us access to the
ideals. It's a dicey game.

Sometimes these ideologies are beneficial; everyone
enjoys feeling attractive, purchasing appealing products, and
having fun. But sometimes the same beliefs are destructive, as
when they undermine self-esteem, encourage us to spend
beyond our means, push us toward unhealthy and unrealistic
goals, or desensitize us to violence and sexual exploitation.
That's why it's important for us to know how to discern the
values that underlie the myths and to make informed decisions about how much or how little to buy into them.

The concept of myth has a long history in media studies,
and media scholars have used it for more than half a century
now to understand how the media work. The idea of myth
was first articulated by the French scholar Roland Barthes, a
literary critic and social theorist. He carefully studied the popular culture of his time and recognized the myths at work in
seemingly trivial areas of life: margarine advertisements,
wrestling matches, magazine covers. Barthes wrote that
"myth has the task of giving an historical intention a natural
justification." By this, he meant exactly what I've discussed
above: that constructed ideas are made to seem natural and
obvious.

We can see the myths of the Lolita Effect working this
way. The images of slender, half-nude young women who
embody the current ideal are almost inescapable in contemporary culture. They are on the giant posters at any shopping
malls, adorning the Victoria's Secret and Abercrombie and
Fitch window displays. They are in music videos, magazines,
advertisements, and movies. Women with Rubenesque bod-

ies—large, fleshy, fat by contemporary standards—are invisible in these media except as objects of ridicule and scorn. Yet four centuries ago, these were the privileged and most desirable female bodies: pale, passive, and portly. But we can't remember that now—the very idea is repulsive. Even the sirens of a few decades ago are unattractive by today's standards: Marilyn Monroe and Jane Russell just wouldn't make it in today's size-0 Hollywood. So of course slenderness is sexy; there's virtually no other way to think about desire, unless you're some kind of pervert who is inexplicably into fatness or oldness. The myth turns a marketer's fabrication into common sense, into nature.

It's the same way with our automatic equating of sexiness with nudity. Could a fully dressed woman be desirable? Given that desire can be sparked by a variety of factors, I'd say yes. But our prevailing myth is that the less clothing worn by the "right type of woman," the sexier she is. It only works for women, though: men don't need to be half-clad to be sexy.

Challenges to the myths are sidelined and minimized. Yes, occasionally a fashion magazine will print a letter to the editor from a reader complaining about the body types in the magazine. Yes, doctors argue in favor of healthy body weights. Yes, scientists might contend that desire is complex and irrational. But these voices are ineffective compared to the prevailing myth, which allows them the space to be heard but easily drowns them out.

Barthes wrote that "myth hides nothing." This is evident when you consider how the five myths of the Lolita Effect are hammered home endlessly in the media, especially in media targeted to youth and children. And the criticisms and challenges to the myths are not hidden either, but they are made to seem foolish, trivial, or nerdy. The mythmakers slyly suggest that conforming to the myths is edgy, hip, and rebellious.

They suggest that criticizing or rejecting the myths is old-fashioned, dull, or censorious.

If you think about it, though, it should be quite the reverse: the highly corporate, profit-motivated, mass-circulated images are the conformist positions. True rebellion lies in challenging, dissecting, and thinking through them—and then living your life according to your own values and ideas, not those of the corporate media.

∞

To do myth analysis, the first thing to be clear about is the motivation behind the myths. In the case of corporate media, the motivation is always profit: bigger audiences mean higher advertising rates, which mean more revenues. For advertisers, bigger audiences mean more potential customers. It's a win-win situation for the media and the marketing companies when they can work to support each other.

But as consumers, we need to ask hard questions. Just how are we being coaxed into spending our money on the advertised products? In the Lolita Effect, the strategy is to create ideals that are impossible to attain and then suggest to audiences that they are attainable if the right products are purchased.

For girls, the myth implies, it's necessary to attain the ideals in order to be sexual. There's no hint that sexuality is an inherent human trait, that both people and animals are de facto sexual, and that sexuality expresses itself in multiple and many-dimensional ways. No: sexiness must be bought.

Ideal sexiness couldn't be a consumer goal, though, if consumers weren't made to feel insecure because they don't inhabit the ideal bodies, or the idealized lives, of the sexy girls in the media. "Keep warm, look hot," urges the tagline for

Ugg boots. "Very irresistible," insists Givenchy Eau de Toilette, with a flirty Liv Tyler pictured beside the bottle of fragrance. "Because you're hot," cajoles an ad for Secret deodorant, picturing a sexy girl. The clever implication of such advertising is that that the reader needs the product in order to be hot. *You're not quite there yet*, goes the rhetoric of the myth, *but you can be if you buy the right stuff.*

In the meantime, if the insecurities run deep enough to provoke eating disorders, crises of self-esteem, teasing by peers, or reckless spending, that's dismissed as a kind of "collateral damage" by the mythmakers. After all, don't people have the sense to turn this stuff off? It's not real, everyone knows that. The media can't *make* people do things. You can't possible take any of this seriously!

But we should. The media industries are multibillion-dollar enterprises that span the globe. The cross-ownership among media and other industries means that the strategies are consolidated in order to maximize profits for increasingly larger transnational entities. The media are part of our lives: the hours that children and adolescents spend consuming media constitute major parts of their days.

In a world like this, media literacy is not optional. It is imperative. Understanding the way the corporate media create myths that have a ripple effect on society is the first step toward taking charge of your relationship with the media, with other people in your life, and with yourself.

What we can do

Media myth analysis is a strategy and a skill that can be quickly learned by 'tweens and teenagers, though it may be too advanced for younger children. But talking with older kids about media allows us to focus on recognizing and dissecting the myths.

• LOOK AT THE MYTH TOGETHER

The first step in any myth analysis is to look carefully at the message: the advertisement, the magazine cover, the CD cover, the film poster, the Web page, etc. (It can be done on videos and films, too, but it's easiest to begin with still images.) Discuss the photograph or artwork in the image.

What kind of person is pictured?
Is he or she attractive?
Why do we think so?
Is the person sexy or hot?
Again, why?
What is it about her that's sexy?

(The typical responses will be vague, or refer to the body or other physical features; that's fine.)

• TALK ABOUT THE TEXT MESSAGE

Look next at any accompanying text. What's the message in the text? Does it contribute to the way we interpret the photograph? It's helpful to use an example here, like a *Cosmopolitan* magazine cover. If the magazine were called *Sleazy* or *Trashy*, might we interpret the image differently? Look at other text. If the cover line reads, "How to have a hot bod!" right next to the cover model, does it encourage us to see the model's body as "hot"?

• TALK ABOUT THE IMPERATIVE OF "HOTNESS"

What about other aspects of life—concern for the environment, a love of art or music, spirituality, sports? Where are those represented? Why are they not represented by the media as being just as important as sex?

Is there an imaginary "he" on the page? Is "he" referred to? Are viewers being subtly coaxed to view the cover the way "he" would? What do these messages tell us about sex and relationships? (This is a good time to explore the restrictive implications of these myths: that only people with ideal bodies can be sexual or find love; that girls need to strive to attract male admiration, but boys don't need to do anything in return; that being bisexual or gay is not an option.) We should also ask: why are the media our manuals for those issues? Can they be trusted? Why or why not? Are there more trustworthy sources, or at least sources that can be used to weigh the information in the media?

• FOCUS ON COLORS

In looking at images, think about colors: they may seem purely aesthetic, but they aren't. Do the colors direct your eye to certain words? Are words like "hot" or "sexy" printed in the same color as the model's lipstick or clothing? Does a subconscious association form there?

• DISCUSS WHERE MAGAZINE "ARTICLES" AND "FEATURES" OVERLAP WITH ADS

On most magazine covers, the makeup and styling products used on the cover are listed on an inside page. These are often the very same products advertised in the magazine. The media scholar Ellen McCracken calls the cover "the first advertisement in the magazine." Talk about that, and about the revenue structure of the media. Explain how advertising is the main source of profit for media industries, contributing billions of dollars a year to them. (In comparison, subscriptions and audience revenues are very small.) Talk about how the content of the magazine or television program has to be compatible with the advertiser's goals. High-end magazines like *Town & Country* contain ads for luxury cars and jewelry, while teen magazines contain ads for Bonne Bell cosmetics and teen clothing lines. It's niche marketing, but it works in tandem with the media content: the two are inseparable, and both are focused on encouraging spending by the reader.

• THINK ABOUT THE EMOTIONAL IMPACT TOGETHER

Finally, talk about how the messages make the reader feel. Good about themselves? Hopeful? Or insecure and inadequate? It's probably a little of both, and this is a great way to talk about both the fun and the problems of media myths. It's also a way to talk about attraction and desire as being more than visual or physical. Sex is complex, rich, and multifaceted, and adults have a responsibility to convey that to kids, even if the media don't—or rather, because the media don't. And adolescents have trouble finding spaces in which to talk openly, unembarrassedly, and nonjudgmentally about sex, which is why they rely on the media in the first place. Myth analysis should offer facts, perspectives, and ideas that counteract the rigidly limited ones the media produce.

• STRATEGIES FOR IDENTIFYING MYTHS WITH YOUNGER CHILDREN

With younger children, more guidance is needed. But even with very young children, you can point out that on TV or in the toys they like, there seems to be only one way to be pretty. Remind them that there are lots of ways to be pretty, pointing to the real-life people they love who are beautiful in their eyes, few of whom probably resemble or dress like the media images. Talk to young children about advertising (I started when my own children were two), explaining how the ads make you want to buy the toys, but that the toys are different in real life—usually not as fun or exciting. Hearing these messages helps children to realize the difference between the way the media portrays life and life itself. When they are older, myth analysis is then easier to show them.

- ### BE CLEAR AND HONEST ABOUT YOUR OWN VIEWS

Be aware of the media your kids are involved with. Talk to them about what they're watching, reading, and listening to, and listen to their opinions with respect. But it doesn't hurt to ask questions or offer your own views. With older kids in particular, it's important not to be harsh or censorious, but to encourage discussion and critique. The goal is to get the wheels turning—to let them know there are many ways to think about these messages, to offer them alternatives, and to encourage them to think critically and independently about these issues.

Be clear about your own values and perspectives, and communicate them to children and teenagers. Explain your reasoning and how you've come to that position. They may argue that things are different now—and they are, but it's still important to be able to live with self-respect, confidence, and clear boundaries, so those are things that should be discussed in relation to the media.

- ### SET POSITIVE BOUNDARIES

Always be affirming and supportive of the child, even if you're not affirming and supportive of her decisions or the media influences behind them. Again, point out the differences between the fantasy world portrayed in the media and the world you live in. If you are concerned about the way a young girl is dressing or behaving, talk about possible real-world repercussions that you're worried about. Help her to think through what she's doing, and set boundaries if you need to. Both children and teenagers need structure and guidance, and adults are responsible for providing it, firmly and thoughtfully. At some point, teenagers need to make their own decisions, but talking through the reasons for those decisions can't hurt, and it may help them gain clarity about their own motivations.

No one is immune to the influence of the media—and no one needs to be. What we do need is a healthy skepticism and a greater critical distance from the media's myths. By understanding and keeping a rein on the myths, we gain perspective and control. By finding ways to reclaim and enjoy reality, we can help children and teenagers navigate the media environment with skill and good judgment.

Chapter 8

SUPERHIGHWAY OF SEX
GIRLS, MEDIA, AND SEXUALITY
AROUND THE WORLD

*I*N 1999, A GROUP OF Harvard anthropologists were on the Pacific Island nation of Fiji when television was first introduced. "The sudden infusion of Western cultural images and values through TV appears to be changing the way Fijian girls view themselves and their bodies," reported Anne Becker, director of research at the Harvard Eating Disorders Center. Eating disorders, virtually unknown before the introduction of television, spiked on the island once *Baywatch* and *Beverly Hills 90210* became staple fare. "Since the characters [on *Beverly Hills 90210*] are slim-built, [my friends] come and tell me that they would also like to look like that. They change their mood, their hairstyles, so that they can be like those characters . . . so in order to be like them, I have to work on myself, exercising, and my eating habits should change," said a Fijian girl in the study, in a direct acknowledgment of the media's role in these developments.

All over the world, Western media are penetrating local communities and spaces, causing seismic cultural shifts, especially in the realm of female sexuality. In Thailand, for example, a study of teenagers in Chiang Mai shows that girls experience stress and depression as a result of the Western media's portrayals of sex and gender roles, which conflict with traditional Thai values: "On the one hand, [the teens] aspired to modern relationships and gender roles, in which boys and girls can date, show public affection, and experiment with sex before marriage. On the other hand, teenagers frequently stated that they valued modesty and virginity (in girls) and respected, and sought to obey, their parents. They were pulled towards traditional norms through their religion, kinship ties, and sometimes school culture; and towards Western norms by mass media influences (especially fashion)," write the study's authors.

News stories report that a "sexual revolution" is occurring among Chinese youth, with an increasing number of China's 240 million adolescents engaging in sex, causing a rise in both abortions and STDs, which the country's health care system is largely unprepared to handle. China is in the early stages of a major HIV/AIDS epidemic. There is virtually no sex education in schools, but the country has recently experienced an influx of Western and European media, which some scholars see as an important factor in these sexual trends.

In Turkey, clashes between Eastern and Western sexual mores are resulting in young girls (some as young as twelve) being murdered by their families in so-called honor killings or forced into suicide—sometimes for nothing more than wearing a miniskirt.

A recent survey in Kenya showed that girls are having sex earlier and engaging in lesbian and group sex, practices called "perverted" in an *Africa News* story; "parents and clerics have blamed the media for carrying too much inappropriate content," the story reports. For African girls, early and unsafe sex is particularly problematic: girls are as much as five times more likely than boys to be infected, and 76 percent of all HIV-infected women live in Africa, a phenomenon being referred to as "the feminization of AIDS." More important, because of the collision of cultural values around female sexual activity, girls are being disciplined and punished for their sexual behavior.

These events are not coincidences. We live in a global village, cross-fertilized and networked by the media; and youth cultures everywhere are attuned to the music, movies, television shows, and Web sites that circulate worldwide. Teenagers in Bombay listen to rappers like Kanye West and 50 Cent; kids in Prague line up to see action movies from Hong Kong; while teens in Chicago clubs dance to Bollywood rhythms and salsa beats. There are wildly popular Chinese and Indian versions of *American Idol*. The fusions and fissions of these global media flows can be energizing and inspiring; entirely new genres of creative art have been inspired by them, like the reggaeton music of Puerto Rico (a blend of hip-hop, electronica, and reggae), the bhangra dancing that melds rural and urban dance forms, or the body art that has become so popular among youth worldwide.

But along with the blossoming of new creative forms come clashes of culture that reverberate in communities grappling with the constructions of sexuality being imported via these media. All over the world, the myths of the Lolita Effect are influencing sexual behaviors and ideas about sexual desirability. The specific instances I've described are examples of global trends. Eating disorders are going global as media ideals of female thinness circulate even in countries where hunger has traditionally been a problem, like Pakistan and the Philippines. Perhaps because of media representations of carefree and impetuous sex, both girls and boys are engaging in sexual activity at younger ages—with serious consequences. Globally, "negative outcomes of early pregnancy and sexually transmitted infections (STIs), including HIV/AIDS, threaten the health of people in the second decade of life more than any other age group," according to the medical journal *Lancet*—and more than three-quarters of those infected are adolescent girls. Seventy thousand girls in the developing world die every year from complications of childbirth and pregnancy. In addition, in many cultures, girls are more often condemned and punished for sexual activity, or for perceived transgressions of cultural values, while boys are not, because of an entrenched sexual double standard that is perpetuated by the Lolita Effect.

The myths of the Lolita Effect promise fun, popularity, self-confidence, and empowerment. For affluent girls with material and emotional resources, this can be true. Fashion and beauty *are* fun; feeling attractive can be a confidence-booster; and sex, at its best, is pleasurable and exciting.

But as we've seen, the Lolita Effect has a very dark side: for girls who don't enjoy upper-class privileges, or for girls whose cultural context is in conflict with the Lolita Effect's myths, or when the Lolita Effect is taken too literally in real life, there can be serious negative repercussions, and we should not ignore or trivialize them.

For example, a news report from South Africa describes girls as young as eleven turning to prostitution to afford the designer fashions and high-tech gadgets touted by "MTV culture." In the Northern Indian village of Nongspun, tribal elders decided that girls wearing pants provoked men into sexual abuse, so girls over twelve are required to wear long skirts or face punishment. In Nigeria, women and girls in trousers and "indecent clothes" have been attacked by street hoodlums and police. In the Iraqi city of Basra, women have been killed for wearing makeup and other "unIslamic behavior." Police in Banda Aceh, Indonesia, monitor women and girls for inappropriate dress, including figure-hugging clothes. The Lolita Effect urges girls to "flaunt it" and display their sexuality by wearing revealing and provocative clothes, but the backlash against them for doing so can be violent and repressive. Even in the United States, the outcomes can be similar: girls are frequently punished by parents for sexual activity, and then punished again by the legal system if they run away or rebel. And in the United Kingdom and other Western countries, the incidence of eating disorders continues to rise, especially among preteen girls—some as young as seven—who cite the media as inspirations for their body ideals.

So the impacts of the Lolita Effect for girls in the global village can be both liberating and devastating. The happy, carefree, sexy-but-not-sexual girl promised by these media myths may be out there, but she's in the minority: for many girls, the pursuit of the Lolita Effect can result in a backlash that they don't have the support or resources to handle. For girls, living up to the myths of the Lolita Effect is a Herculean labor: projecting sexuality without engaging in sex, or engaging in sex without suffering any social, emotional, or physical consequences, is unrealistic in real life. Expecting girls to deal with these issues before they have reached adulthood, with no guidance and no help, is unconscionable. Societies judge them, but extend no helping hands: they must struggle with these situations on their own.

It's important, therefore, for adults in society to take the Lolita Effect seriously: not to police or condemn girls, but to work in collaboration with girls to help them gain a critical and informed perspective on sexuality and its representations, so that they can make responsible choices about their sex lives. The Lolita Effect promises sex without strings attached: it's a purely pleasurable, consumerist fantasy that reaps profits for the media industries, but pays no heed to the real world that girls inhabit. It is up to the rest of us, then, to recognize the Lolita Effect as a series of myths that need to be rejected rather than pursued as an ideal.

But for legions of girls worldwide, this kind of power cannot be exercised because they are living the Lolita Effect in its most extreme form: their sexualized bodies *are* the commodities for sale. The enormity of this reality is played down, discounted, and repudiated when it is brought up in this context: many of us are unwilling to make any connection between sexy little girls in the relatively sanitized world of media and marketing and the commodified sexualization of girls in worldwide trafficking and pornography. The easiest argument to make is that they aren't the same thing: a twelve-year-old fashion model in stiletto heels and fishnet hose in an advertisement isn't the same thing at all as a twelve-year-old prostitute in the same attire on a Bangkok or New Orleans street corner. After all, one is just an image, and a lucrative one—a media construction, not a reality; and the plight of the child prostitute is not necessarily caused by the first image. Ergo, they have no relation to each other. Or so the argument goes.

But I have to suggest otherwise. The sexualization of young girls in the seemingly safe, unrealistic, make-believe worlds of media and marketing works to legitimize, and even glamorize, the use of girls' sexuality for commercial purposes. It may not cause it, but it makes it acceptable—even fun and trendy. And because the signs of sexiness—the thong underwear, the push-up bras, the fishnet hose, the spiky high heels, the revealing clothing, the French-maid outfits sold at Halloween time in toddler sizes—are the easily recognized costumes of sex work, they send the powerful message that sexualizing girls' bodies in the commercial realm is just fine.

Again, I want to make it clear that this is not a rejection of girls' right to be sexual, to develop sexually, or to explore sexuality safely and satisfyingly. In fact, I am fully in favor of those things. In critiquing the way girls' sexuality is commodified through the filter of sex work, I am in fact defending girls' rights to be sexual in healthy ways—ways that are not motivated by profit, that have no connection with the commercial enterprises that capitalize on the Lolita Effect, from marketing to prostitution. Sexuality should be safe, self-directed, and free of violence and coercion. Girls need to have social and cultural support for their sexual growth and well-being.

None of this is true in the Lolita Effect, especially in the realm of child sex trafficking, where we find its most powerful form. Dressed up in the clothing made cute and seemingly innocuous by the Bratz, the Pussycat Dolls, and the juniors' styles bedecked with sleazy slogans, child sex workers are living embodiments of Lolita. They take the implications of the Lolita Effect to the ultimate conclusion: that young girls' bodies are an appropriate element of sexual commerce. The scale of this enterprise is monstrous: child sex trafficking is a multibillion-dollar industry that involves more than a million children a year; the United Nations Office on Drugs and Crime describes child sex trafficking as the world's fastest-growing criminal enterprise. The children involved are as young as toddlers, sometimes even babies. As Matthew Robb writes in *Social Work Today*, "Against a backdrop of high-risk sex, HIV, hepatitis, street drugs, and pathologically abusive men, these children can expect a life prophesied long ago by English philosopher Thomas Hobbes: 'solitary, poor, nasty, brutish, and short.'"

The filmmaker Guy Jacobson describes five-year-old girls in Thailand offering to perform oral sex for money; so does an NBC *Dateline* report that actually shows video of little girls in brothels using childish words like "yum yum" for oral sex and "boom boom" for intercourse. Sometimes these children wear rags or ordinary children's clothing, but more often they are garmented in the skimpy skirts, bustiers, thong underwear, and transparent tops of the Lolita Effect. Peter Landesman of the *New York Times Magazine* describes child prostitutes in Mexico "in stilettos and spray-on-tight neon vinyl and satin or skimpy leopard-patterned outfits." The *New York Times* journalist Nicholas Kristof writes about "Chai Hour" in Phnom Penh, Cambodia, where young teenage girls "in skimpy white outfits" stand in glass cages to be rented for sex. An *Economist* story depicts young Vietnamese girl prostitutes in heavy makeup and Gucci high-heeled sandals. Lisa Ling's documentary *Slave Girls of India* shows a madam in an Indian brothel bragging about her "baby beauties." It's no wonder, then, that when we see these outfits in the children's sections of department stores, or in Halloween costume catalogs, or in media targeted to kids, some of us are creeped out. There are obvious visual connections there that give some of us pause.

These sexy clothes, and the concept of girls' sexuality underlying them, are adult projections onto girls' lives. Kids didn't come up with these markers of female sexuality. These are adult fantasies being sold to children, and to the rest of us. Wanting to reject the accoutrements of sex work as symbols of girls' sexuality is not the same thing as wanting to curb or censor girls' sexuality. Rather, my critique is geared to finding new, progressive, dynamic visions of girls' sexuality that are not in bondage to sex work. We need versions of girls' sexuality that are completely disconnected from commercial sex.

Right now, the sexualization of girls is a high-dollar, worldwide industry. Child prostitution and sex work are thriving, not just in the Third World, but in the United States, Europe, Canada, Australia, and Japan, as countless news stories and government reports attest. Atlanta, Georgia, for example, is a hub of child sex work: the juvenile prostitution problem there is "a lot bigger than anyone would really like to know," according to Kaffie McCullough, director of the Juvenile Justice Fund in that city. In New York City, "child prostitution is clearly growing," says Julie Schwartz, bureau chief of the sex crimes division of the Brooklyn district attorney's office. The United States Department of Justice estimates that between 100,000 and three million children are involved in sex work in this country. Winnipeg, Manitoba, is a thriving site of child prostitution.

In France, sixty-two adults were recently convicted of selling children (including their own) for sex. Two years ago, police seized thousands of pornographic pictures and videos of children from computers in eight European countries, including Norway, Italy, and the Netherlands. Romania is a primary source for children sold into sex work. Stories like this appear in newspapers all over the world, every day. The writer Kathryn Farr points out that it is a crime that operates "almost everywhere with relative impunity." The Internet is a "child pornography superhighway," with millions of photographs and videos of the sexual assault of children transmitted daily. A quarter of all sex tourists in developing countries are estimated to be American, with others coming from a variety of First World countries.

The real-life Lolita Effect is global.

These girls' stories don't involve fun, glamour, or pleasure. "Andrea" was four years old when she was abandoned by her mother, perhaps in the United States, perhaps in Mexico: she doesn't remember. She was seven when she first had sex with a john in a hotel in Juarez. She and other children were beaten, abused, and starved during their sexual training as prostitutes, according to a *New York Times Magazine* story. When they were hooked up with johns, they were told to say, "I've been looking for you, Daddy!" Twelve-year-old "Heena" was prostituted by her uncle in India, and locked up and beaten if she resisted. In Toronto, five-year-old Masha Allen was chained in a basement and subjected to sexual abuse by her adoptive father; her abuse was pictured and distributed in his child pornography operation. In New York, thirteen-year-old Lucilia was gang-raped and beaten before being put on the street by her pimps. These stories are not isolated instances: millions of girls are exploited in these ways in the sex industry today.

These Lolitas do not voluntarily enter sex work. Most young girls (and boys) are sold into prostitution by parents because of sheer economic necessity, or forced into sex work because they had to leave unbearable and abusive home lives, or simply taken, like Masha. The few that enter the sex industries without force do so because they have no other options: sex work is their only viable means of economic survival. For girls this is especially true, as in many countries girls are denied the education that could give them other choices. Sometimes they are not paid at all: they are sex slaves. In either case, they become addicted to drugs, ravaged by disease, victims of daily violence; and they die young.

The familiar myths of the Lolita Effect take shape and coalesce in these realities. The media's sexualization of young girls positions them as willing and appropriate participants in sex work. Healthy, responsible, ethical sexuality is not a prevalent feature of the Lolita Effect, as we've seen; rather, the rhetoric of girls' empowerment is used to promote a subjugated and commercialized version of female sexuality that is aligned with the distorted value systems of sex work.

Girls' bodies are clad in the familiar garments of the Lolita Effect when they are sold on the streets. And in many cases, these girls, posed and dressed in these ways, are fodder for an underground but flourishing media industry that circulates child pornography worldwide and exploits children unrelentingly for obscene profits. The line between these media industries and the "legitimate" ones that relay disturbingly similar images is becoming increasingly blurred. The Lolita Effect pops up in kids' magazines, in television shows, in malls, in pornography, and on the streets. Sometimes it's hard to tell these images apart.

The real problem with the Lolita Effect is that girls are not in control. The Lolita Effect is an adult male fantasy of girls' sexuality, just as Lolita was the object of Humbert Humbert's fantasies. In the Lolita Effect, the girl has no choices: sexuality for her is limited to the realm of an imaginary Lolita. The girl's body is an object on display for others' sexual pleasure. She must either voluntarily work on it to render it suitable for display in the Lolita mold, or give it up to be used by others for profit. In the meantime, she cannot safely explore other modes of sexuality, for there are none available in the public discourses about girls and sex. She has no authority over her own sexuality.

The Lolita Effect operates within a corporate, commercial sphere. Because of this, there are no ethics at work: the Lolita Effect is driven by profit motives. The creators and promoters of the Lolita Effect are those who benefit financially from it. The adults who head up the fashion, diet, fitness, cosmetics, plastic surgery, and media industries profit legally; pornographers, pimps, and human traffickers profit illegally. In either case, girls' best interests are not at the heart of these constructions of sexuality.

At its root, then, the Lolita Effect is a human rights issue and an ethical issue. It's about girls' freedom to have safe, self-directed, and healthy sexual lives, free of coercion and exploitation. This requires facing up to the constraints and perils that circumscribe girls' sex lives today—in the mainstream media, in our culture, in our attitudes—and opening up public discussions of the subject, in collaboration with girls themselves. It's about thinking through sexual ethics, which are complicated and always evolving.

An ethics of girls' sexuality puts girls first. Girls need to be guaranteed the right to a safe and happy sex life that progresses in ways they feel comfortable with and in control of. Girls should not be catapulted into sexuality by a media-driven hard-sell that works as a cover for the more exploitative prostitution and porn industries. Discussions about sex should happen apart from the commercial sphere, in as many safe and responsible spaces as possible; sexual awareness should come with no threats and no illusions, in ways aimed at helping girls make good decisions for themselves and protecting them from violence and exploitation. This may sound utopian, but my firm belief is that if safe sexuality becomes an important public health issue, then girls will have access to knowledge from multiple sources, many of which will challenge the harmful consequences of the Lolita Effect.

To confront and combat the Lolita Effect, we need to figure out alternatives that offer girls the tools to understand and define their own sexuality. We need to make girls' sexual safety a priority everywhere in the world. We need to deal with issues of power and prejudice, analyzing how they play out in girls' sexual lives. We need to celebrate girls' bodies, in their natural and diverse forms, without exploiting them. The way girls are treated now, and the way they treat themselves, tells us something about their social value. This has to change.

This goal applies to girls in the First World who are pressured by media culture into body ideals, behaviors, and situations that can (and do) hurt them, as well as to girls in poverty whose sexuality is the sole reason for their denigration and exploitation. It applies to the way we think about mainstream media images as well as the way we deal with child pornography and prostitution. If we approach girls' sexuality from the perspective of sexual ethics and human rights, we gain valuable and far-reaching tools for understanding and negotiating this crucial issue.

The ideals of human rights aim to protect people from abuses and from the loss of worth and dignity. Human rights goals include promoting social progress and protecting people—especially vulnerable groups of people—from oppression and exploitation. Freedom is a core principle of human rights movements; so is personal safety. If we make these ideals a priority for girls, then sex will become an arena for defining and defending these principles. By doing so, we open up the possibility of reinventing girls' sexuality—of finding positive, progressive, humane concepts of female sexuality that energize and enrich girls' everyday lives.

Today, we have no words or concepts for dealing with girls' sexuality in a positive and forward-thinking way. As child psychiatrist Dr. Lynn Ponton points out, children's first introduction to sex is usually through sex-ed programs that focus on the negative and scary aspects of sexual behavior. "How different these first programs would be," she writes, "if they focused on normal sexual development, encouraging self-exploration and sexual curiosity." How much better things would be if we could openly discuss girls' sexuality within an ethical framework, instead of allowing the corporate media to monopolize the issue.

Although these discussions seem to involve a private realm, they are public, and they call on the public sector: health care, social work, public information campaigns, legal aid, public schooling. These are institutions that are severely underfunded and politically constrained everywhere. Public support, both fiscal and ethical, has been withdrawn from these crucial arenas. If we are to help girls succeed in an environment that uses their sexuality against them, we must talk about how we can shape public policy and cultivate institutional resources that truly work *for* girls. Pro-girl activism needs to engage debates on reproductive rights, health care reform, and media ownership regulations that impinge on the way girls' sexuality is lived out in society.

In its Universal Declaration of Human Rights in 1948, the United Nations recognized "that childhood is entitled to special care and assistance," and in 1990 adopted the Convention on the Rights of the Child. Though controversial, the convention is a good-faith attempt to focus on children's well-being in an increasingly unstable and violent world, and more countries have ratified this convention than any other human rights treaty in history—192 as of November 2005. The articles of the Convention recognize the important role of the media as well as the prevalence of sexual abuse and sexual commerce in children's lives today. A central goal of the Convention is to "ensure that all children . . . grow up in an environment of happiness, love and understanding; and are informed about and participate in, achieving their rights in an accessible and active manner."

The goals of myth analysis and challenging the Lolita Effect are exactly the same. Moreover, it's critical to understand that the Lolita Effect is global: it cuts across borders, race, and class via a network of multinational media that spans the planet. In her book *No Logo*, Naomi Klein has pointed out that the world is intricately interconnected: the expensive sneakers purchased in U.S. malls originate in abusive Vietnamese sweatshops; cute little Barbie outfits are made by child laborers in Sumatra; Starbucks lattes come from the exploitation of impoverished laborers in Guatemala; Shell oil pollutes and impoverishes villages of the Niger Delta. Her point is that we are all inexorably intertwined on this fragile planet; every move each of us makes causes reverberations and ripple effects in far-flung places, affecting people we will never know, but whose lives are linked with ours. Similarly, representations of girls' sexuality produced in one country, culture, or context are disseminated worldwide, impacting girls in various contexts powerfully and differently; girls' bodies are the targets of marketing and merchandising that manipulate race, class, and physical difference in their own interests; girls' bodies are trafficked across borders and sold on streets and in brothels; girls' sexualized images are streamed through Internet portals to buyers all over the globe.

So how we learn to understand girls' sexuality in First World settings must take into consideration girls' sexuality in Third World spaces: in an era of globalized media, issues of sexuality are necessarily international and cross-cultural. The issues are not the same everywhere, but the human rights goals are.

The World Congress against the Commercial Sexual Exploitation of Children declared in 1996 that child prostitution "constitutes a form of coercion and violence against children, and amounts to forced labor and a contemporary form of slavery." This Congress convenes again in 2008, and the problem of child sex work has only escalated in the intervening years, a fact that should push us to think hard about the reasons. Why are children, especially young girls, the main targets of the sex industries today? What are the beliefs, values, and ideologies at work in the world that have caused this situation? And what can we do about it?

We can do a lot—and the first step is opening up the discussion. Although there are laws in place, clearly they're inadequate to tackle the range of problems that have arisen in this context; sex is still taboo and unfamiliar terrain for legal bodies (for example, although rape has been a by-product of war for millennia, the UN General Assembly is only now considering a resolution recognizing rape as a war crime). But we can't wait for institutions to take the lead: it's time for us to move from being passive consumers of the Lolita Effect to being active citizens with a voice in the matter. Some of this is happening already: for example, a coalition of civil rights, religious, and antiracist groups have protested images of women in rap videos and initiated televised town-hall meetings and Congressional hearings on the issue. We need more open dialogue and public exchange of ideas around these issues, without moralizing or political polarization along liberal/conservative lines. We have to take a holistic view and understand that if we quibble about semantics, splitting hairs about whether commercial representations are or are not pornographic, we're missing the forest for the trees: we have to put girls first, and work for a world that's in their best interests.

Most important, girls need to be part of these discussions. Their voices must be heard. Their perspectives must be at the forefront of these debates—not just educated, privileged girls, but girls of all backgrounds and experiences, so that their diverse understandings, struggles, and knowledge are brought to bear on the process.

The support of boys and men would boost these efforts, and many recognize the problems and want to help with them. Although the Lolita Effect seems to benefit men and boys, there are in fact attendant harms that perceptive boys and men recognize and want to change: the angst that many girls experience as a result of the Lolita Effect; the pervasive violence against girls and women in the world; the racism and classism at work; the way the Lolita Effect lures girls away from other things that matter—politics, intellectual life, art, music, spirituality, charitable work, community action. Girls are the sisters, daughters, friends, and lovers of boys and men, and many of them care about the girls in their lives enough to want to join this discussion. They should be welcome.

Such relationships of caring are at the crux of developing an ethics of girls' sexuality. Thinking about sexuality allows us to consider our interrelatedness with others, the impulses that urge us to seek physical and other forms of intimacy, and even our connections with our bodies and ourselves. The Reverend Anne Bathurst Gilson, a prominent Episcopalian minister and theologian, has written that sexuality is "a yearning for embodied connection [and] a movement toward embodied justice. . . . We cannot help but care about those with whom we are intimate, and caring about them gives us energy to challenge institutions, social trends, or individuals which threaten or oppress them." Sex, then, offers a lens for seeing a larger picture: it's not just about bodies or a physical act; it has meanings far beyond those crude basics.

"Justice," writes the theologian Marvin Ellison, "means . . . a fair distribution of intangible goods, such as respect, compassion, and care. Above all, it means that those with greater personal and social power, typically adults, should use their power in the interests, and for the benefit, of those with lesser power, namely, children and adolescents. In fact, justice demands that adult power be morally accountable to the well-being of youth." This is a concept of justice that has as its starting points compassion, respect and equality, and these values should apply when we consider sexuality as well as all other aspects of human experience.

What would a positive, progressive, socially responsible, proactive concept of girls' sexuality look like? Right now, we don't have good models for this. What we need is first, a concept of girls' sexuality that is inclusive, diverse, and affirming, rather than negative and punitive. Sexuality is a characteristic of all people, though it is infinitely varied in its expression and manifestations. Girls' desires and sexuality need to be recognized as natural, multifarious, and socially relevant. From here, we need to begin formulating ideas about sexual ethics that would give us guidelines that would help girls to experience sexuality fearlessly, responsibly, and unhurriedly, at a pace that's in line with their physical and cognitive development. These ethics should be used to develop social, educational, and medical policies as well; and they could be drawn upon by religious institutions seeking to rethink their moral tenets in a rapidly changing world.

"To be effective in implementing social change, it often requires looking at the world from a different vantage point," write the policy analysts Andrea Parrott and Nina Cummings. Media literacy education can offer this new viewpoint: it is a crucial component of formulating an ethics of girls' sexuality. As the sociologist Virginia Olesen has argued, "Rage is not enough." Unless both kids and adults learn to skillfully analyze and contemplate the myths at work in media representations of girls' sexuality, there is no basis for critique or change. When I spoke recently to a group of pediatricians in Iowa, it became clear that many of us with a stake in girls' well-being— doctors, teachers, media scholars, parents, counselors—could combine our efforts to make media literacy required in the K-12 curriculum. It's as important as math or reading: more important, really, in today's media-clogged climate.

Recognizing the Lolita Effect and understanding its far-reaching implications can motivate awareness, and then social transformation. It can point us toward the kinds of dialogues about sexual ethics that we have never had, but that should begin immediately.

Chapter 9

CONFRONTING THE LOLITA EFFECT
STRATEGIES FOR RESISTANCE

*M*Y SIX-YEAR-OLD DAUGHTER Loves to play dress-up. She'll layer on gauzy garments, sling a tool belt across her shoulder, slip on plastic high-heeled shoes, and crown it all with a cowboy hat or a chef's toque. Then she'll stand in front of the mirror and preen. She knows she's gorgeous—not because she's conforming to some media-inspired ideal, but because she's taking pure sensuous pleasure in the joy of self-adornment without self-consciousness.

As she grows older, the Lolita Effect will rob her of this pleasure, the pleasure of femininity and sensuality without self-criticism or anxiety. The Lolita Effect promises girls that they can experience joyful sexuality and femininity, but only at a price: the price of conforming to the restrictive ideals it imposes on the entire landscape of female sexuality. So if a girl is not slender-yet-voluptuous, if she is "too" dark-skinned or light-skinned or freckled or birthmarked, if she is modest about flaunting her body, if she has a physical or mental disability, if she doesn't strive to measure up to the imaginary standards of the imaginary male gaze, if she is concerned about violence in her life, if she thinks sex is not a commodity to be traded, bought and sold . . . then she's out of luck, as far as the Lolita Effect is concerned.

The Lolita Effect is not an affirmation or celebration of girls' sexuality, in all its diverse and blossoming forms. On the contrary, it is a restrictive, hidebound, market-driven set of impositions on girls' sexuality. And it's virtually inescapable, because it's the only definition of girls' sexuality that's represented in the globally circulating mainstream media.

The feel-good the Lolita Effect promises is a consumer fantasy, and it's designed to be short-lived, because the Lolita Effect needs to fuel constant consumerism in order to support the interconnected web of industries, from diet aids to pornography, that depend on it. So any sense of genuine, self-loving, unfettered sexual pleasure is inimical to it. It needs girls (and later, women) to feel the anxieties it generates about sex enough to spend exorbitant amounts of money in its pursuit. But it offers a façade of sexual empowerment as a powerful lure. The Lolita Effect is a sexual Venus flytrap, seducing unwary victims with promises of nectar, then devouring them.

The Lolita Effect has toxic side effects that are manifested in girls' everyday lives. From eating disorders and body image issues to dating violence, teen pregnancy, sexual abuse, and sexual exploitation, girls everywhere grapple with the fallout from the Lolita Effect. For some girls, the side effects aren't significant. They can move past them and experience fulfilled, potent girlhoods and adult lives. But for others, the impacts are significant, long-term, and devastating. The Lolita Effect operates on a continuum, affecting some girls much more negatively and brutally than others. But no girl is immune to it.

I'm convinced that the Lolita Effect is a major factor in the high rates of teen pregnancy and STDs in the United States and many other countries, as it purveys a version of sexuality that erases all notions of girls' rights and responsibilities in sexual activity. It doesn't encourage girls to gain fact-based sexual knowledge. Instead, it glamorizes and fictionalizes sex. It offers girls a nefarious mixed message: be sexy but not sexual. Flaunt your sexuality (*if* you've "got it")—but don't act on it. Attract male attention, but fend off sexual advances. Think "abstinence only," take pledges of virginity and chastity, but know that the best sex is passionate and spontaneous. Good girls, according to the Lolita Effect, don't feel desire, but they need to transmit the playful message that they are "sluts" or "hotties," as their glittering T-shirts attest. These contradictory messages can only result in confusion and rash decision making. Nowhere in the Lolita Effect are girls' feelings, needs, developmental capabilities, or, most important, boundaries, acknowledged or addressed. Nowhere in it is sex taken seriously or thoughtfully.

In the United States (and elsewhere), we are squeamish about children's sexuality, so we have allowed the media to dominate this important discourse. We cling to notions of childhood innocence, but look away when our kids gain sexual knowledge via the sexual media messages that surround and target them. Abandoning children's sexual education to the media means allowing the Lolita Effect to predominate. But sex and sexuality are so much more than a corporate, mass-media commodity.

At its best, sex is about ethical and positive human connections. In my own view, sex is richest in the context of a loving, meaningful, deeply felt relationship, but I realize that for many people, good sex is defined in other ways. After all, sex is infinitely complex. People are drawn to each other in desiring relationships for all kinds of reasons—sometimes something as simple as the curve of a jawline or a gesture can inflame desire. The people we desire don't have to conform to the beauty ideals of the Lolita Effect: King William of Orange's mistress Elizabeth Villiers reportedly had a wandering eye and a bad complexion, but the king doted on her; "The breath . . . from my mistress reeks," wrote Shakespeare wryly, going on to describe his lover's physical inadequacies in a well-known love sonnet; the lyrics to the classic Rodgers and Hart song "My Funny Valentine" are a testament to desire beyond the Lolita Effect: *Your looks are laughable / Unphotographable / Yet you're my favorite work of art . . .*

Many factors influence sexual desire, from physical attractiveness to adventurousness to pheromones; we have a sketchy and incomplete understanding of what draws people to one another. But it's a rich and multidimensional aspect of being human, so it's tragic that the Lolita Effect narrows it down and flattens it out so completely. By maintaining that sex and desirability are the prerogatives only of girls who conform to the restricted criteria of the Lolita Effect, a whole range of possibilities and potential joys are being implicitly denied to millions of others. And even for those who come close to meeting the Lolita Effect's grueling criteria, the stress of measuring up surely makes it hard to enjoy a relaxed, pleasurable sexual experience. Even as it dominates, the Lolita Effect is actually antithetical to girls' sexual fulfillment.

This is because it eliminates the possibilities of sex outside of a commercial context. "Sex sells" goes the old adage, but only very specific definitions of sex can be used to sell, because only those definitions will move products and maximize profits, as we've seen. The sex that sells is a corrupted version of human sexuality, because it denies and negates so many aspects of it, and because sexual ethics are not even considered. Kids—indeed, all of us—need to seek out richer, deeper, more humane, and more ethical concepts of sexuality if we are to make any progress at all toward healthy, inclusive, unoppressive sexuality.

The American Psychological Association identifies a clear distinction between sexualization and healthy sexuality; in a recent report, they write that sexualization occurs when:

- a person's value comes only from his or her sexual appeal, or behavior, to the exclusion of other characteristics;
- a person is held to a standard that equates physical attractiveness (narrowly defined) with being sexy;
- a person is sexually objectified—that is, made into a thing for others' sexual use, rather than seen as a person with the capacity for independent action and decision-making;
- and/or sexuality is inappropriately imposed upon a person.

The Lolita Effect meets all four of these criteria: the commodified version of girls' sexuality is not conducive to girls' healthy sexual growth and development. Instead, it works against girls' best interests to create a pervasive idea of sexuality that objectifies, undermines, and exploits girls, and narrows their options.

The APA also points out, correctly, that developmental age has a great deal to do with how girls are able to deal with and process the sexual messages in the media: a six-year-old's responses and reactions are different from a sixteen-year-old's. But the Lolita Effect treats them all the same way. Because it is so widespread, it pervades the media—it's present in the media targeted to toddlers as well as in R-rated films and M-rated video games intended for older adolescents. The Lolita Effect is intended to induce a conception of ideal girlhood, focused on female sexuality, that creates consumer consciousness and aspirations at a very early age. So the Bratz and Trollz dolls, with their fishnet hose and hot-tub parties and "bling," are the baby versions of the hypersexualized women in music videos: the construction of female sexuality is the same.

Many girls grow increasingly aware of these issues as they get older; the girls I've talked with who are in middle and high school are often well aware of the fictions and fabrications of the media industries, but they feel caught in them; many of them struggle to find a middle ground where they can enjoy the benefits and pleasures of mainstream sexuality without falling prey to its harms. But younger children, I've found, are wholly unaware: they gasp when I show them videos of computer manipulations of images of magazine images. "But Miley Cyrus is real," a boy protested when I talked about digital editing in a sixth-grade classroom. He and other children in the class were having a hard time grasping what I was telling them. "Yes," I explained, "she is real, but she doesn't look like this picture in real life. No one could, because of how much the computer changes things." I had to go over this several times, because they had never imagined that the seemingly "real" images in the media were not faithful representations of reality. No one had ever told them this. They knew that cartoons and certain special effects weren't real, but they didn't know that realistic images were constructed and modified, too.

Many kids are innocent about the media, but thankfully, that is changing as they become more technologically savvy, and as the apparatus for filmmaking, editing, digital photography, and music recording becomes more accessible and affordable. But still, for many kids, this kind of knowledge is not part of their everyday experience. No one has taught them to be wary or skeptical of the media. No one has taught them to analyze what they see or question its relevance to their lives.

Of course, the capacity for critical thinking is different at different ages. Childhood progresses gradually and in stages. Every child is different in his or her capacities and cognitions. In the contemporary era, we can't simply ignore the ways in which children are largely unequipped to deal with the adult world. Scholars have argued that childhood is a social construction, and that is true: prior to the twentieth century, childhood was not a concept—child laborers were not treated as different from adults; child sexual abuse was not defined as a crime; children were not required to go to school; children were not a protected category of people. But we can see things differently now, because the world is a different place. Just as you couldn't hand a three-year-old a copy of *Moby Dick* and expect her to make sense of it, and you couldn't expect a ten-year-old to perform brain surgery, you can't expect a child to be able to make informed, fully cognizant, clear decisions about sex. So why do we seem to think they can handle this aspect of adult life without guidance or social support?

"At this moment in our history, young women develop earlier than ever before, but they do so within a society that does not protect or nurture them," writes the historian Joan Jacobs Brumberg in her groundbreaking book *The Body Project*. "Given what we know about the deep commercial investment in girls' bodies, and also the tenor of our contemporary culture, it seems unrealistic to think that young girls can operate independently, without parental or adult assistance, or that they should be expected to."

We have a responsibility to girls, to ensure that they grow up in safety, and to ensure that they have the wherewithal to make good decisions about their sex lives as well as about all other aspects of their being. "Empowerment" is a word that has been too much bandied about in the media, used to sell everything from deodorant to pop music. Because of this, it has lost its meaning. But there are real ways to give girls more power, to help them gain the strength to confront the Lolita Effect. There are tools we can give them that will help them in these aims. This is not the same thing as curbing them, breaking their spirits, or cordoning them off from the real world. On the contrary, giving them these tools and the information to use them well will encourage them to use their intelligence, critical capabilities, and courage to forge their own way in the world.

These tools include:

1. MEDIA LITERACY EDUCATION. This book is geared to fostering informed critical analyses of media messages. Media literacy education can be formal or informal; the ability to achieve critical distance from the media's constructions of the world is a lifelong resource. This book gives you a start on raising these issues and talking about them with kids. The ideas, questions, and strategies outlined in previous chapters can be used by parents, teachers, counselors, or anyone who works with and cares about kids. Media literacy can happen in after-school programs, in the classroom, in mother-daughter groups, or one-on-one. It can begin with children as young as two, who can understand make-believe.

Ideally, media literacy education would be a required part of the K-12 curriculum. In a media-saturated world, children need to learn how to dissect and understand this pervasive aspect of their environment, just as they learn to understand the seasons or Newton's laws of motion. Media economics, technologies, and representations should be an essential part of learning to navigate the world. This is a discussion that's only just beginning to happen. People outside the small world of media studies—doctors, psychologists, teachers, counselors— are just beginning to understand the role of the media in children's lives. We need more dialogues among these groups to begin to develop and lobby for media literacy education.

But in the meantime, media literacy can happen informally and easily in the home or among friends. The seeds of analysis and critique can be planted. Parents and teachers can educate themselves so that they can open up discussions with children. As kids grow into and through adolescence, these discussions need to become more frequent and more rigorous. It's important to respect and value children's opinions during these talks, and it's equally important to voice your own, as well as the reasoning behind it. Kids model the adults in their lives; they learn a great deal from us. In my own discussions with girls, they credit their parents (especially their mothers) with helping them see things clearly and critically. These efforts won't result in overnight, or even radical, changes, but they do initiate new ideas and perspectives. As one of my students told me, "Once that light bulb goes on, it never goes off."

2. CREATIVITY. Girls' creative energies are awe-inspiring. The girls I know are instinctive and prolific artists, writers, poets, actresses, filmmakers, photographers, Web designers, and musicians, especially in the preteen years. They are bursting with ideas, talent, and creative impulses—and they are technologically savvy and unafraid. It's crucially important to foster these activities and nurture their vitality in these areas, as they can produce media that challenge, counter, and reimagine femininity and sexuality in response to the Lolita Effect. Ophira Edut's "Adios Barbie" Web site (http://www.adiosbarbie .com/) is a wonderful example of a bright, funny counter to the Lolita Effect; Kiri Davis's short documentary "A Girl Like Me" is another. Encourage girls to take classes in video production and editing, Web site construction, writing, and art. Many summer camps focus on teaching these skills, like FemmeFilmTexas in Austin, which "teaches the nuts and bolts

of filmmaking" to teenage girls (www.femmefilmtexas.org /programs/camp.html). It is vitally important that we feed girls' creative energies and support their visions. Girls need to become active media producers, not passive media consumers. Through creating and sharing their ideas about being a girl, they can begin to talk back to the media.

3. MULTIDIMENSIONALITY. Help girls to recognize the value of their abilities in areas other than sex and sex appeal. Sex is an important part of human life, but it is not the only one that matters. In a way, the Lolita Effect both overvalues and undervalues sex: it overemphasizes the need for girls to be sexy, but it doesn't take sex seriously enough to provide good information about handling it in real life. By overemphasizing sex, though, it also undervalues all the other aspects of human existence that matter. We need to fight back by giving girls credit for being smart, talented, scientifically curious, musically gifted, artistic, strong leaders, caring, or athletic. We have a responsibility to make sure they feel really good about their achievements in these other areas, all of which contribute to their worth as human beings.

The American Psychological Association's task force report on girls' sexualization points out that parents, teachers, and other adults implicitly buy into the Lolita Effect. They tend to favor girls who physically meet the Lolita Effect criteria and react negatively to girls with larger bodies or unconventional features. It's important that we all take a good hard look at whether we are unconsciously perpetuating these patterns. Let's make sure we recognize the importance of girls' achievements in other arenas, regardless of their success at achieving the Lolita Effect. Girls need not to be one-dimensional Barbie dolls whose allure will diminish as they age. They need to be nurtured into full-fledged, accomplished, complex people whose sense of self-worth is not totally dependent on the media's skewed criteria for successful girlhood.

4. CONSUMER ADVOCACY AND ACTION. We can and must engage actively with the media. We have the ability to critique, analyze, challenge, and affirm media messages, and we also have the option of turning off, boycotting, and disengaging from media that denigrate or insult girls. This is not the same as censorship, though the media producers often call it that. But in fact, it is free speech. Just as media producers have the right to create and distribute messages they see as valuable, ordinary people have the right to discuss, debate, and challenge them. It's called "democracy."

We can also talk back to the media. These days, it's easy to contact corporations via their Web sites. A little Internet searching, or an hour with a reference librarian in a public library, and companies' contact information is readily found. We can, and should, send e-mails and letters to companies when they use images that condone violence against women or girls or otherwise malign or insult us. Already, watchdog groups publicize such events—for example the University of Michigan's Sexual Assault Prevention and Awareness Center has a Web site that showcases degrading and sexist advertising (www.umich.edu/~sapac/sia/2007/). If you want to protest media that degrade women and girls, you should. Companies are typically loath to give up the Lolita Effect—it's so profitable—but they are sensitive to their customers' views, and challenges can sometimes be effective. At any rate, it is crucial for our voices to be heard. Girls must learn to be active, aware consumers in the context of a free-market economy.

5. SOCIAL ENGAGEMENT AND ACTIVISM. All over the world, girls are denied access to independence, economic security, and

good health, especially reproductive health. This is because of gender discrimination that operates at multiple levels. In many countries and cultures, girls don't even have a fighting chance at life, because of culturally sanctioned female infanticide. If they do make it to childhood, poverty and disease may cut their lives short. Many girls can't get an education, which limits their options and forces them into sex work at early ages. Many girls' lives are marred by violence. Many girls have no choices insofar as their sex lives, marital status, or childbearing options are concerned. "In every part of the world," writes Graça Machel in the UNICEF report *Because I Am a Girl*, "families and societies treat girls and boys differently, with girls facing greater discrimination and accessing fewer opportunities and little or sub-standard education, health care and nutrition."

As I've said earlier in this book, the lives of girls throughout the world are linked. It's simply unacceptable to condone the denigration of any girls, anywhere, as girls everywhere face discrimination and restrictions simply because of their gender, though these issues are (of course) complicated by other factors, such as race, class, sexual orientation, and religion. We need to accept the fact that in this global village, our lives are intertwined. The fashionable jeans we buy may have been made by a preteen girl in a sweatshop. The teen Web site we visit may also own pornographic portals. To what extent do our actions and consumer behaviors contribute to girls' exploitation?

We need to examine our responsibilities in these areas. The German scholar Rosi Braidotti calls on us to recognize the "relations of responsibility" among women of different backgrounds, cultures, and situations. Because girls and women are suffering, we have to think about our role as agents in working to prevent these ongoing atrocities. What can we do to help? How can we ensure that the world moves toward being a safer, healthier, more promising place for girls? Fortunately, there are many agencies working to change girls' lives for the better, from global initiatives like UNICEF and Plan International to local efforts in various cities throughout the world. It would be impossible to list them all, but a selection is listed in the Resources section of this book, and they all welcome contributions and support. Their work, and the publications they disseminate, can be shared and discussed with teenage girls, many of whom are passionate about social justice. Girls need to become full-fledged citizens of the world; they need to be socially aware, thoughtful, analytical. They need to compare their lives to those of other girls and talk about the problems they see and their possible solutions. Girls can initiate fund-raisers, public information campaigns, and other action-based efforts to raise awareness of these issues as a step toward facilitating social change. Girls, too, must realize their "relations of responsibility" to other girls.

∽

The Lolita Effect is everywhere. It has gradually become our only framework for understanding girls' sexuality. It's invisible and familiar, and it goes largely unchallenged because it is so widespread. But it distorts girls' sexuality into a commercialized, commodified travesty. It affects girls' relationships with one another, with boys, and with themselves. It also skews the way boys see them. It impedes girls' healthy sexual development, and interferes with the possibility of more responsible, open-minded, and beneficial concepts of female sexuality.

Fortunately, many girls are keenly aware of the problems and of the ways in which it impinges on their lives. They need a place where they can explore the issues, and they need to be encouraged when they want to ask questions or reflect on them. They also need adult guidance in thinking through these complicated issues. The insights from media studies can offer clear and structured and clear approaches to these subjects. This book is a starting point for such analyses and discussions, which are becoming increasingly crucial as the Lolita Effect becomes more pervasive and enters girls' lives at younger and younger ages.

If we want to combat the Lolita Effect, those of us who care about girls need to make the time to talk to them about it. Because the Lolita Effect is designed to appeal to girls, we can't (and shouldn't) force them to be critical or reject it outright (though many girls do, anyway). What we can (and should) do is provide safe spaces where alternative viewpoints can be discussed, where ideas that counter the Lolita Effect can be expressed and explained, where values can be evaluated. Parents and guardians are the most likely facilitators in this sphere, but many girls don't have a home environment that can foster reflection or safe resistance. This is where schools, after-school programs, and social service agencies can step in. Anyone who works with children and cares about them can initiate these discussions and deliberations. What's lacking right now is a way and a place for girls to talk and think about these issues in collaboration and dialogue with adults.

Girls need to know that the media profit from certain fictions, that there are problems as well as delights in the Lolita Effect, that it's important for girls to feel good, comfortable, and safe about sex, and that they need to take wise precautions as they become sexually aware and active. The goal is for girls to see sex as a responsibility and an area of real empowerment. The Lolita Effect bandies the word "empowerment" around, but empowerment can't be realized in a commerce-bound context. Real power goes beyond the Lolita Effect. It has to be defined in real-world terms of girls having the freedom and knowledge to make clear decisions that are good for them in the long run, to understand biological realities, to understand consequences, and to understand how to analyze the media in relation to these things.

"In an ideal culture," writes the psychologist Mary Pipher, "sexual decisions should be the result of intentional choices." This is a goal to work toward, for all girls, everywhere. This is the goal of recognizing, and renouncing, the Lolita Effect.

Resources

*I*T WOULD BE IMPOSSIBLE to compile a comprehensive list of all the resources offering information and activism against the Lolita Effect, as there are so many—but here is a selection of my favorite recent reports, useful Web sites, and nonprofit organizations that offer relevant education and practical guidelines for parents, teachers, counselors, and girls.

REPORTS

American Bar Association. *Teen Dating Violence Facts*. Washington, DC: ABA, 2006. Available online at www.abanet.org/unmet/teen-dating/facts.pdf.

American Psychological Association. *Report of the Task Force on the Sexualization of Girls*. Washington, DC: APA, 2007. Available online at www.apa.org/pi/wpo/sexualization.html.

ECPAT International. *ECPAT Report on the Implementation Of The Agenda For Action Against The Commercial Sexual Exploitation Of Children 2002–2003*. Bangkok, Thailand: ECPAT International,

2004. Available online at www.ecpat.net/eng/A4A02-03_online /ENG_A4A/ECPAT_7th_A4A_2003-ENG.doc.

Human Rights Watch. *Hatred in the Hallways: Violence and Discrimination Against Lesbian, Gay, Bisexual and Transgender Teens in US Schools.* New York: Human Rights Watch, 2001. Available online at www.hrw.org/reports/2001/uslgbt/toc.htm.

Phillips, Lynn. *The Girls Report: What We Know and Need to Know About Growing Up Female.* New York: National Council for Research on Women, 1998. Information on the report is available at www.ncrw.org/research/girlsrpt.htm.

Plan International. *Because I Am a Girl.* Woking, Surrey, UK: Plan International, 2007. Available online at www.plan-international.org/pdfs/becauseiamagirl.pdf.

Priebe, Alexandra, and Cristen Suhr. *Hidden in Plain View: The Commercial Sexual Exploitation of Girls in Atlanta.* Atlanta, GA: Atlanta Women's Agenda, 2005. Available online at www.womensagenda.com/Child_Prostitution.pdf.

Ross, David A., Bruce Dick, and Jane Ferguson, eds. *Preventing AIDS in Young People.* Geneva, Switzerland: World Health Organization, 2006.

UNICEF. *The State of the World's Children 2007: Women and Children.* New York: UNICEF, 2007. Available online at www.unice.org /sowc07/index.php.

United Nations. *United Nations Secretary General's Task Force on Women, Girls, and HIV/AIDS in Southern Africa.* Gaborone, Botswana: United Nations in Botswana, 2004. Available online at womenandaids.unaids.org/regional/sgtaskforce.html.

In addition, a number of well-documented, thorough reports on adolescent reproductive and sexual health are available from the Guttmacher

Institute at www.guttmacher.org/ and the Kaiser Family Foundation at www.kff.org. By searching these organizations' Web sites using key words such as "sex," "media," "adolescents," or "children," in varying combinations, or more specific topics like "teen pregnancy," you will find many fact sheets and information based on many excellent studies.

INTERNET RESOURCES

Adios, Barbie. www.adiosbarbie.com/

> This site is definitely for older teens, because it contains a bit of salty language and somewhat adult themes. Unlike most of the other sites listed here, this one is a commercial operation, but the spirit and motivations behind it are in line with the goals of this book. With games like "Feed the Model," virtual stickers, videos, and thoughtful commentaries on sizeism and sexism in the media, the site is lots of fun for teens as well as adults.

Advocates for Youth. www.advocatesforyouth.org/index.htm

> This is a very informative site with a great deal of accurate, up-to-date sexual and reproductive health information for adolescents and their parents (in English and in Spanish). It's busy and hard to read, but a valuable resource. The organization offers workshops and trainings, too.

Break the Cycle. www.breakthecycle.org/

> This site focuses on helping youth to achieve nonviolent, healthy relationships and to work against domestic violence. It focuses on teen dating violence as well as other domestic violence issues.

Center for Media Literacy. www.medialit.org/

> Exactly what it sounds like—a Web site dedicated to developing critical thinking and media literacy skills, especially among young

people. The site offers downloadable "kits" for media literacy lesson plans and strategies; it has a "best practices" section with case studies and examples of student-made media; and it offers speakers and consultations for schools and other groups.

Coalition for Positive Sexuality. www.positive.org/

Again, definitely a resource for older teens, as it focuses on teens who are sexually active, providing nonjudgmental, factual information about sex. "No one can punish us for liking sex," is one of its slogans. The FAQs and forums may be helpful for many teens who have questions about sex and sexuality.

ECPAT International. www.ecpat.net/

The acronym stands for "End Child Prostitution, Pornography and Trafficking," and the group is a coalition of agencies combating these issues. The Web site has reports, action plans, and resources. The organization is supported by UNICEF and won the 1998 Rafto human rights award.

Girls For a Change. girlsforachange.typepad.com/national/

This nonprofit agency encourages girls to get involved in community action and social change. "GFC provides girls with professional female role models, leadership training and the inspiration to work together in teams to solve persistent societal problems in their communities," according to its Web site. It draws on girls as key resources for solving social problems, including homelessness and gang violence. It sponsors annual "Girl Summits" in California.

Girls, Inc. www.girlsinc.org/

A nonprofit organization with chapters in many U.S. cities, this group is dedicated to "inspiring all girls to be strong, smart, and bold." Their "Girls' Bill of Rights" is terrific, and they have interesting links to sections on the media, sexuality, violence. and other topics, as well as resources for parents and teachers. A plus is their information for Latina girls. Another plus is that they organize after-school programs in many areas.

Girls, Women + Media Project. www.mediaandwomen.org/

This is a Web site developed by the American Psychological Association; it contains great resources on the way girls are represented in popular culture. A vital part of it is the I-Can Network, a consumer action organization.

Media Awareness Network. www.media-awareness.ca/english/

This Canadian Web site is all about media literacy education and awareness, and it features educational resources, games, and research, as well as special sections for parents and teachers. If you click on "Issues" and then "Stereotyping," you will find wonderful information about sexism and sexualization in the media.

Media Education Foundation. www.mediaed.org/

A fantastic resource for educators, in particular, with many videos (and accompanying study guides) for sale on a variety of media topics, from globalization to adolescent sexuality. Jean Kilbourne's Killing Us Softly series, on representations of women in advertising, are contemporary classics.

Mind on the Media. www.tbio.org/

This nonprofit group's "Turn Beauty Inside-Out" project is aimed at countering the unhealthy and unrealistic images of beauty in the media. The TBIO action kit is aimed at raising awareness of media literacy and sexism in the media, with action items and organizing strategies.

New Moon Media. www.newmoongirlmedia.com/

> This Web site began in Duluth, Minnesota, and has burgeoned into a national phenomenon for younger girls (ages eight to fifteen). Its magazine New Moon and online club, the Luna Vida Club, foster intelligent, multicultural, progressive approaches to issues of importance to girls. Its new Web site features a parents' blog and networking opportunities.

The Ophelia Project. www.opheliaproject.org/

> Relational aggression and safe social climates for girls are the focus of this group, which received the 2007 Eleanor Roosevelt Award from the American Association of University Women. The site contains a wealth of resources, from speakers to research to school programming guidelines.

Teaching Tolerance. www.tolerance.org/

> This is the Southern Poverty Law Center's terrific antibias curriculum focusing on promoting diversity in schools and communities. With sections for parents, teachers, and kids, the site is full of easy-to-implement ideas and valuable information about social justice.

GOOD BOOKS

Brumberg, Joan Jacobs. *The Body Project: An Intimate History of American Girls*. New York: Vintage, 1997.

Griffin, Starla. *Girl, 13: A Global Snapshot of Generation E*. New York: Hylas Publishing, 2004.

Kilbourne, Jean. *Deadly Persuasion: Why Women and Girls Must Fight the Addictive Power of Advertising*. New York: Free Press, 1999.

Lamb, Sharon, and Lyn Mikel Brown. *Packaging Girlhood: Rescuing Our Daughters from Marketers' Schemes.* New York: St. Martin's, 2006.

Levin, Diane. *Remote Control Childhood?: Combating the Hazards of Media Culture.* Washington, DC: NAEYC, 1998.

Levy, Ariel. *Female Chauvinist Pigs: Women and the Rise of Raunch Culture.* New York: Free Press, 2005.

Martin, Courtney E. *Perfect Girls, Starving Daughters: The Frightening New Normalcy of Hating Your Body.* New York: Free Press, 2007.

Parrott, Andrea, and Nina Cummings. *Forsaken Females: The Global Brutalization of Women.* Lanham, MD: Rowman & Littlefield, 2006.

Pipher, Mary. *Reviving Ophelia: Saving the Selves of Adolescent Girls.* New York: Anchor, 1994.

Ponton, Lynn. *The Sex Lives of Teenagers.* New York: Plume, 2001.

Postman, Neil. *The Disappearance of Childhood.* New York: Vintage, 1994.

Quart, Alissa. *Branded: The Buying and Selling of Teenagers.* New York: Basic Books, 2004.

Rimm, Sylvia. *See Jane Win! How 1000 Girls Became Successful Women.* New York: Three Rivers, 1999.

Schor, Juliet B. *Born to Buy: The Commercialized Child and the New Consumer Culture.* New York: Scribner, 2005.

Shandler, Sara. *Ophelia Speaks!* New York: Harper Perennial, 2000.

Simmons, Rachel. *Odd Girl Out: The Hidden Culture of Aggression in Girls.* New York: Harcourt, 2002.

Thompson, Sharon. *Going All the Way: Teenage Girls' Tales of Sex, Romance, and Pregnancy.* New York: Hill & Wang, 1996.

Tolman, Deborah L. *Dilemmas of Desire: Teenage Girls Talk About Sexuality*. Cambridge, MA: Harvard University Press, 2005.

White, Emily. *Fast Girls: Teenage Tribes and the Myth of the Slut*. New York: Berkley Books, 2003.

Wiseman, Rosalind. *Queen Bees and Wannabees: Helping Your Daughter Survive Cliques, Gossip, Boyfriends & Other Realities of Adolescence*. New York: Three Rivers, 2002.

Wolf, Naomi. *The Beauty Myth: How Images of Beauty Are Used Against Women*. New York: Anchor, 1991.

Notes

Page 23, *fierce, fun independence* Jennifer Baumgardner and Amy Richards, "Feminism and Femininity: Or, How We Learned to Stop Worrying and Love the Thong," in *All About the Girl*, ed. Anita Harris (New York: Routledge, 2004), 61.

Page 23, *Eye Candy* Bella English, "The Disappearing Tween Years: Bombarded by Sexualized Cultural Forces, Girls are Growing Up Faster Than Ever," *Boston Globe*, Mar. 12, 2005.

Page 23, *Lacy briefs to preteens* Olinka Koster, "What possessed BHS to sell 'provocative' underwear for girls as young as seven?" *Daily Mail* (London), Mar. 26, 2003.

Page 23, *it's still on the market* "Pole-dancing set removed from Tesco toy site," *Birmingham Post* (UK), Oct. 25, 2006.

Page 25, *the most obvious ways, attractive* Alyssa Harad, "Reviving Lolita; or, because junior high is still hell," in *Catching a Wave: Reclaiming Feminism in the 21st Century*, ed. Rory Dicker and Alison Piepmeier (Boston: Northeastern University Press, 2003), 85.

Page 26, *sexy schoolgirl fashions* Colin Randall, "Bring back school uniforms for little Lolitas, say French," *Daily Telegraph*, June 21, 2006.

Page 26, *evoke male Lolita fantasies* Stephanie Rosenbloom, "Good girls go bad, for a day," *New York Times*, Oct. 19, 2006.

Page 26, *animé cartoon characters*   Sawa Kurotani, "Behind the paper screen: Japanese beauty fit for global consumption," *Daily Yomiuri*, Sept. 14, 2006.

Page 26, *wanton home-wrecker*   Sheryl Connelly, "You, too, may be raising a Long Island Lolita," *New York Daily News*, Sept. 26, 2004.

Page 26, *Lolita of sacred architecture*   Will Self, "Psycho Geography: Teenage Daydreams," *The Independent*, Aug. 12, 2006.

Page 28, *eight times that of Japan*   Teen pregnancy and abortion data are taken from the National Campaign to Prevent Pregnancy, www.teen-pregnancy.org/resources/teens/facts/fact3.asp, retrieved on Aug. 23, 2006. These data are supported in a report from the Sexuality Information and Education Council of the United States (SIECUS); see www.siecus.org/pubs/fact/fact0010.html, accessed Aug. 23, 2006.

Page 28, *including sexual violence*   The information about Shai's online porn campaign was in a story by Claire Hoffman and Chris Gaither, "Web ads show just how sexy these clothes make you feel," *Los Angeles Times*, Aug. 13, 2006; the Harvard story is in Jeremy Caplan, "Pornography for preppies," *Time*, Mar. 1, 2004, 20; the video game story was by Joseph Pereira, "Games get more explicit," *Wall Street Journal*, Sept. 25, 2003.

Page 28, *television, and the movies*   Mary Pipher, *Reviving Ophelia: Saving the Selves of Adolescent Girls* (New York: Anchor, 1994), 27, 38.

Page 29, *girls all over the world*   Manveet Kaur, "Young and dressed to kill," *New Straits Times* (Malaysia), Nov. 11, 2003. Monique Polak, "Teaching parents to talk back to their teenagers," *The Gazette* (Montreal, Canada), Mar. 4, 2004.

Page 29, *to poor school performance*   The information in this section is drawn from the following sources:

> Kristen Harrison and Veronica Hefner, "Media exposure, current and future body ideals, and disordered eating among preadolescent girls: A longitudinal panel study," *Journal of Youth & Adolescence* 35, no. 2 (2006): 146–56.

> Meghan Sinton and Leann L. Birch, "Individual and sociocultural influences on pre-adolescent girls' appearance schemas and body

dissatisfaction," *Journal of Youth & Adolescence* 35, no. 2 (2006): 157–67.

Pipher, *Reviving Ophelia*.

Daniel Clay et al., "Body image and self-esteem among adolescent girls: Testing the influence of sociocultural factors," *Journal of Research on Adolescence* 15, no. 4 (2005): 451–77.

Monique Ward et al., "Wading through the stereotypes: Positive and negative associations between media use and black adolescents' conceptions of self," *Developmental Psychology* 40, no. 2 (2004): 284–94.

Emma Renold, "'Square-girls': Negotiation of academic success in the primary school," *British Educational Research Journal* 27, no. 5 (2001): 577–88.

Peggy Orenstein, *Schoolgirls: Young Women, Self-Esteem and the Confidence Gap* (New York: Doubleday, 1994).

American Academy of Pediatrics, "Children, adolescents and television," *Pediatrics* 107, no. 2 (2001): 423–26. Retrieved from aappolicy.aappublications.org/cgi/content/full/pediatrics;107/2/423, accessed Sept. 1, 2006.

Victor Dwyer, "Eye of the beholder," *MacLean's*, Feb. 22, 1993, 46–47.

Page 29, *levels of sexual content*   Recent large-scale studies indicate that young adolescents who watch media with sexual content are more likely to begin sexual activity early; studies of this include Jane Brown et al., "Sexy media matter: Exposure to sexual content in music, movies, television, and magazines predicts black and white adolescents' sexual behavior," *Pediatrics* 117, no. 4 (2006): 1018–27; and Kelly Ladin L'Engle et al., "The mass media are an important context for adolescents' sexual behavior," *Journal of Adolescent Health* 38, no. 3 (2006): 186–92. Studies also show that the sexual content of children's and teen media is rising; see, for example, Aletha C. Huston, Ellen Wartella, and Edward Donnerstein, "Measuring the effects of sexual content in the media: A report to the Kaiser Foundation" (1998). Retrieved from www.kff.org /entmedia/1389-content.cfm, accessed Sept. 1, 2006.

Page 29, *aspect of their lives*   Bradley S. Greenberg, "Sex content on soaps and prime-time television series most viewed by adolescents," in *Media, Sex and the Adolescent*, ed. Bradley S. Greenberg, Jane D. Brown, and Nancy Buerkel-Rothfuss (Creskill, NJ: Hampton Press, 1993), 29–44. Greenberg et al., "Sex content in R-rated films viewed by adolescents," in *Media, Sex and the Adolescent*, 45–58.

Page 29, *embarrassed to ask your parents*   Girl quoted in Debbie Triese and Alyse Gotthoffer, "Stuff you couldn't ask your parents: Teens talking about using magazines for sex information," in *Sexual Teens, Sexual Media: Investigating Media's Influence on Adolescent Sexuality*, ed. Jane D. Brown, Jeanne R. Steele, and Kim Walsh-Childers (Mahwah, NJ: Lawrence Erlbaum, 2002), 173–90.

Page 29, *I know it's just TV*   Julie Backson of Westport, Connecticut, quoted in Betsy Streisand, "Doing it in prime time," *U.S. News & World Report*, Oct. 10, 2005, 50.

Page 32, *youth as "mediavores"*   The data in these paragraphs are drawn from a variety of sources, including:

L. Monique Ward, Edwina Hansbrough, and Eboni Walker, "Contributions of Music Video Exposure to Black Adolescents' Gender and Sexual Schemas," *Journal of Adolescent Research* 20:2 (2005): 143–66.

Ron Erickson, "Text TV's interactivity can lure youths back," *TelevisionWeek*, June 26–July 3 2006, 16.

"Teen clout shows no sign of diminishing," *Teen Marketing*, July 18, 2005, 31.

Harris Interactive, "Generation Y earns about $211 and spends $172 billion annually," Sept. 23, 2003. Retrieved from www.harrisinteractive.com/news/allnewsbydate.asp?NewsID=667, accessed Sept. 13, 2006.

Kaiser Family Foundation, *Generation M: Media in the lives of 8–18 year olds*, (Mar. 2005). Publication No. 7250. PDF file retrieved from www.kff.org/entmedia/entmedia030905pkg.cfm, accessed Sept. 13, 2006.

"Advertising to which teens pay most attention are ranked by media," *Cable World*, Jan. 31, 2000, 26.

"Feeling of control makes web medium of choice for millennial generation," *Youth Markets Alert*, Sept. 2003, 1.

Yahoo! "And Carat unveil research results showing teens are truly 'born to be Wired,'" press release from Yahoo! Media Relations (July 24, 2003), retrieved from docs.yahoo.com/docs/pr/release1107 .html, accessed Sept. 13, 2006.

Rowan Callick, "Chinese teens more conservative than their elders," *The Australian*, July 6, 2006, 22.

Jonathan Watts, "Shanghai opens shelter for young Internet addicts," *The Guardian* (London), Aug. 25, 2006.

Robin Hicks, "Young planet," *Campaign KIDS*, May 5, 2006, 10.

Manjeet Kripalani, "India's youth," *BusinessWeek*, Oct. 11, 1999, 74. Compare the numbers with those of Elissa Moses in her book *The $100 Billion Allowance* (John Wiley & Sons, 2000), 24, where she ranks India as having the second-highest teen spending rate in the world, after the United States—much higher than developed countries like Germany and France.

Suman Verma and Reed W. Larsen, "Television in Indian adolescents' lives: A member of the family," *Journal of Youth and Adolescence* 31, no. 3 (2002): 177–83.

Dirk Smilie, "Tuning in first global TV generation," *Christian Science Monitor*, June 4, 1997, 1.

Elissa Moses, *The $100 Billion Allowance: Accessing the Global Teen Market* (New York: John Wiley & Sons, 2000).

Page 34, *archetypal female roles*   Lakshmi Chaudhry, "Babes in Bush World," *In These Times* Nov. 21, 2005, 40.

Page 36, *of the virus*   Steven Sternberg, "To get federal funds, groups that fight AIDS must sign pledge," *USA Today*, June 10, 2005; "Ideology and AIDS," *New York Times*, Feb. 26, 2005.

Page 36, *with those of PPFA*   www.plannedparenthood.org; see also the Religious Coalition for Reproductive Choice Web site at www.rcrc.org.

Page 36, *pedophilia worldwide*   Judith Levine, *Harmful to Minors: The Perils of Protecting Children from Sex*, (Minneapolis: University of Minnesota Press, 2002). James R. Kincaid, *Erotic Innocence: The*

Culture of Child Molesting. (Durham, NC: Duke University Press, 1998). Kurt Eichenwald, "With child sex sites on the run, nearly nude photos hit the web," *New York Times*, Aug. 20, 2006. Kurt Eichenwald, "From their own online world, pedophiles extend their reach," *New York Times*, Aug. 21, 2006.

Page 37, *understand their significance* Rosa Brooks, "Thongs for kids, and other scary stuff," *Los Angeles Times*, Aug. 25, 2006.

Page 37, *music television, and the Internet* Bella English, "The Disappearing Tween Years: Bombarded by Sexualized Cultural Forces, Girls Are Growing Up Faster Than Ever," *Boston Globe*, Mar. 12, 2005.

Page 39, *are girls under eighteen* Centers for Disease Control, "Health risk behaviors by sex," National Youth Risk Behavior Survey (Atlanta, GA: CDC, 2005). The reason for the statistical discrepancy is that girls are frequently sexually involved with older men rather than with their peers. National Victim Center, *Rape in America: A Report to the Nation* (Charleston, SC: University of South Carolina, 1992).

Page 44, *as young as eleven* Katie Zezima, "Not all are pleased at plan to offer birth control at Maine middle school," *New York Times*, Oct. 21, 2007.

Page 45, *in a recent interview* John Schlitt in an interview with Claudio Sanchez, "Birth Control in Middle Schools Debated," *Weekend Edition*, National Public Radio, Oct. 21, 2007.

Page 45, *together after practice* Abigail Jones and Marissa Miley, *Restless Virgins: Love, Sex and Survival at a New England Prep School* (New York: William Morrow/HarperCollins, 2007).

Page 45, *has had sex* The Henry Kaiser Family Foundation, "National Survey of Adolescents and Young Adults: Sexual Health Knowledge, Attitudes and Experiences" 2003, www.kff.org, accessed Oct. 7, 2007; The National Campaign to Prevent Teen Pregnancy, "14 and Younger: The Sexual Behavior of Young Adolescents," 2003, www.teenpregnancy.org, accessed Oct. 7, 2007.

Page 45, *campaigns in schools* Rob Stein, "Teen sex rates stop falling, data show," *Washington Post*, July 22, 2007.

Page 45, *rates of teen pregnancy* Rob Stein, "Teen birth rate rises in U.S., reversing a 14-year decline," *Washington Post* (December 6, 2007), p. A1

Page 45, *transmitted disease every year* Kaiser Family Foundation, "U.S. Teen Sexual Activity," Report No. 3040-02, Jan. 2005, www.kff.org, accessed Oct. 7, 2007.

Page 45, *year in these regions* Susan Mayor, "Pregnancy and childbirth are leading causes of death of teenage girls in developing countries," *British Medical Journal*, May 15, 2004, www.bmj.com/cgi/content/full /328/7449/1152-a, accessed Oct. 7, 2007.

Page 45, *teenagers and young adults* Karl L. Dehne and Gabriele Riedner, "Sexually transmitted infections among adolescents: the need for adequate health services" *Reproductive Health Matters* 17 (2001): 170–83.

Page 46, *their parents thought otherwise* Thomas L. Young and Rick Zimmerman, "Clueless: parental knowledge of risk behaviors of middle school students," *Archives of Pediatric and Adolescent Medicine* 152 (Nov. 1998): 1137–39.

Page 47, *adolescents watch the most* Monique Ward, "Talking about sex: Common themes about sexuality in the prime-time television programs children and adolescents view most," *Journal of Youth and Adolescence* 24, no. 5 (1995): 595–615.

Page 47, *and in their explicitness* Aletha C. Huston, Ellen Wartella, and Edward Donnerstein, *Measuring the effects of sexual content in the media*, Kaiser Family Foundation Report No. 1389 (1998). Retrieved from www.kff.org/entmedia/1389-content.cfm, accessed Oct. 30, 2007.

Page 47, *depicted or strongly implied* Dale Kunkel, Kirstie M. Cope, and Carlyn Colvin, *Sexual messages on family hour television: Content and context*, Kaiser Family Foundation Report No. 1209 (1996), retrieved from www.kff.org/entmedia/1209-index.cfm, accessed Oct. 29, 2007.

Page 47, *identified with the main characters* L. Monique Ward, Benjamin Gorvine, and Adena Cyron, "Would that really happen? Adolescents' perceptions of sexual relationships according to prime-time TV," in *Sexual Teens, Sexual Media*, ed. Jane D. Brown, Jeanne R. Steele, and Kim Walsh-Childers, 95–123. (Mahwah, NJ: Erlbaum, 2006).

Page 48, *followed, questioned, or rejected* Michael J. Sutton, Jane D. Brown, Karen M. Wilson, and Jonathan D. Klein, "Shaking the tree of knowledge for forbidden fruit: Where adolescents learn about sexuality and contraception," in *Sexual Teens, Sexual Media* ed. Jane D. Brown, Jeanne R. Steele, and Kim Walsh-Childers, 26 (Mahwah, NJ: Erlbaum, 2006).

Page 50, *care services or birth control*   bid.

Page 51, *early as kids who don't*   Jane D. Brown, Kelly L. L'Engle, Carol Pardu, Guang Guo, Kristin Kenneavy, and Christine Jackson, "Sexy media matter: Exposure to sexual content in music, movies, television and magazines predicts black and white adolescents' sexual behavior," *Pediatrics* 117, no. 4 (2006): 1018–27.

Page 51, *abstinence-only approach to adolescent sex*   Peter Sprigg, "A promising vaccine . . . but Gardasil should not be mandatory," *Washington Times*, July 17, 2006.

Page 51, *kids defer sexual activity*   "Issues and answers: Fact sheet on sexuality education," Sexuality Education and Information Council of the United States (SIECUS), Report 29, No. 6. (Aug./Sept. 2001), www.siecus.org /pubs/fact/fact0007.html, accessed Oct. 21, 2007. Jane Friedman, "Teen sex," CQ Researcher Online 15 (Sept. 16, 2005), pp. 761–84, library.cqpress .com/cqresearcher/cqresrre2005091600, accessed Oct. 21, 2007.

Page 51, *more unsafe sex among teens*   "Study: Abstinence classes don't stop sex," *Cedar Rapids Gazette*, Apr. 14, 2007; "Abstinence-only fails to stop pregnancies, diseases," *USA Today*, Apr. 16, 2007; "$1bn abstinence program 'a waste,'" *The Times* (London), Apr. 16, 2007.

Page 51, *problem on their own*   "Parental consent/notification for teen abortions: All viewpoints," ReligiousTolerance.org, www.religioustoler-ance.org/abo_pare.htm#menu, accessed Oct. 21, 2007.

Page 52, *12 percent in France*   Heather Boonstra, "Teen pregnancy: trends and lessons learned," Guttmacher Report on Public Policy 5, no. 7 (2002): 7–10, available at www.guttmacher.org/pubs/tgr/05/1 /gr050107.html, accessed Jan. 8, 2008.

Guttmacher Institute, "U.S. Teenage Pregnancy Statistics National and State Trends and Trends by Race and Ethnicity" (New York: Guttmacher Institute, 2006), 1–24.

Jacqueline E. Darroch et al., "Teenage Sexual and Reproductive Behavior in Developed Countries: Can More Progress Be Made?"

(New York: Guttmacher Institute, 2001), 1–122, available at www
.guttmacher.org/pubs/covers/euroteen_or.html, accessed Jan. 8, 2008.

Page 52, *greater access to contraception*   Friedman, "Teen sex."

Page 53, *and the education communities*   Lisa L. Lottes, "Sexual Health
Policies in Other Industrialized Countries: Are There Lessons for the
United States?" *Journal of Sex Research* 39, no. 1 (Feb. 2005): 79–83.

Page 53, *and can set up a household*   Stephen G. Wieting, "The Icelandic
Family," in *The International Handbook of Marriage and Families*, ed.
Karen Altergott (Westport, Conn.: Greenwood Publishing Group, 1996).

Page 53, *and in the health care settings*   Maureen Kelly and Michael
McGee, "Teen sexuality education in the Netherlands, France and
Germany," SIECUS Reports 27/2 (Dec./Jan. 1999), 11–14.

Page 53, *integration into the community*   Margaret Mead, *Coming of
Age in Samoa: A Psychological Study of Primitive Youth for Western
Civilization* (New York: Morrow, 1928).

Page 55, *seeming naïve or inexperienced*   Kerry Vincent, "Teenage pregnancy and sex and relationship information: Myths and (mis)concep-
tions," *Pastoral Care in Education* 25, no. 3 (Sept. 2007): 16–23.

Page 55, *Common Sense Media, puts it*   Friedman, "Teen Sex."

Page 55, *social historian of teen sexuality*   Ibid.

Page 56, *hurt by her dating partner*   "Teen Dating Violence Facts,"
American Bar Association, www.abanet.org/unmet/teendating/facts.pdf
(2006), accessed Oct. 23, 2007.

Page 57, *recent* New York Times *story*   Julian Sher and Benedict Carey,
"Debate on child pornography's link to molesting," *New York Times*,
July 19, 2007.

Page 57, *involving seventy-seven countries*   Craig S. Smith, "Child
pornography on Vienna computer prompts worldwide hunt," *New York
Times*, Feb. 8, 2007.

Page 57, *to be abused than boys*   UNICEF, "The state of the world's children 2007: Women and children, the double dividend of gender equality,"
24, available online at www.unicef.org/sowc07/index.php, accessed Oct.
23, 2007.

Page 58, *known to work as prostitutes*   UNICEF, "Child protection from violence, exploitation and abuse," www.unicef.org/protection /index _exploitation.html, accessed Oct. 23, 2007.

Page 58, *myths about girls and sex*   "South Africa's child sex trafficking nightmare," BBC World Service, Nov. 23, 2000, news.bbc.co.uk/2/hi /africa/1037215.stm, accessed Oct. 23, 2007.

Page 58, *as young as three years old*   Jeffrey Gettleman, "Savage rapes stoke trauma of Congo war," *New York Times*, Oct. 7, 2007.

Page 58, *more recently in circuses*   *Global Monitoring Report on the Status of Action Against Commercial Sexual Exploitation of Children* (2006) (Bangkok: ECPAT International).

Page 60, *myth of the slut*   Emily White, *Fast Girls: Teenage Tribes and the Myth of the Slut* (New York: Berkley Books, 2002).

Page 61, *constitute a common culture*   Douglas M. Kellner, "Cultural studies, multiculturalism and media culture," in *Gender, Race and Class in Media*, ed. Gail Dines and Jean M. Humez (Thousand Oaks, CA: Sage, 1995), 5.

Page 64, *as one of them explained*   Sara Rimer, "For girls, it's be yourself, and be perfect, too," *New York Times*, Apr. 1, 2007.

Page 65, *good for others at age four*   Deborah Roffman, quoted in Stacy Weiner, "Goodbye to girlhood," *Washington Post*, Feb. 20, 2007.

Page 65, *among middle schoolers today*   Sylvia Rimm, *Growing Up Too Fast: The Rimm Report on the Secret World of America's Middle-Schoolers* (Emmaus, PA: Rodale, 2005), 31.

Page 65, *since 1850*   Ibid.

Page 67, *won't bat an eyelid*   Sharon Lamb and Lyn Mikel Brown, *Packaging Girlhood: Rescuing Our Daughters from Marketers' Schemes* (New York: St. Martin's Press, 2006), 143.

Page 67, *Ariel Levy puts it*   The historian Joan Jacobs Brumberg has charted these changes in her book *The Body Project: An Intimate History of American Girls* (New York: Vintage, 1998); the quote from Ariel Levy is taken from her book *Female Chauvinist Pigs: Women and the Rise of Raunch Culture* (New York: Free Press, 2005), 145.

Page 67, *for perceived promiscuity* Compare the descriptions of middle-school girls' sexual exploits in the chapter "Pigs in Training" from Ariel Levy's *Female Chauvinist Pigs* and the rejection and persecution of perceived teenage sluts in Emily White's *Fast Girls*, both cited above.

Page 68, *girls look hotter* Rebecca Haines, "Negotiating Girl Power: Girlhood on Screen and in Everyday Life," Ph.D. dissertation, Temple University (Philadelphia: Temple University Press, 2007), 276.

Page 68, *behavior in young children* Sally Lloyd Davies, Danya Glaser, and Ruth Kossoff, "Children's sex play and behavior in preschool settings," *Child Abuse and Neglect*, 24, no. 10 (2000): 1329–43.

Page 69, *pedophiles on a corporate platter* Rosa Brooks. "Thongs for kids and other scary stuff," *Los Angeles Times*, Aug. 25, 2006, Metro section.

Page 69, *dressed as sex bait* Jill Parkin, "Trash the plastic slappers," *Courier Mail*, Mar. 20, 2007.

Page 70, *for one another?* Kerry Howley, "Invasion of the prostitots," ReasonOnline, posted Mar. 5, 2007, www.reason.com/news/show /118939.html, accessed Aug. 19, 2007.

Page 70, *self-expression, self-identity* Bratz product designer Paula Treantafelles, quoted in Tess Stimson, "Brazen Bratz," *Daily Mail*, Oct. 19, 2006, 56.

Page 73, *sophistication and glamour* Ellen McCracken, *Decoding Women's Magazines: From Mademoiselle to Ms.* (New York: St. Martin's Press, 1993), 27.

Page 74, *work at a gentlemen's club* Margaret Talbott, "Little hotties" *New Yorker*, Dec. 4, 2006, 72.

Page 74, *hypersexual body display* Winx club Web site, www.winxclub .tv/alfea.php, accessed Aug. 19, 2007.

Page 76, *by much younger viewers* Julie Salamon, "The rating says PG, but is that guidance enough?" *New York Times*, Jan. 7, 2005.

Page 77, *are fully clothed* Kiyomi Kutzusawa, "Disney's Pocahontas: Reproduction of gender, Orientalism, and the strategic construction of racial harmony in the Disney empire," *Asian Journal of Women's Studies* 6, no. 4 (2000): 39. Kathy Maio, "Disney's dolls," *New Internationalist*

38 (1998): 12. Mia Towbin et al., "Images of gender, race, age and sexual orientation in Disney animated films," *Journal of Feminist Family Therapy* 15, no. 4 (2003): 19–44.

Page 77, *men act and women appear*   John Berger. *Ways of Seeing* (London: BBC/Penguin, 1972), 55.

Page 79, *or sit as ordered*   Saartje (Sara) Bartman, www.blackhistorypages .net/pages/sbaartman.php, accessed Aug. 8, 2007.

Page 80, *men looking at them*   Quoted in Margaret Eagan, "Spicy schoolgirl outfits give parents fits," *Boston Herald*, June 15, 1999.

Page 81, *of gender and sexuality*   Gregory Stone, "Appearance and the self," in *Human Behavior and the Social Processes: An Interactionist Approach*, ed. Arnold Rose (Boston: Houghton Mifflin, 1962), 86-118. Joanne B. Eicher, "Dress, gender and the public display of skin," in *Body Dressing*, ed. Joanne Entwistle and Elizabeth Wilson (Oxford: Berg, 2001), 233–52. Ruth Holliday, "Fashioning the queer self," in *Body Dressing*, ed. Joanne Entwistle and Elizabeth Wilson (Oxford: Berg, 2001), 215–31.

Page 81, *the psychologist Susan Kaiser*   Susan Kaiser, *The Social Psychology of Clothing: Symbolic Appearances in Context*, 2nd ed., rev. (New York: Fairchild, 1997), 2.

Page 82, *to his passional nature*   Elizabeth Cady Stanton, 1857, quoted in F. E. Russell, "A brief survey of the American dress reform movements of the past, with views of representative women," *Arena* 33 (1892): 325–39.

Page 82, *over the pachucos*   Ruth P. Rubinstein, *Dress Codes: Meanings and Messages in American Culture,* 2nd ed. (Boulder, CO: Westview, 2001), 263.

Page 83, *for a butch dyke*   David Carter, *Stonewall: The Riots That Sparked the Gay Revolution* (New York: St. Martin's Press, 2004), 150.

Page 89, *individual counseling sessions*   Nancy Khattab and Cathy P. Jones, "Growing up girl: Preparing for change through group work," *Journal for Specialists in Group Work* 32, no. 1 (2007): 41–50; see also M. Bolognini, B. Plancherel, W. Bettshart, and O. Halfon, "Self-esteem and mental health in early adolescence: Development and gender differences," *Journal of Adolescence* 19 (1996): 233–45.

Page 89, *trust and air out problem* One such mother-daughter group that has been sustained over a period of years was featured on NPR's *Morning Edition* on Aug. 2, 2007. The now decade-old Ophelia Project, which works to create "safe social spaces" for girls, uses peer groups and peer mentoring to educate adolescents about a variety of issues, including relational aggression.

Page 90-1, *younger siblings being affected* These exercises are taken from Shari Graydon, "Overcoming Impossible Bodies: Using Media Literacy to Challenge Popular Culture," *Emergency Librarian* 24, no. 3 (Jan./Feb. 1997): 15–18.

Page 96, *strong, and courageous* Abby Jones, "Long live Barbie," *New Moon*, Sept./Oct. 2007, 24.

Page 96, *body as "perfect"* Tara L. Kuther and Erin McDonald, "Early adolescents' experiences with, and views of, Barbie," *Adolescence* 39, no. 153 (2004): 39–51.

Page 96, *like in a bathing suit* David Hiltbrand, "Hold the sugar: Teen TV is getting meatier," *Philadelphia Inquirer*, June 18, 2006.

Page 97, *tripled in the last five years* A news story about "pro-ana" (pro-anorexia) groups on social networking sites was broadcast by the BBC on Aug. 8, 2007; it was retrieved from news.bbc.co.uk/2/hi /uk_news /magazine/6935768.stm on Sept. 3, 2007. The breast implant statistics are taken from Sandra G. Boodman's article "For more teenage girls, adult plastic surgery," which ran in the *Washington Post* on Oct. 26, 2004.

Page 97, *bodies should look like* Renee A. Botta, "Television images and adolescent girls' body image disturbance," *Journal of Communication* 49, no. 2 (Spring 1999): 22–41.

Page 97, *flesh must not "wiggle"* Susan Bordo, *Unbearable Weight: Feminism, Western Culture and the Body* (Berkeley: University of California Press, 1993), 191.

Page 98, *for an eating disorder* "Global Body Image Survey," *Cosmo Girl*, Feb. 2006.

Page 98, *upholding the large breast size* Kristen Harrison, "Television viewers' ideal body proportions: The case of the curvaceously thin woman," *Sex Roles* 48, no. 5/6 (2003): 255–64.

Page 99, *because of men's preferences*   Maya A. Poran, "The politics of protection: Body image, social pressures, and the misrepresentation of young black women," *Sex Roles* 55, no. 11/12 (Dec. 2006): 739–55. Information was also drawn from Zondra Hughes's "Dying to be thin: Deadly disorders are killing some sisters," *Ebony*, July 2005, 72; and Denise Brodey's "Blacks join the eating disorders mainstream," *New York Times*, Sept. 20, 2005.

Page 99, *size between 2 and 4*   Nanci Hellmich, "Do thin models warp girls' body image?" *USA Today*, Sept. 25, 2006.

Page 100, *weighs 163 pounds*   National Center for Health Statistics, Women's Health, www.cdc.gov/women/natstat/overwght.htm, accessed Sept. 5, 2007.

Page 101, *of almost $77 million*   Nat Ives, "Where have all the girls gone?" *Advertising Age*, July 16, 2007, 1–2.

Page 101, *between $80,000 and $300,000*   Jessi Hempel, "MySpace keeps getting bigger," *Business Week*, Nov. 7, 2005, 9.

Page 101, *high proportion of young users*   Brian Morrissey, "Beyond clicks: Measuring effects of social net ads," *Adweek*, Apr. 23, 2007.

Page 101, *prime-time TV in 2006*   Tony Case, "Special report: Health and beauty," *Adweek*, Apr. 30, 2007.

Page 102, *parents for spray-on tans*   "Teenagers turning to Botox to stay young," www.kfoxtv.com/health/9717417/detail.html, accessed Sept. 9, 2007.

Page 102, *and weekly spa appointments*   Diana Appleyard and Sadie Nicholas, "Preteen beauty addicts," *Daily Mail*, Aug. 6, 2007.

Page 102, *skin-bleaching creams*   Leela Jacinto, "Ouch! Western beauty norms head east," *ABC News*, Nov. 14, 2005, abcnews.go.com /International/story?id=84642&page=1, accessed Sept. 9, 2007.

Page 103, *their racial characteristics*   Laurel R. Davis, *The Swimsuit Issue and Sport: Hegemonic Masculinity and* Sports Illustrated (Albany, NY: SUNY Press, 1997), 92.

Page 104, *"Chemistry" is over*   Ynestra King, "The other body: Reflections on difference, disability and identity politics," *Ms.*, Mar./Apr. 1993.

Page 105, *women spend more each year* "Pots of promise—the beauty business," *The Economist*, May 24, 2003, 69.

Page 105, *cost of a house* Janine Bennetts, "Kiwi women spend more on looking good," *The Press* (Christchurch, New Zealand), Apr. 29, 2006.

Page 105, *billion in 2006* Jane Cunningham, "The beauty big spenders," *The Express*, Nov. 23, 2006.

Page 105, *beauty and clothing* Emily Lek and Melody Zacheus, "Hey, big spender! Some teenagers have no qualms about spending top dollar to look and feel good," *Singapore Times*, Aug. 12, 2007.

Page 105, *billion a year* "Pots of promise," 69.

Page 105, *women outspend men despite earning less* "Single loaded female," *In-Store*, Oct. 2003, 25.

Page 105, *rate of 12 percent* Robin Goldwyn Blumenthal, "Baubles versus beer," *Barron's*, Mar. 5, 2007, 16.

Page 106, *research firm Euromonitor* Alana Semuels, "Applying cosmetics to budding markets," *Los Angeles Times*, Nov. 26, 2006.

Page 106, *double digit growth in Asia* Andrea Pawlyna, "Beauty and the best of treatments," *South China Post*, Nov. 13, 2006.

Page 106, *5 million Euros in 2004* "China consumer growth led by cosmetics," CosmeticDesign.com, Sept. 14, 2004, www.cosmeticsdesign .com/news/ng.asp?id=54709-china-consumer-growth, accessed Sept. 23, 2007.

Page 106, *campaigns aimed at women* Kristen Ghodsee, "Potions, lotions and lipstick: The gendered consumption of cosmetics and perfumery in socialist and post-socialist urban Bulgaria," *Women's Studies International Forum* 30, no. 1 (Jan.–Feb. 2007): 26–39.

Page 106, *darkening of skin viewed as a sign of aging* Sharmila Devi, "The dark side of a lighter skin," *Financial Times*, Nov. 10, 2001, 8.

Page 107, *$800 for the procedure* Chisu Ko, "Peer pressure plastics," *Time Asia*, www.time.com/time/asia/covers/1101020805/plastics.html, accessed Sept. 27, 2004.

Page 107, *important for success* Ibid.

Page 113, *called her "Lolita-inspired"* Susan Donaldson James, "Lolita-lipped model creates uproar on Australian runway," ABCNews.com, Sept. 19, 2007, www.abcnews.go.com/US/story?id=3620910&page=1, accessed Nov. 13, 2007.

Page 113, *kitten of the catwalk* Eloise Parker, "13-year-old Maddison Gabriel is the kitten of the catwalk," NYDailyNews.com, www.nydailynews.com/lifestyle/2007/09/19/2007-09-19_13yearold_maddison _gabriel_is_the_kitten-1.html, accessed Nov. 13, 2007.

Page 114, *the nurse uniform* Glenn O'Brien and Sante D'Orazio, *Katlick School* (New York: teNeues Publishing Company, 2006), www.amazon .com/Katlick-School-Glenn-OBrien/dp/3832791639, accessed Nov. 8, 2007.

Page 114, *the uniform signifies* Lianne George, "Why are we dressing our daughters like this?" *Maclean's*, Jan. 1–8, 2007, 36.

Page 115, *and we continued* Jenny Eliscu, "Britney takes (it) off." *Rolling Stone*, May 18, 2006, 202–3.

Page 115, *as young as seven* "Outrage as children learn pole dancing," reported at "Pole dancing classes for kids," reported by National Nine News, news.ninemsn.com.au/article.aspx?id=303248, accessed Jan. 8, 2008, and "Pole dancing classes for kids," www.ananova.com/news/story /sm_2116649.html?menu=news.quirkies.badtaste, accessed Jan. 8, 2008.

Page 116, *in a film review* Marianne Sinclair, *Hollywood Lolita* (London: Plexus, 1988).

Page 117, *sociologist Wendy Chapkis* Wendy Chapkis, *Beauty Secrets: Women and the Politics of Appearance* (Boston: South End Press, 1986), 8.

Page 118, *Johnson and Tommy Hilfiger* Sandra Lee, "Thin models? Be outraged instead at catwalk kiddies," *Sunday Telegraph* (Australia), Feb. 18, 2007.

Page 118, *efficacy of youth* Lauren Tucker, "The framing of Calvin Klein: A frame analysis of media discourse about the Aug. 1995 Calvin Klein advertising campaign," *Critical Studies in Media Communication* 15 (1998): 141–57.

Page 119, *"sexy" and "hot"* Matthew Philips, "Eye candy," *Newsweek*, Oct. 29, 2007, www.newsweek.com/id/62474/page/1, accessed Nov. 8, 2007.

Page 119, *Philippe Aries has noted*   Philippe Aries, *Centuries of Childhood*, trans. Robert Baldrick (New York: Random House, Vintage Books, 1962), 103.

Page 120, *terrorized and sexually abused* Lloyd deMause, *The History of Childhood* (New York: Psychohistory Press, 1974), 1.

Page 120, *in a few modern nations*   Lloyd deMause, "The history of child abuse," speech given at the National Parenting Conference in Boulder, Colorado, Sept. 25, 1997, www.psychohistory.com/htm/05_history.html, accessed Nov. 19, 2007.

Page 120, *to the sixteenth century*   Michel Foucault, *The History of Sexuality: An Introduction*, vol. 1 (New York: Random House, Vintage Books, 1978), 29.

Page 120, *of consent to twelve* Judith Levine, *Harmful to Minors: The Perils of Protecting Children from Sex* (Minneapolis: University of Minnesota Press, 2002); Judith Levine, "Teen sex with adults is not harmful," in *Teenage Sexuality: Opposing Viewpoints*, ed. Ken R. Wells (Detroit: Greenhaven Press, 2006), 103–9.

Page 122, *sanctioned form of child prostitution*   "The Darker Side of Cuteness," *The Economist*, May 8, 1999, 32; "She's Only a Little Schoolgirl," *TimeAsia* (2001), www.time.com/time/asia/features/sex/sexenjo.html, accessed Jan. 8, 2008.

Page 122, *medical journal* Lancet   Samuel Siringi, "East Africa to tackle high rates of child prostitution," *Lancet* (May 18, 2002): 1765:359.

Page 124, *about "forbidden fruit"*   Quotes are from the "Pedophilia and the movies" forum, www.movieforums.com/community/showthread.php?t=4165, accessed Nov. 15, 2007.

Page 125, *children's media corporations*   Rosa Brooks, "Thongs for kids, and other scary stuff," *Los Angeles Times*, Aug. 25, 2006.

Page 126, *intended for their elders*   Ruth La Ferla, "Fashion aims young," *New York Times*, Aug. 24, 2006.

Page 126, *for the entire generation* Jayne O'Donnell, "Marketers keep pace with tweens," *USA Today*, Apr. 11, 2007.

Page 127, *in the* Journal of Sex Research   John Delamater and William

N. Friedrich, "Human sexual development," *Journal of Sex Research* 39, no. 1 (Feb. 2002): 10–14.

Page 128, *sexual desire until adolescence* Pamela C. Regan, "Hormonal correlates and causes of sexual desire: A review," *Canadian Journal of Human Sexuality* 8, no. 1 (Spring 1999): 1–16.

Page 128, *well as their sexual arousal* Cynthia Graham, Stephanie Sanders, Robin R. Milhausen, and Kimberly R. McBride, "Turning On and Turning Off: A Focus Group Study of the Factors That Affect Women's Sexual Arousal," *Archives of Sexual Behavior* 33, no. 6 (Dec. 2004): 527–38.

Page 128, *during the prime childbearing years* Elizabeth G. Pillsworth, Martie G. Buss, and David M. Haselton, "Ovulatory Shifts in Female Sexual Desire," *Journal of Sex Research* 41, no. 1 (Feb. 2004): 55–65.

Page 128, *was the aggressor* "Rape nightmare," *Spare Rib*, May 1982, 118, 13.

Page 130, *$57 billion a year* Michael Kirsch, "Facing up to those lines and wrinkles," *The Times* (London), Feb. 16, 2007.

Page 130, *$7 billion a year in profits* Ken Dilanian, "Victims of globalization's seamy side," *Philadelphia Inquirer*, Dec. 3, 2005.

Page 130, *at $100 million annually* All these statistics are from Donna M. Hughes's paper, "The Demand for Victims of Sex Trafficking," www.uri.edu/artsci/wms/hughes/demand_for_victims.pdf, accessed January 8, 2008.

Page 130, *which are consumed immediately* David R. Hodge and Cynthia A. Leitz, "The International Sexual Trafficking of Women and Children: A Review of the Literature," *Affilia: Journal of Women & Social Work*, 22, no. 2 (Summer 2007): 163–74.

Page 138, *appreciated, dose of nudity* Adam Rockoff, *Going to Pieces: The Rise and Fall of the Slasher Film 1978–1986* (Jefferson, NC: McFarland, 2002), 14.

Page 138, *is when the girls are assaulted* Jackson Katz, *Tough Guise: Violence, Media and the Crisis in Masculinity* [DVD] (Northampton, MA: Media Education Foundation).

Page 139, *being inherently sexual* Amy Holden Jones, in the documentary film *Going to Pieces* (New York: Thinkfilm, 2006).

Page 139, *up vanquishing the killer* Carol J. Clover, *Men, Women, and Chainsaws: Gender in the Modern Horror Film* (Princeton, NJ: Princeton University Press, 1992), 35.

Page 139, *products of the better studios* Carol J. Clover, "Her Body, Himself: Gender in the Slasher Film," *Representations* 20 (1987): 187–228.

Page 139, *their drugs and their sexuality* Adam Rockoff, in the documentary film *Going to Pieces* (New York: Thinkfilm, 2006).

Page 141, *studio budgets and backing* "Horror porn" of this type has been around for a long time—e.g., the Japanese "Guinea Pig" films that show young women being tortured and dismembered—but they were previously underground and "art house" films, not in wide distribution.

Page 141, *even more restrictive rating* Carrie Rickey, "A more adult way to rate films," *Philadelphia Inquirer*, Jan. 25, 2007. See also Ron Leone, "Contemplating Ratings: An Examination of What the MPAA Considers 'Too Far for R' and Why," *Journal of Communication* 52, no. 4 (2002): 938–54.

Page 141, *detailed depiction of sadism* Richard Corliss, Rebecca Winters Keegan, and Lisa McLaughlin, "Blood in the Streets," *Time*, Apr. 9, 2007, 128. Also, see the study "Adolescent exposure to extremely violent movies," by James D. Sargent, Todd F. Heatherton, M. Bridget Ahrens, Madeline A. Dalton, Jennifer J. Tickle, and Michael L. Beach, published in the *Journal of Adolescent Health* 31, no. 6 (Dec. 2002): 449–54, which indicates that most middle-school students have seen extremely violent films.

Page 141, *violence than about sexual content* Ron Leone and Lynn Osborn, "Hollywood's Triumph and Parents' Loss: An Examination of the PG-13 Rating," *Popular Communication* 2, no. 2, (2005): 85–101.

Page 142, *and girls down gender barriers* Linda Williams, "Film Bodies: Gender, Genre, and Excess," *Film Quarterly* 44, no. 4 (Summer 1991): 2–13.

Page 142, *wielded against the female form* Jay McRoy, "Simulating torture, documenting horror: The technology of nonfiction filmmaking in *Devil's Experiment* and *Flowers of Flesh and Blood*," in *Horror Film: Creating and Marketing Fear*, ed. Steffen Hanke (Jackson: University Press of Mississippi, 2004), 143.

Page 142, *enjoy them the most*   These findings are taken from several sources:

> Mary Beth Oliver and Meghan Sanders, "The appeal of horror and suspense," in *The Horror Film*, ed. Stephen Prince (New Brunswick, NJ: Rutgers University Press, 2004), 242–59.

> Cynthia A. Hoffner and Kenneth J. Levine, "Enjoyment of Mediated Fright and Violence: A Meta-Analysis," *Media Psychology* 7, no. 2 (2005): 207–37.

> Justin M. Nolan and Gery W. Ryan, "Fear and Loathing at the Cineplex: Gender Differences in Descriptions and Perceptions of Slasher Films," *Sex Roles* 42, no. 1/2 (Jan. 2000): 39–56.

Page 142, *focus group research with teenagers*   Jeanne R. Steele, "Teens and movies: Something to do, plenty to learn," in *Sexual Teens, Sexual Media: Investigating Media's Influence on Adolescent Sexuality*, ed. Jane D. Brown, Jeanne R. Steele, and Kim Walsh-Childers (Mahwah, NJ: Lawrence Erlbaum, 2002), 227–52.

Page 142, *their number one pastime*   Nick Madigan, "For Teens, Movies Are a Big Deal, Really Big," *Variety*, Nov. 2–8, 1998, 3–4. "Reality Check—What's Up with All the Hot Teen Movies?" *Seattle Times*, Apr. 4, 1999.

Page 142, *viscerally, emotionally*   Steele, "Teens and movies."

Page 143, *self-mutilation and emotional withdrawal*   Gabor Maté, "We should be alarmed that our children are not alarmed," *Globe and Mail* (Canada), Jan. 14, 2006.

Page 143, *the car and run her over*   Tom Zeller Jr., "Cruelty: It's Only a Game," *New York Times*, Feb. 20, 2006.

Page 143, *prostitutes expected to be raped*   David Jackson and Jonathan Salisbury, "Why should secondary schools take working with boys seriously?" *Gender and Education* 8, no. 1 (1996): 103–15.

Page 143, *global smash hit*   "Grand Theft Auto: Vice City," *Financial Times*, Nov. 26, 2002, 32.

Page 144, *played violent video games*   Cheryl K. Olson, Lawrence Kutner, Dorothy E. Warner, Jason B. Almerigi, Lee Baer, Armand M.

Nicholi II, and Eugene V. Beresin, "Factors Correlated with Violent Video Game Use by Adolescent Boys and Girls," *Journal of Adolescent Health* 41, no. 1 (July 2007): 77–83.

Page 144, *M-rated/violent video games*   Paul Kearney and Maja Pivec, "Sex, lies and video games," *British Journal of Educational Technology* 38, no. 3 (May 2007): 489–501.

Page 144, *more aggressive behavior*   L. B. Cohn "Violent video games: Aggression, arousal, and desensitization in young adolescent boys," Ph.D. diss., University of Southern California (1995). Dissertation abstracts international 57 (2-B), 1463. University Microfilms No. 9616947.

Page 144, *be involved in physical fights*   Douglas A. Gentile, Paul J. Lynch, Jennifer Ruh Linder, and David A. Walsh, "The effects of violent video game habits on adolescent hostility, aggressive behaviors, and school performance," *Journal of Adolescence* 27, no. 1 (Feb. 2004): 5–22.

Page 144, *increased hostility and aggression*   Christopher P. Barlett, Richard J. Harris, and Ross Baldassaro, "Longer you play, the more hostile you feel: examination of first person shooter video games and aggression during video game play," *Aggressive Behavior* 33, no. 6 (Nov/Dec 2007): 486–97.

Page 146, *conform to the script*   Erik Eckholm, "Rap fan asks hard questions about the music he loves," *New York Times*, Dec. 24, 2006.

Page 146, *accepting of teen dating violence*   James D. Johnson, Mike S. Adams, Leslie Ashburn, and William Reed, "Differential gender effects of exposure to rap music on African American adolescents' acceptance of teen dating violence," *Sex Roles* 33 (1995): 597–605.

Page 146, *life violence seem more acceptable*   Stacy L. Smith, "From Dr. Dre to 'Dismissed': Assessing Violence, Sex and Substance Abuse on MTV," *Critical Studies in Media Communication* 22, no. 1 (Mar. 2005): 89–98.

Page 146, *six violent acts every hour*   Kaiser Family Foundation, "Key facts on TV violence" (Spring 2003), Report No. 3335.

Page 147, *than in any other category*   Ibid.

Page 147, *by what they see and hear*   Robert H. DuRant, Heather Champion, and Mark Wolfson, "The Relationship Between Watching Professional Wrestling on Television and Engaging in Date Fighting Among High School Students," *Pediatrics* 118, no. 2 (2006): e265–e272.

Page 147, *there were no such effects on girls*   Dmitri A. Christakis and Frederick J. Zimmerman, "Violent Television Viewing During Preschool Is Associated With Antisocial Behavior During School Age," *Pediatrics* 120, no. 5 (Nov. 2007): 993–99.

Page 147, *twelve- to seventeen-year-old girls*   "Nielsen media research reports television's popularity is still growing," *Nielsen Media Research* (Sept. 21, 2006), www.nielsenmedia.com/nc/portal/site/Public/menuitem.55dc65b4a7d5adff3f65936147a062a0/?vgnextoid=4156527aacccd010VgnVCM100000ac0a260aRCRD.

Page 150, *they were thirty years ago*   Evan Stark, *Coercive Control: The Entrapment of Women in Personal Life* (New York: Oxford University Press, 2007), 7.

Page 150, *be the victims in these cases*   Callie M. Rennison, *Intimate partner violence and age of victim, 1993–99: Special report* (Washington, DC: Bureau of Justice Statistics, 2001), retrieved from www.ojp.usdoj.gov/bjs/pub/pdf/ipva99.pdf, accessed Nov. 30, 2007.

Page 150, *physical or sexual dating violence*   Jay G. Silverman, Anita Raj, Lorelei A. Mucci, and Jeanne E. Hathaway, "Dating Violence Against Adolescent Girls and Associated Substance Use, Unhealthy Weight Control, Sexual Risk Behaviour, Pregnancy and Suicidality," *Journal of the American Medical Association* 286, no. 5 (Aug. 1, 2001): 572–79.

Page 150, *experienced violence in a relationship*   "Fifty percent of young people in Japan subject to dating violence," *Mainichi Daily News*, Nov. 10, 2007.

Page 150, *suffered violence in a romantic relationship*   Bojana Stoparic, "Dating violence warnings candy-wrapped in Croatia," *Women's E-News*, www.ncdsv.org/images/dating%violence%20Warnings%20Candy-Wrapped%20in%20Croatia.pdf, Sept. 26, 2007.

Page 150, *both partners as perpetrators*   "Physical dating violence among high school students—United States, 2003," Centers for Disease

Control, *Morbidity and Mortality Weekly Report 55*, no. 19 (May 19, 2006): 532–35. See also Murray Straus's publications drawn from his International Dating Violence Study, pubpages.unh.edu/~mas2/IDV-Proj-Descript.htm, accessed Nov. 30, 2007.

Page 150, *to be seriously injured because of it* Donna E. Howard, Min Qi Wang, and Fang Yan, "Psychosocial factors associated with reports of physical dating violence among U.S. adolescent females," *Adolescence* 38 (June 22, 2007): 311–24.

Page 150, *than against boys or men* National Institute of Justice and Centers for Disease Control, *Extent, nature and consequences of intimate partner violence* (Washington, DC: U.S. Department of Justice, 2000).

Page 150, *one of his students claimed* Bonnie Miller Rubin, "When domestic violence starts young," *Chicago Tribune*, Feb. 8, 2007.

Page 150, *someone known to her* Amnesty International, "Making violence against women count: Facts and figures—a summary." Mar. 5, 2004, news.amnesty.org/index/ENGACT770342004, accessed Nov. 30, 2007.

Page 150, *attempted rape in her lifetime* Ibid.

Page 151, *violence in their jobs* Melissa Ditmore and Catherine Poulcallec-Gordon, "Human rights violations: The acceptance of violence against sex workers in New York" (New York: Urban Justice Center Sex Workers Project, 2003), www.sexworkersproject.org/downloads /DitmorePoulcallec200312.pdf, accessed Nov. 30, 2007. "Murders in Atlantic City Highlight Violence Against Sex Workers," press release from the Urban Justice Center's Sex Workers Project, Nov. 30, 2006.

Page 151, *that encourage their victimization* World Health Organization, "Violence against sex workers and HIV prevention," Information Bulletin Series No. 3 (2005), www.who.int/entity/gender /documents/sexworkers.pdf, accessed Nov. 30, 2007.

Page 152, *not easily explained* Stephen Prince, "Introduction: The Dark Genre and its Paradoxes," in *The Horror Film*, ed. Stephen Prince (New Brunswick, NJ: Rutgers University Press, 2004), 4.

Page 158, *wearing a perfume he likes* The quotations are taken from the following issues of *Seventeen* magazine in 2006: Feb., p. 51; Oct., p. 82; and Dec., pp. 7 and 130).

Page 159, *go at least 10 percent* *Seventeen*, Dec. 2007/Jan. 2008, cover, and pp. 157–59.

Page 159, *they found sexy in girls* *Seventeen*, Aug. 2006, 144.

Page 159, *pick you out of a crowd* *Seventeen*, July 2006, 74.

Page 159, *perfume she's wearing* Ibid., 75.

Page 159, *practical advice in these matters* Dawn Currie, *Girl Talk: Adolescent Magazines and Their Readers* (Toronto: University of Toronto Press, 1999), chapter 6.

Page 160, *informed consumers of boys* Kristen B. Ferminger, "Is He Boyfriend Material?" *Men & Masculinities* 8, no. 3 (Jan. 2006): 298–308.

Page 160, *wave of women's emancipation* Currie, *Girl Talk*, 7.

Page 161, *themselves as they did men* Ana Garner and Helen M. Sterk, "Narrative analysis of sexual etiquette in teenage magazines," *Journal of Communication* 48, no. 4 (1998): 59–78.

Page 161, *3 regrets her first time* *Seventeen*, Aug. 2006, 137.

Page 162, *destroyed my self-esteem* *Seventeen*, Nov. 2006, 68.

Page 162, *sleeping with him* *Seventeen*, Aug. 2006, 167.

Page 163, *that is, if they're interested* Quoted in Lynn Ponton, *The Sex Lives of Teenagers* (New York: Plume, 2000), 15.

Page 163, *from their desire for attention* Ariel Levy, *Female Chauvinist Pigs: Women and the Rise of Raunch Culture* (New York: Free Press, 2005), 162.

Page 164, *clinical facts of sex* Josie A. Weiss, "Let us talk about it: Safe adolescent sexual decision making," *Journal of the American Academy of Nurse Practitioners* 19, no. 9 (2007): 450–58. Kerry Vincent, "Teenage Pregnancy and Sex and Relationship Education: Myths and (mis)Conceptions," *Pastoral Care in Education* 25, no. 3 (Sept. 2007): 16–23.

Page 164, *that demonized lesbianism* *Seventeen*, Feb. 2006, 58–59.

Page 164, *celebrated a lesbian relationship* *Seventeen*, July 2006, 110–11.

Page 165, *to manage their lives* Currie, *Girl Talk*, chapter 6.

Page 165, *doing and undoing of the reading subject* Ibid., 248.

Page 166, *woman is designed to flatter him* John Berger, *Ways of Seeing* (London: BBC Books/Penguin), 64.

Page 166, *an object of vision: a sight* Ibid., 47.

Page 167, *cruising a porn theater* Michael Amico, "Gay Youths as 'Whorified Virgins,'" *Gay and Lesbian Review Worldwide* 12, no. 4 (July/Aug. 2005): 34–36.

Page 168, *groundbreaking like this is an honor* From Episode 1 of *A Shot At Love With Tila Tequila*, "Surprise! I Like Boys and Girls," www.mtv.com/overdrive/?id=1571193&vid=180299, accessed Dec. 13, 2007.

Page 169, *provide a lifeline for queer youth* Gay and Lesbian Alliance Against Defamation, "Where We Are on TV," Aug. 24, 2006, www.glaad.org/eye/ontv/06-07/overview.php, accessed Dec. 11, 2007.

Page 170, *against the gay and lesbian community* Southern Poverty Law Center, "Ten Ways to Fight Hate," www.tolerance.org/10_ways/index .html, accessed Dec. 13, 2007.

Page 170, *norms are less accepted by their peers* Staccy S. Horn, "Adolescents' Acceptance of Same-Sex Peers Based on Sexual Orientation and Gender Expression," *Journal of Youth & Adolescence* 36, no. 3 (Apr. 2007): 363–71.

Page 170, *sexually harassed and victimized* SIECUS, "Lesbian, gay, bisexual and transgender youth issues," www.siecus.org/pubs/fact /fact0013.html, accessed Dec. 11, 2007. Susan Fineran, "Sexual minority students and peer sexual harassment in high school," *Journal of School Social Work* 11 (2001): 50–69.

Page 170, *consequently attempted suicide* Human Rights Watch, "Hatred in the Hallways," www.hrw.org/reports/2001/uslgbt/Final-05 .htm#TopOfPage, accessed Dec. 11, 2007.

Page 170, *attempt suicide than other people* Paul Gibson, "Gay Male and Lesbian Suicide," www.lambda.org/youth_suicide.htm, accessed Dec. 11, 2007.

Page 170, *gay teen suicide and depression*   Carol Goodenow, Laura Szalacha, and Kim Westheimer, "School Support Groups, Other School Factors, and the Safety of Sexual Minority Adolescents," *Psychology in the Schools* 43, no. 5 (May 2006): 573–89.

Page 171, *own emerging sexual desires*   Rich Savin-Williams, *The New Gay Teenager* (Cambridge, MA: Harvard University Press, 1995), 18.

Page 175, *risk-reduction counseling about sex*   American Academy of Pediatrics Committee on Adolescence, "Contraception and Adolescents," *Pediatrics* 120, no. 5 (Nov. 2007): 1135–48.

Page 181, *holding themselves to it anyway*   Rosalind Wiseman, *Queen Bees and Wannabees: Helping Your Daughter Survive Cliques, Gossip, Boyfriends, and Other Realities of Adolescence* (New York: Three Rivers Press, 2002), 77.

Page 182, *svelte, beautiful, and sexy*   Nanci Hellmich, "Do thin models warp girls' body image?" *USA Today*, Sept. 26, 2006.

Page 182, whose bodies develop early   Lynn Ponton, The Sex Lives of Teenagers (New York: Penguin Putnam, 2000). Emily White, Fast Girls: Teenage Tribes and the Myth of the Slut (New York: Berkley Books, 2000).

Page 182, *their body image later in life*   Thomas F. Cash, "Developmental teasing about physical appearance: Retrospective descriptions and relationships with body image," *Social Behavior and Personality* 23, no. 2 (1995): 123–30.

Page 182, *involve young girls as victims*   Rape, Abuse and Incest National Network, "The Victims of Sexual Assault," www.rainn.org/statistics/victims-of-sexual-assault.html, accessed Dec. 20, 2007.

Page 182, *mediated by images*   Guy Debord, *Society of the Spectacle* (Detroit: Black & Red, 1967/1977), thesis 4.

Page 184, *positive vice in the mature*   Peter Stearns, *Fat History* (New York: NYU Press, 1997), 8.

Page 184, *above all with good health*   Roberta Seid, *Never Too Thin: Why Women Are At War With Their Bodies* (New York: Prentice-Hall, 1989), 5.

Page 184, *imitation of Art Nouveau aesthetics*   Marianne Thesander, *The Feminine Ideal* (London: Reaktion Books, 1997), 91.

Page 185, *every year since 1959*   David M. Garner, Paul E. Garfinkel, Donald Schwartz, and Michael Thompson, "Cultural expectations of thinness in women," *Psychological Reports* 47 (1980): 483–91. Also see Sharon Rubinstein and Benjamin Caballero, "Is Miss America an Undernourished Role Model?" *Journal of the American Medical Association* 283, no. 12 (Mar. 22, 2000): 1569.

Page 185, *decrease in body size over time*   Brett Silverstein, Barbara Peterson, and Lauren Perdue, "Some correlates of the thin standard of bodily attractiveness for women," *International Journal of Eating Disorders* 5, no. 5 (1986): 895–905. Brett Silverstein, Lauren Perdue, Barbara Peterson, and Eileen Kelley, "The Role of the Mass Media in Promoting a Thin Standard of Bodily Attractiveness for Women," *Sex Roles* 14, no. 9/10 (1986): 519–32.

Page 185, *appetite suppressants*   Larry Rohter, "In The Land of Bold Beauty, A Trusted Mirror Cracks," *New York Times*, The Week In Review, Jan. 14, 2007.

Page 186, *Singapore's Asian Civilisations Museum*   Sonia Kolesnikov-Jessop, "Asian Beauty: Beyond Skin Deep," *Newsweek* (international edition), May 28, 2007.

Page 186, *though not usually on the face*   Gail Anthony, "The Quest for Beauty," *The West Australian*, July 31, 2007.

Page 186, *beauty as the new standard*   Annaleigh Vallie, "The measure of beauty is a measurement of the hips," *Business Day* (South Africa), May 6, 2006.

Page 187, *assertiveness than unattractive people*   Megumi Hosoda, Eugene F. Stone-Romero, and Gwen Coats, "The effects of physical attractiveness on job-related outcomes: A meta-analysis of experimental studies," *Personnel Psychology* 56, no. 2 (2003): 431–62. Donn Byrne and Joel H. Neuman, "The implications of attraction research for organizational issues," in *Issues, Theory and Research in Industrial/Organizational Psychology*, ed. K. Kelly (Amsterdam: North-Holland-Elsevier, 1992), 29–70. Alan Feingold, "Good-looking people are not what we think," *Psychological Bulletin* 111 (1992): 304–41.

Page 189, *intention a natural justification*   Roland Barthes, *Mythologies*, trans. Annette Lavers (New York: Hill and Wang, 1952/1972), 142.

Page 194, *first advertisement in the magazine*   Ellen McCracken, *Decoding Women's Magazines: From Mademoiselle to Ms.* (New York: St. Martin's Press, 1993), 14.

Page 199, *role in these developments*   Peta Gillyat and Tom Reynolds, "Sharp Rise in Eating Disorders in Fiji Follows Arrival of TV," press release from the Harvard Medical School Office of Public Affairs, www.hms.harvard.edu/news/releases/599bodyimage.html, May 17, 1999, accessed Dec. 21, 2007.

Page 200, *norms by mass media influences*   Uraiwan Vuttanont, Trisha Greenhalgh and Petra Boynton, "'Smart boys' and 'sweet girls'—Sex education needs in Thai teenagers: a mixed-method study," *Lancet* 368:9552 (Dec. 9, 2006–Dec. 15, 2006), 2068.

Page 200, *China is in the early stages*   Cesar Chalala, "Abortions up in China as taboos weaken," *Japan Times*, Aug. 7, 2006. Lilian Zhang, "Hospital caters to rising demand for abortions from teenagers," *South China Morning Post*, Aug. 6, 2007.

Page 200, *an important factor in these sexual trends*   Wang Feng and Yang Quanhe, "Age at Marriage and the First Birth Interval: The Emerging Change in Sexual Behavior Among Young Couples in China," *Population and Development Review* 22, no. 2 (June 1996): 299–320.

Page 200, *for nothing more than wearing a miniskirt*   Helena Smith, "Honour suicides: When wrong boyfriends or clothes lead daughters to kill themselves," *The Guardian* (London), Aug. 23, 2007.

Page 200, *parents and clerics have blamed . . .*   "Underage sex: New survey unveils open decadence," *Africa News*, Feb. 8, 2007.

Page 201, *feminization of AIDS*   "Why We Are Failing African Girls," BBC World Service (Nov. 30, 2004), available at news.bbc.co.uk/2/hi/africa/4052531.stm, accessed Jan. 8, 2008. Also see "Away from the headlines," *Africa News*, July 17, 2006.

Page 201, *where hunger has traditionally been a problem*   Sonni Efron, "Women's Eating Disorders Go Global," *Los Angeles Times*, Oct. 18, 1997.

Page 202, *three-quarters of those infected*   Linda H. Bearinger, Renee E. Sieving, Jane Ferguson, and Vinit Sharma, "Global perspectives on the sexual and reproductive health of adolescents: patterns, prevention, and potential," *Lancet* 369:9568 (Apr. 7, 2007), 1220–31. Amnesty International, *Because I Am a Girl: The State of the World's Girls, 2007* (London: Plan UK, 2007), www.crin.org/docs/becauseiamagirl.pdf, accessed Dec. 24, 2007, 6.

Page 202, *complications of childbirth and pregnancy*   Amnesty International, *Because I Am a Girl*, 29.

Page 202, *perpetuated by the Lolita Effect*   Janie Victoria Ward and Jill MacLean Taylor, "Sexuality Education for Immigrant and Minority Students: Developing a Culturally Appropriate Curriculum," in *Sexual Cultures*, ed. Janice Irvine (Philadelphia: Temple University Press, 1994), 51–70. Marie Klingberg-Allvin, Nguyen Thu Nga, Anna-Berit Ransjö-Arvidson, and Annika Johansson, "Perspectives of midwives and doctors on adolescent sexuality and abortion care in Vietnam," *Scandinavian Journal of Public Health* 34, no. 4 (Aug. 2006): 414–21. "Execution of a teenage girl," BBC World Service News, July 27, 2006, news.bbc.co.uk/2/hi/programmes/5217424.stm, accessed Dec. 22, 2007.

Page 202, *MTV culture*   "Hip kids blackmail parents," *Africa News*, Aug. 27, 2006.

Page 202, *wear long skirts or face punishment*   "Village council decrees girls over 12 to wear skirts to stop sexual abuse," BBC Monitoring South Asia, Nov. 23, 2006.

Page 202, *street hoodlums and police*   "Stripping of women in trousers condemned in Abia state," *Africa News*, Sept. 29, 2007.

Page 202, *for wearing makeup and*   "Women live in terror as Iraq's new hardliners enforce Islamic law," *The Advertiser* (Australia), Dec. 8, 2007, 66.

Page 203, *figure-hugging clothes*   Cindy Wockner, "Caned in the name of God," *Sunday Mail* (Southern Australia), Dec. 17, 2006.

Page 203, *legal system if they run away or rebel*   Ruth Egel Khowais, *Bad Girls: The Criminalization of Female Sexuality* (Ph.D. dissertation, Massachusetts School of Professional Psychology, Oct. 2001).

Page 203, *inspirations for their body ideals*   Kamahl Cogdon, "Younger Anorexics," *Herald Sun* (Australia), Sept. 8, 2006. Fiona Macrae, "Anorexics age seven: Girls falling prey to stick-thin celebrities," *Daily Mail* (London), Feb. 6, 2007, ED IRE 27. Caroline Marcus, "Anorexia begins at five: Children starving to be thin," *Herald Sun* (Australia), Nov. 26, 2006. Courtney E. Martin, *Perfect Girls, Starving Daughters: The Frightening New Normalcy of Hating Your Body* (New York: Free Press, 2007). Also see anorexia statistics in Amnesty International, *Because I Am a Girl*, 70.

Page 205, *fastest-growing criminal enterprise*   Matthew Robb, "International Child Sex Trafficking—Ravaged Innocence," *Social Work Today* 6, no. 5 (2007): 22, www.socialworktoday.com/archive/swsept 2006p22.shtml, accessed Dec. 24, 2007.

UN statistics quoted in John Anderson, "Little Girl Sold, And Other Tales of the Sex Trade," *New York Times,* Nov. 11, 2007, Arts & Leisure.

Page 205, *nasty, brutish, and short*   Robb, "International Child Sex Trafficking."

Page 205, *boom boom*   Guy Jacobson is quoted in John Anderson, "Little Girl Sold, And Other Tales of the Sex Trade," *New York Times*, Nov. 11, 2007, Arts & Leisure. The NBC news story is "Children for sale," reported by Chris Hansen for *Dateline,* Sept. 5, 2006, www.msnbc.msn.com/id/14483961/, accessed Dec. 24, 2007.

Page 206, *skimpy leopard-patterned outfits*   Peter Landesman, "The Girls Next Door," *New York Times Magazine*, Jan. 25, 2004, 30.

Page 206, *glass cages to be rented*   Nicholas D. Kristof, "Cambodia, Where Sex Traffickers Are King," *New York Times*, Jan. 15, 2005.

Page 206, *Gucci high-heeled sandals*   "The children in Gucci shoes," *The Economist*, Nov. 22, 2003, 42.

Page 206, *baby beauties*   Lisa Ling, *Slave Girls of India*, a documentary in Oxygen's "Who Cares About Girls?" series, 2007.

Page 207, *a lot bigger than anyone would really like to know*   Bob Herbert, "Young, Cold and For Sale," *New York Times*, Oct. 19, 2006. Also see Nancy A. Boxill and Deborah J. Richardson, "End Sex Trafficking of

Children in Atlanta," *Affilia: Journal of Women and Social Work* 22, no. 2, 2007, 138–49.

Page 207, *Brooklyn district attorney's office*   Leslie Kaufman, "Is the Answer to Child Prostitution Counseling, or Incarceration?" *New York Times*, Sept. 15, 2004.

Page 207, *Winnipeg, Manitoba*   Global March Against Child Labour, "Child Prostitution and Pornography: Countrywise Report," www.globalmarch.org/worstformsreport/world/childprostitutionandpornography.html, accessed Jan. 8, 2008. Joe Friesen, "Hundreds of young girls work Winnipeg's sex trade," *Globe and Mail* (Canada), Feb. 21, 2007.

Page 207, *62 adults were recently*   John Tagliabue, "Heavy Prison Terms in France for 62 Pedophiles," *New York Times*, July 28, 2005.

Page 207, *Norway, Italy, and the Netherlands*   John Tagliabue, "Child Pornography Raid in 8 Countries," *New York Times*, May 7, 2005.

Page 207, *Romania is a primary source*   Adrian Humphreys, "For the sake of children," *Financial Post* (Canada), Dec. 8, 2007.

Page 207, *with relative impunity*   Kathryn Farr, *Sex Trafficking: The Global Market in Women and Children* (New York: Worth Publishers, 2005), xvii.

Page 207, *child pornography superhighway*   Ernie Allen, "In Child Pornography, Fight Harder," *Christian Science Monitor*, Nov. 26, 2007, 9.

Page 207, *variety of First World countries*   Dawn Herzog Jewell, "Child Sex Tours," *Christianity Today* 51, no. 1 (Jan. 2007): 32–33.

Page 207, *I've been looking for you*   Andrea's story is told in Peter Landesman, "The Girls Next Door."

Page 208, *locked up and beaten*   Heena's story is in Raekha Prasad, "Child Poverty: What Children Need Now," a supplement in *The Guardian* (London), Oct. 27, 2007.

Page 208, *five-year-old Masha Allen*   Masha's story is in Peter Small, "Abused Girl's Harrowing Tale Heard at Child-Porn Trial," *Toronto Star*, Jan. 10, 2007.

Page 208, *thirteen-year-old Lucilia*   Jessica Lustig, "The 13-Year-Old Prostitute: Working Girl or Sex Slave?" *New York*, Apr. 2, 2007, nymag.com/news/features/30018/, accessed Dec. 26, 2007.

Page 211, *exploration and sexual curiosity*   Ponton, *The Sex Lives of Teenagers*, 213.

Page 212, *accessible and active manner*   UNICEF, "Convention on the Rights of the Child," www.unicef.org/crc/index_30229.html, accessed Dec. 25, 2007.

Page 212, *villages of the Niger Delta*   Naomi Klein, *No Logo* (New York: Picador, 2000), xx.

Page 213, *contemporary form of slavery*   Michelle Kuo, "Asia's Dirty Little Secret," *Harvard International Review* 22, no. 2 (Summer 2000): 42.

Page 214, *recognizing rape as a war crime*   "War's Other Victims," *The Economist*, Dec. 8, 2007, 70–71.

Page 214, *Congressional hearings on the issue*   Felicia Lee, "Protesting Demeaning Images in Media," *New York Times*, Nov. 5, 2007, Arts & Culture.

Page 215, *a yearning for embodied connection*   Anne Bathurst Gilson, *Eros Breaking Free: Interpreting Sexual Theo-Ethics*. (Cleveland, OH: Pilgrim Press, 1995), 109.

Page 215, *a fair distribution of intangible goods*   Marvin M. Ellison, "Advocating Sexual Justice for Children," *Conscience* 23, no. 2 (Summer 2002): 28.

Page 216, *to be effective in implementing social change*   Andrea Parrott and Nina Cummings, *Forsaken Females: The Global Brutalization of Women* (Lanham, MD: Rowman & Littlefield, 2006), 201.

Page 221, *clear distinction between sexualization and healthy sexuality*   American Psychological Association, *Report of the Task Force on the Sexualization of Girls* (Washington, DC: APA, 2007), 2.

Page 223, *At this moment in our history*   Joan Jacobs Brumberg, *The Body Project: An Intimate History of American Girls* (New York: Vintage, 1997), 197 and 209.

Page 226, *parents, teachers, and other adults implicitly buy into*   American Psychological Association, *Report of the Task Force on the Sexualization of Girls* (Washington, DC: APA, 2007), 16–17.

Page 228, *treat boys and girls differently*   Graça Machel, "Foreword," *Because I Am a Girl* (Woking, Surrey, UK: Plan International, 2007), 8.

Page 228, *the teen Web site we visit may also own pornographic portrayals*   In fact, the popular social networking site Stickam, open to users under eighteen, is owned by the Japanese businessman Wataru Takahashi, who also owns Web sites offering live sex shows, according to a *New York Times* story (Brad Stone, "Accuser Says Web Site Has X-Rated Link," *New York Times*, July 11, 2007, Business).

Page 228, *relations of responsibility*   Rosi Braidotti, "On the feminist female subject or from she-self to she-other," in *Beyond Equality and Difference: Citizenship, Feminist Politics and Female Subjectivity*, ed. Gisela Bock and Susan James (New York: Routledge, 1992), 176–92.

Page 231, *sexual decisions should be*   Mary Pipher, "Introduction to the Perennial Classics Edition" of Margaret Mead's *Coming of Age in Samoa* (New York: Perennial, 2001), xvi.

274 /

Index